Alan
Shrugged

Books by the Author

Radical Libertarianism

It Usually Begins with Ayn Rand

Here Comes Immortality

Everything the Beginner Needs to Know to Invest Shrewdly

Who's Afraid of 1984?

The Optimist's Guide to Making Money in the 1980s

Mind over Money

Dynamic Investing

How to Profit from the Wall Street Mergers

The New Tax Law and You

Inside the Underground Economy

Kingdom

Trump

Wall Street Blues

Rupert Murdoch

The Mission (with Philip Sayetta Jacobs)

Politics as a Noble Calling (with F. Clifton White)

It Still Begins with Ayn Rand

Dominick's Van Gogh

War of the Werewolf (with Gary Greenberg)

Alan Shrugged

*The Life and Times of Alan Greenspan,
the World's Most Powerful Banker*

JEROME TUCCILLE

John Wiley & Sons, Inc.

This book is printed on acid-free paper. ∞

Published by John Wiley & Sons, Inc., Hoboken, New Jersey
Published simultaneously in Canada

Design and production by Navta Associates, Inc.

Photo credits: Page 143 top: AP Photo/Nick Ut; page 143 bottom: AP Photo/ Barry Thumma; page 144 top: AP Photo/Marcy Nighswander; page 144 bottom: AP Photo/Doug Mills; page 145 top: AP Photo/Wilfredo Lee; page 145 bottom: AP Photo/Ruth Fremson; page 146 top: AP Photo/Adam Nadel; page 146 bottom: AP Photo; page 147 top: AP Photo/Ryan Remiorz; page 147 bottom: AP Photo/Joe Marquette; page 148 top: J. Scott Applewhite; page 148 bottom: AP Photo/Rick Bowmer.

For general information about our other products and services, please contact our Customer Care Department within the United States at (800) 762-2974, outside the United States at (317) 572-3993 or fax (317) 572-4002.

Wiley also publishes its books in a variety of electronic formats. Some content that appears in print may not be available in electronic books.

ISBN 0-471-39906-X

Printed in the United States of America

10 9 8 7 6 5 4 3 2 1

To my wife, Marie,
who has been at my side through eternity

CONTENTS

CONTENTS

ACKNOWLEDGMENTS

I would like to thank Alan Greenspan for his assistance with this book. While the Fed chairman has refused to be interviewed directly by the media since the late 1980s, he did respond to questions through his press secretary, Lynn Fox, and he agreed to check for accuracy the sections of my manuscript pertaining to his earlier years. The chairman made it clear from the outset that he would not comment on content reflecting the author's personal opinions—for instance, the author's critical views about Greenspan's role as chairman of the National Commission on Social Security Reform.

In many ways, I began researching this book in 1969, although I did not know it at the time. It was in the late 1960s that I came in contact with many of the people who knew Greenspan intimately through his association with philosopher and novelist Ayn Rand. Some of these individuals went on to work in various capacities for the Ford, Reagan, and the first Bush administrations, and I interviewed most of them over the years in connection with my own political and literary activities.

The people whose contributions were indispensable to my

research for this book are listed in roughly chronological order according to the dates I interviewed them or sources close to them, corresponded with them, or reviewed their personal papers and Web sites. The danger in composing such a list is that, while I have tried to make it as comprehensive as possible, some individuals who deserve credit may have been inadvertently overlooked. To them I apologize in advance. I take full responsibility for any unintended oversights.

Thanks are in order to the following people and organizations: Murray Rothbard, Leonard Peikoff, George Reisman, Nancy Reagan, F. Clifton White, Bill Rusher, George H. Bush, Barbara Branden, Nathaniel Branden, Joan Mitchell Blumenthal, Barbara Walters, Harry Belafonte, Andrea Mitchell Greenspan, Pierre A. Rinfret, Herbert Stein, James Baker, Gerald Ford, Leonard Garment, Henry Jerome, Henry Kissinger, Jack Kemp, Milton Friedman, Martin Anderson, Bill Archer, William Simon, William Seidman, Jude Wanniski, Henry Gonzalez, Paul Sarbanes, Alphonse D'Amato, Andrea Millen Rich, Robert S. Getman, Lawrence B. Lindsey, the Washington Heights–NYC Committee, the George Washington High School Alumni Association, Rupert Murdoch, Wesley Halpert, Mark Lutsky, Johnny Mandel, Prestige Records, Historysplash.com, The Juilliard School Board of Trustees, David E. Joyce, the Federal Bureau of Investigation, the Social Security Administration, Robert Kavesh, the Conference Board, the National Baseball Hall of Fame, John B. Taylor, the American-Israeli Cooperative Enterprise, Nicholas F. Brady, Milo Schield, Jim Surowiecki, R. W. Bradford, Wyatt C. Wells, the Nobel Foundation, Father James Sadowsky, Andy Thibeau, the Cato Institute, Michael J. Boskin, Gerald Corrigan, the National Center for Policy Analysis, Robert Rubin, Al Gore, Larry Summers, the Union League of Pennsylvania, J. Bradford DeLong, Steve Forbes, Lawrence Chimerine, Lawrence Kudlow, Ed Yardeni, Stephen Moore, Declan McCullagh, Andrew West, and many others who chose to remain anonymous.

Several books and articles provided important background material. Among them were *The Passion of Ayn Rand* by Barbara Branden; *Judgment Day* by Nathaniel Branden; "Nathaniel Branden

Speaks," *Liberty*, September 1999; *Back from the Brink* by Steven K. Beckner; "The Fountainhead: Alan Greenspan Faces the Biggest Challenge of His Career" by John Cassidy, *The New Yorker*, May 1, 2000; *Crazy Rhythm* by Leonard Garment; *Secrets of the Temple* by William Greider; *Economic Puppetmasters* by Lawrence B. Lindsey; *Greenspan* by Justin Martin; *The Bankers* by Martin Mayer; *Reagonomics* by William A. Niskanen; *The Greenspan Effect* by David B. Sicilia and Jeffrey L. Cruikshank; and *Maestro* and *The Agenda* by Bob Woodward.

PREFACE

Alan Greenspan was born in a decade not unlike the 1990s. During the 1920s, the stock market was booming, the good times were rolling along, people had more than enough money to burn, and many believed the bubble would never burst. But burst it did, and when it finally deflated, the hopes, dreams, and fortunes of millions of people were dashed to smithereens.

The 1990s ended differently. In 1999, stocks turned in their fifth straight year of returns in excess of 20 percent, with technology shares actually doubling in value during the final year of the decade. While many stood on the sidelines predicting that this bubble would also burst, millions of speculators ignored them and grew rich buying the stocks of companies with no hope of turning a profit in the foreseeable future. Most observers gave the credit for this decade of unprecedented prosperity to the man who had been controlling the nation's money spigot for the past thirteen years, Alan Greenspan.

As 2000 got under way, Greenspan had become a household name. The last name alone was enough to identify the man behind it. There was no question that *Greenspan* meant Alan Greenspan, the highly respected chairman of the Federal Reserve. By then he was internationally recognized as the world's most powerful banker, perhaps second in absolute power to the U.S. President. After serving as an economic adviser to three presidents—Richard M. Nixon, Gerald R. Ford, and Ronald Reagan—Greenspan had replaced the venerable Paul Volcker at the helm of the Federal Reserve in 1987. President Clinton appointed him to a rare fourth term in January 2000.

Despite his tenure as perhaps the most powerful financial figure in the world, even more influential than the U.S. Treasury Secretary, little is known about the private life of the man behind the headlines. His evolution from a shy, gawky musical protégé growing up in the Washington Heights section of New York City to the Delphic oracle of U.S. monetary policy is an epic saga that could only have taken place in the United States of America.

Much has been written about Greenspan's early years as a disciple of Ayn Rand, the best-selling novelist and champion of freewheeling individualism, but the true story of what actually took place in Rand's inner circle rivals some of the more fanciful chapters in Rand's colorful fiction. The young Greenspan was so somber in appearance and manner that Rand gave him the nickname "The Undertaker" when he joined her Saturday night soirées in the early 1950s. His philosophical underpinnings were so muddled that he often maintained he couldn't be absolutely certain that he existed. "Alan's psycho-epistemology is completely warped," Rand often complained to her chief apostle and lover, Nathaniel Branden. "How can I discuss philosophy with a man who doesn't know whether or not he exists?"

Yet Greenspan's brilliance with figures and economic data was undeniable, and he eventually earned his place as the most promising acolyte in her inner circle, the one whom Rand predicted was destined to have the brightest future.

Rand's forecast was right on target. After establishing his own financial firm on Wall Street, Greenspan became an economic adviser to Nixon, chairman of the Council of Economic Advisers under Ford, and chairman of the National Commission on Social

Security Reform as well as chairman of the Federal Reserve during the Reagan administration. President Bush reappointed him Fed chairman with some reservations when Greenspan's first term expired, and President Clinton reappointed him twice during his own two terms in the White House. A lifelong Republican, Greenspan has been flexible enough to work with Democrats as well, despite his Randian background.

As Fed chairman, Greenspan is the number-one arbiter of U.S. monetary policy. How the Fed regulates money to keep the economy growing, while simultaneously holding inflation down, is a mysterious topic for many, but it is not all that complicated. One of the goals of this book is to demystify Fed policy and explain it in a way everyone can understand. The key to deciphering monetary policy is to understand *money*—what it is, how the Fed maintains its value, how interest rates come into play, and other pertinent details.

While Greenspan's tenure at the Fed has spanned part or all of three decades, it came at the end of a long history of success—and some pitfalls—in both the public and private sectors. He was already sixty-one when he first accepted the job, an age when many are thinking of retiring. Greenspan's life as a public figure has been well covered, but he has managed to veil his personal life from the scrutiny of the media. The man behind the dour personage who speaks in a language few understand is actually a colorful, complicated individual with a sharp sense of humor. How he was raised, the defining incidents in his life, the major influences on his thinking, and his personal idiosyncrasies constitute an exciting drama with a strong undercurrent of comedy running beneath the surface.

Greenspan would be the first to admit that it took him a while to evolve into the all-but-infallible guardian of the nation's financial health. As chairman of the National Commission on Social Security Reform, he had perhaps a once-in-a-lifetime opportunity to transform the Social Security System into at least a quasi-privatized retirement program. There was much impetus for him to do so at the time. Milton Friedman and his Chicago School economists had already helped privatize the Chilean system, with excellent results.

The United States was in the midst of the so-called Reagan Revolution, which—flawed as it was—nonetheless provided Greenspan with the ideological environment needed to wean Social Security from government control. Instead, Greenspan adopted a piecemeal solution by raising taxes and boosting the retirement age in stages to keep the existing system viable for an additional twenty years or so.

Reagan himself was appalled when Greenspan turned in his report. He had thought that Greenspan and his team would give him the cover to call for at least the partial privatization of the system, but he was left with little choice but to go along with Greenspan's proposals, which he found inadequate and temporary at best. Many of the key people around Reagan, including F. Clifton White, Jim Baker, Don Regan, Jack Kemp, Mike Deaver, and many others, were astonished that Greenspan failed to provide the President with the intellectual weapons required to give Social Security a permanent private-sector structure.

This book presents an even mix of Greenspan's personal and public life. In writing it, I have attempted to reveal the man behind the public face. To fully understand how a shy, self-effacing youth without privilege grew up to become the most powerful financial figure in the world, it is necessary to go back to his roots as a boy growing up in New York City during the worst depression of the twentieth century.

PART ONE

All That Jazz

CHAPTER 1

You know how it was in the early days, before the population explosion and urbanization covered the natural beauty of Manhattan with a hard shell of concrete and brick. Only Native Americans lived in the finger of land on the northern rim of the island, with its lush wilderness of hills, valleys, and cliffs. The cliffs sloped sharply downward toward two of New York City's three great rivers, the Hudson to the west and the Harlem to the east. In 1626, the Native Americans sold their birthright to European colonists who turned the fecund soil into a patchwork of farms within half a century. The most famous among them was Dyckman Farm, three hundred acres of farmland owned by a Dutch settler named William Dyckman in the mid-eighteenth century.

The War for Independence, and particularly the Battle of Fort Washington, brought an abrupt end to the bucolic life of the colonists in Upper Manhattan. A fort, named after General George Washington, was built in the summer of 1776 on the heights overlooking the Hudson, and occupied what is now the intersection of West 183rd Street and Fort Washington Avenue. On November 16,

1776, a ragtag, woefully outnumbered band of colonists fought a losing battle with an overpowering force of British troops. It would take seven bitter, bloody years before the Americans were finally able to hoist their flag over the fort after they forced the British to evacuate.

After the war, the city entered an era of economic growth and prosperity that drew newly rich merchants northward in search of land on which to build their estates. They were attracted to the area because of the panoramic views from the sweeping hills and cliffs towering above the rivers. The city's oldest surviving residence is the Morris-Jumel Mansion, which is furnished with priceless pieces from the colonial period. It takes its name from the original owner, Roger Morris, and Stephen Jumel, a rich wine merchant who bought the mansion and farm in 1810 for his wife Eliza.

Other great relics of an era lost in the mists of history have been preserved in the clutter of noisy streets and crowded apartment buildings that began to characterize the area when Alan Greenspan was born. The Cloisters, a medieval museum comprising reassembled sections of French and Spanish monasteries, sits on top of a hill in Fort Tryon Park overlooking the Hudson. The museum is a repository of five-hundred-year-old art treasures, including a set of six handwoven tapestries depicting the Hunt of the Unicorn. The gardens on the site are still redolent with the aroma of herbs similar to types grown in the Middle Ages.

Fort Tryon Park itself sprawls over sixty-six acres along the eastern bank of the Hudson from West 193rd to Dyckman Street. The entrance to, and drive through, Fort Tryon Park is named after Revolutionary War hero Margaret Cochran Corbin, who fought beside her husband during the Battle of Fort Washington. The Promenade in the park runs northward past the Heather Garden, filled with shrubs and flowers, to the Upper Terrace with its view of the Palisades from the George Washington to the Tappan Zee bridges. Just north of Fort Tryon Park is Inwood Hill Park, blanketing 196 acres along the river to Spuyten Duyvil at the confluence of the Hudson and Harlem Rivers. Urban explorers can still rummage through caves that once housed the Algonquins, and climb over rocks rich with wildflowers and striations from the last glacial era.

New generations of merchants and financiers followed in the wake of Jumel and his contemporaries. During the second half of the nineteenth century, they built a string of magnificent estates along the river all the way up to Washington Irving country in Irvingon-on-the-Hudson. The high cliffs and surrounding terrain are dotted with homes that once belonged to John D. Rockefeller and other industrialists.

They in turn were followed by tides of Germans, Irish, Jews, and Eastern Europeans looking for their own foothold on American soil. With the completion of the IRT subway in 1904, many of them traveled north to the land between the banks of the rivers. The sprawl of farms, fields, and large country estates gradually gave way to an expanding shell of brick and concrete as tenements, houses, and small apartment buildings sprouted like mushrooms during the first two decades of the twentieth century.

Churches and synagogues took root between the rows of residential dwellings and crowded out the shrinking countryside. Yeshiva University, the first Jewish parochial school in North America, was built in 1886. The Episcopal Church of the Intercession, across from Audubon Terrace, went up in 1915. In the graveyard alongside the church lie the bones of John James Audubon, who captured birds on canvas better than anyone; Philip Livingston, signer of the Declaration of Independence; Alfred Tennyson Dickens, son of Charles; the original Madame Jumel; Clement C. Moore, author of *'Twas the Night before Christmas*; and other early Americans. The area also became home to Frances Xavier Cabrini Chapel, built in honor of the Mother Teresa of her day, Italian immigrant Mother Cabrini, who founded schools, hospitals, and the Missionary Sisters of the Sacred Heart religious order.

Museums sprung up beside the houses of worship. Philanthropist Archer Milton Huntington founded the Hispanic Society of America in 1904 and built a museum that opened four years later. During the next twenty years, the American Numismatic Society Museum, the Museum of the American Indian, and the American Institute of Arts and Letters were erected in the northern section of Manhattan that had come to be known as Washington Heights.

Alan Greenspan entered the world in the midst of this urban stew of diverse ethnic and religious groups. He was born on March 6, 1926, a blustery late-winter New York day with raw winds blowing in from the Hudson River. Young Alan didn't know it at the time, but he would learn later that the year of his birth was the same year that a Yale economist named Irving Fisher identified a trade-off between unemployment and inflation.

Fisher's theories, along with those of a British economist named A. W. Phillips, would hold sway for the next seventy years and would profoundly influence the thinking of several generations of politicians and economists, including the adult Alan Greenspan. It would take the boom years of the 1990s with their record-breaking streak of dynamic economic growth, combined with low inflation, to cast doubts on Fisher's theories. However, that was still many decades, filled with countless economic and political battles, in the future. Interestingly enough, just days before the Crash of 1929, Fisher proclaimed that "stock prices have reached what looks like a permanently high plateau," but what the hell, the reputations of many economic gurus have been built on worse forecasts than that.

Alan's father, Herman Herbert Greenspan, was a successful, self-educated stockbroker and Wall Street trader during a decade of powerful stock market advances. For a long time it seemed the great bull market of the 1920s would never end. Herbert was born in 1900 in Scranton, Pennsylvania, the son of David and Anna Greenspan, who came from Germany. As a young man Herbert was slim, about five feet eight inches tall. Alan's mother, Rose Goldsmith Greenspan, was short, dark-haired, pretty, and vivacious, with a love for music, singing, and ballroom dancing. She was two years younger than her husband, the daughter of Nathan Toluchko and Anna Edelstein, Polish-Russian Jews who emigrated to the United States from Hungary shortly after Rose was born. Nathan "Americanized" his name to Goldsmith at Riker's Island when he entered the country.

"She was a young, beautiful, talented woman," recalled Rose's nephew Wesley Halpert. "She had a beautiful voice. She was very short and a little on the plump side, but really adorable. She was my favorite aunt, and Alan really loved her."

The great stock market crash of 1929 and the Great Depression that followed ended the prosperity that Alan's parents and others of their generation had enjoyed. Alan's safe and secure world crashed along with the market when Herbert and Rose divorced when Alan was only three. Rose later told her son that she was too young when they were married; she was only seventeen years old. She and Herbert were totally different kinds of people—Herb more serious and somewhat somber, Rose high-spirited and fun-loving—and the collapse of the financial house of cards that had sheltered them was more than their fragile marriage could possibly handle.

Rose and her young son moved back from their own apartment to her parents' six-story, solidly built apartment building in Washington Heights on the corner of Broadway and 163rd Street, a neighborhood where most of the Jewish residents gravitated. The four of them lived cramped together in the one-bedroom apartment, as many working-class families did in those days. The Irish, Germans, and later waves of Greeks, Hispanics, and African Americans congregated in their own enclaves. Rose found a job selling furniture in a retail store named Ludwig-Bauman across the Harlem River at 149th Street and Third Avenue in the Bronx. It was not her first choice of a job, but she was happy to be employed at a time when armies of destitute men and women loitered in the surrounding parks and streets with little or nothing to do. Alan remembered his grandfather as an imposing presence in the house, a towering, bearded disciplinarian who was an Orthodox cantor and rabbi. Rose was not particularly religious, which caused some contention with her father, but she was strong and independent and brought sorely needed money home, so an uneasy truce of sorts prevailed between daughter and father.

The urbanization of the city continued apace, further altering the landscape of Washington Heights and other areas of the city. The A subway train, immortalized in song by Duke Ellington, was completed as a continuation of the Eighth Avenue IND subway when Alan was a boy. The extension of the subway led to a new migration of city residents further northward and to the construction of more apartment buildings in the streets above Isham Park. When Alan was five, city engineers completed the world's longest suspension structure at the time, the George Washington Bridge, which was the most ambitious urban project of its day. The glistening steel bridge connected the western end of 178th Street to the cliffs of Fort Lee, New Jersey, on the other side of the Hudson.

The financial wreckage of Herbert Greenspan's life dealt him a devastating blow, and he seems to have fallen off the face of the earth for a long period after his divorce from Rose. Then, suddenly, he reappeared in Alan's life, although his visits were infrequent and sporadic. Alan was happy to see him, but he missed having a permanent father figure to look up to and suffered as a result. As a small boy he was as shy and withdrawn as his mother was cheerful and gregarious.

"Being a child without a father was hard on Alan," remembered his cousin Wesley Halpert, who would go on to become a prominent New York City dentist with a Madison Avenue practice and a side business giving expert witness testimony at trials. Wesley's mother, Mary, was Rose's sister, and they lived only half a block away from Alan and his mother. "My father served as a pretty good surrogate. He loved kids and took us out for ice cream and walks through the parks in the neighborhood. My sister Marianne would hold one hand, I would hold the other, and Alan would squeeze in between us and try to grab a hand because he wanted a daddy. When he did see his father, Alan was ecstatic."

Alan recalled that his father worshiped Franklin D. Roosevelt and became a staunch supporter of the New Deal. When Alan was eight years old, his father wrote a book entitled *Recovery Ahead* and inscribed a copy to his son with the message, ". . . at your maturity, you can look back and endeavor to interpret the reasoning behind these logical forecasts and begin a like work of your own. Your dad." Herbert was prophetic in that Alan did, indeed, become a world-famous economic forecaster as an adult, but he was abysmally off the mark in his characterization of his son's economic orientation. Alan's right-wing laissez-faire approach to economics would take root in his twenties and remain with him throughout his life.

Rose evolved into an accomplished singer and musician who gravitated immediately toward the piano when she visited someone's home. Through her influence, Alan developed a love of music, classical as well as be-bop and jazz, which shocked middle-class America the way rock and roll did a generation later. Social conservatives of the period considered jazz to be suggestive and immoral, but fortunately for Alan, Rose did not share that view and encouraged her son to ignore the opinions of others.

There was barely enough money available for food in the Goldsmith household, let alone for private education, so Alan attended the local public elementary school serving his neighborhood. At P.S. 169, located at 169th Street and Audubon Avenue, Alan demonstrated an aptitude for math and English. His talent with numbers was so extraordinary that before Alan was ten, he could multiply triple-digit figures in his head and come up with the right answer every time. Rose was as delighted with his proficiency for figures as she was with his gift for music, and she trotted him out in front of friends and neighbors to show him off. Alan, however, was more interested in putting his mathematical ability to a better use— compiling batting averages and other statistics for his favorite team, the Brooklyn Dodgers.

"He was very much into baseball, as most kids were at that age, and he knew everybody's baseball average and all their stats," recalled Wesley Halpert.

Alan spent most summer weekends at the Halperts' bungalow at Rockaway Beach, a Queens oceanfront community for working-class New Yorkers. The Irish had their enclave on the water, and the Jews gravitated to their own. One of Alan's greatest pleasures was riding on the subway from Washington Heights all the way out to Ebbets Field in Brooklyn, an hour-and-a-half trip each way. The Polo Grounds and Yankee Stadium were both a quick subway ride to the Bronx just over the Harlem River, but for Alan, the Brooklyn Dodgers were baseball. The New York Yankees and New York Giants were mere teams, while the Dodgers were a *religion*. Going to Ebbets Field on the train was like going to church or synagogue. Alan lived and died with the Dodgers' victories and defeats, mostly defeats at that time, and followed them through their many incarnations. Early on they were known by different names—the Flock, the Robins, the Daffiness Boys—and it wasn't until Alan was seven that they officially became the Brooklyn Dodgers after their manager, Wilbert "Uncle Robbie" Robertson, dodged a question about player salaries for a newspaper story.

Alan told stories about the day three players wound up on third base at the same time, and about the game when a fly ball landed on Babe Herman's head. There was also the time Dodger pitcher Billy Loes blamed an error that cost his team a World Series game on the sun that got in his eyes. The problem with that explanation was that Loes had not dropped a pop fly; he had fumbled a ground ball. But this was the same Billy Loes who also said he never wanted to win twenty games in one season because "If you do it once, they expect you to do it again."

Alan loved to play baseball as much as he enjoyed watching his favorite team engaged in combat on the diamond. A nearsighted lefthander without great speed or the ability to hit the long ball, he was usually picked to play first base in neighborhood games of pickup baseball. Alan went almost every day to the parks that blanketed Washington Heights, particularly Inwood Hill Park with its baseball diamonds and basketball courts settled in among the rolling green hills. He spent long hours after school running with his friends through the wild patches of woods that isolated them from the city noise and smells just a few hundred yards away. They enjoyed going down by the river to watch the never-ending string of traffic wending east and west over the great, arching bridge that linked New York and New Jersey. Alan's grandparents thought he was becoming a bit wild, but his mother recognized herself as the source of his adventurous spirit and was his steadfast ally.

"Rose was a great mother," said Alan's cousin Wesley. "She was not a typical Jewish mother who was on top of him every minute: 'Why don't you do this? Why don't you do that?' She left him alone, and Alan appreciated that and was very close to her."

The Jewish kids lived in terror of the Irish gangs that spilled over from Inwood into their own neighborhood, but Alan was not afraid to stand his ground against them. Wesley remembered a time when he and Alan were playing handball and the schoolyard was invaded by a band of mostly older and bigger Irish toughs. Alan sailed into them with his fists until they went off looking for easier prey.

The streets of Washington Heights were filled with the smells of hot bagels, first boiled and then baked in the Jewish bagel factory; pungent potato knishes thickly coated with breading; and garlicky hot dogs and sharp sauerkraut steaming in the wagons of street vendors along Broadway and St. Nicholas and Amsterdam avenues. There was also the heady aroma of beer and whiskey emanating from Irish and German saloons in Inwood, and the shouts of beefy men lined up along the bars.

Those who could find any work at all before World War II put an end to the Depression drove buses and subway cars; hauled garbage from houses, shops, and restaurants; and shaped up daily at the docks in Manhattan and Brooklyn, hoping to load and unload ships bound for Europe. The luckier among them got steady work and an eventual pension on the police force or fire department, or a higher-paid job in the construction trades. The Jews became cutters in the garment industry downtown in the West Thirties, and went to school at night to get a free education at City College. The inhabitants of Washington Heights and Inwood were working-class people from every ethnic background imaginable. They clustered in crowded enclaves mostly with their own kind. They didn't particularly like their neighbors who were somehow different. But they lived cheek by jowl with strange people from alien religious and cultural backgrounds in an atmosphere of mutual toleration.

Alan breathed this air every day, listened to the raucous shouts and urban clamor, steered clear of the fights that spilled out onto the sidewalks from the bars, and stepped gingerly through the trash that littered the gutters. New York has always been a dirty town, and it was dirtier when Alan was a teenager than it is today.

Fortunately for young Alan, he inherited his father's slim physique, but he was a bit taller. In his mid-teens, he was already approaching his full adult height, an inch or two under six feet. He had a full mat of dark, straight hair that he combed back away from his forehead, and he wore large, thick glasses to correct his myopia. Even then he was somber in appearance, favoring white shirts and dark slacks, a style he picked up from the main male influence in his life, his rabbi grandfather. He adored the bright, pretty, spirited girls in the neighborhood, but he was painfully shy and afraid to approach them. It would take another decade or so before he was able to impress the women he fancied with the power of his intellect.

CHAPTER 2

I n 1939 New York City hosted one of the great events of the century, the New York World's Fair, in Queens on the other side of the East River from Manhattan. Alan was thirteen years old when Rose took him for a long subway ride to see "The World of Tomorrow," which was the theme of the fair. Alan was spellbound as he and his mother took in the Perisphere and the Trylon, towering motion machines straight out of science fiction, and entered a vast hall to see General Motors' Vision of 1960. Alan did a quick calculation to see if he would be alive in 1960, seemingly so far off in the future, and decided he would probably make it.

Rose's enthusiasm was catching as she and her son got their first glimpse of a television set, a small box hardly bigger than a radio that actually transmitted pictures on a screen. It would take another decade or so before television became available to the public. Entire neighborhoods descended on the first family on the block that could afford one to watch distorted images of Arthur Godfrey and Milton Berle on a screen about as big as a medium-sized clock. The mathematician in Alan was particularly impressed by a device so sensitive it measured the thickness of a hair, by his first look inside the cockpit of a real airplane, by the chilling sight of a gas mask, and by elaborate displays of mighty Railroads on Parade.

Many who went to the fair said afterward that it changed their lives forever. It gave them a good perspective on man's nature as a dreamer, a builder, a planner of the future. Alan was no different. His memories of everything he saw there made him aware of the full dimensions of the human spirit and its great potential.

As Hitler's troops invaded Poland and the movie *Gone With the Wind* captivated audiences across the country, Alan began to prepare for the next phase of his educational development, the transition from junior high to high school. After elementary school, he had attended the Edward W. Stitt Junior High School at 164th Street and Edgecombe Avenue, which he was able to complete in two years instead of the usual three. As a gangly pubescent boy, he had his share of crushes on several classmates, particularly a pretty dark-haired girl named Corinne, but none of them amounted to much.

"Alan never talked much," said another one of his junior high friends, named Leila. "He was a very quiet person."

But Alan had an independent streak even then, which he demonstrated by refusing to be bar mitzvahed—an unthinkable act of resistance for the grandson of a prominent neighborhood rabbi. "I believe it was our grandparents who turned him off," said Wesley Halpert. "Our grandfather was rigid and authoritarian, and our grandmother was overemotional and prone to hysteria. Alan hid in his room a lot, listening to music with the door shut to tune them out. Fortunately for him, Rose defended Alan against her father in particular, who was beside himself with rage."

Going to a private high school was out of the question, leaving him with one alternative: the public high school up the street. The public elementary schools in New York City funnel their graduates into a regional high school, as they do in most urban areas around the country.

High school was the end of the educational line for the great majority of kids in those days. When the United States entered World War II following the "sneak attack" on Pearl Harbor in 1941, almost all teenagers turning eighteen years of age were drafted into the armed forces or volunteered for action in the army, navy, or marine corps. Aside from the demands of war, college was not on the horizon for most working-class gentiles; the boys tended to follow their fathers into one of the blue-collar trades, and the girls generally shopped around for an early marriage. Jewish parents, in contrast, were more interested in taking advantage of opportunities that were denied Jews in Europe, and pressured their offspring to go on to college. Rose was no exception in that regard. She allowed Alan his freedom to do what he wanted, but she made it clear that she expected him to earn a college degree after high school.

George Washington High School came into existence as the Washington Heights Annex of the Morris High School on February 2, 1917, on a plot of land above Dyckman Street that had been donated to the city by Isaac Dyckman. The city had built a three-story building on the site that had remained mostly empty since its construction in 1858. Over time, the farms and rambling woods in the neighborhood gave way to residential housing, paved streets, and a growing population of culturally diverse immigrants. John Whalen, chairman of the High School Committee of the Board of Education and a graduate of the Inwood School, a local private school, selected the building on the old Dyckman land for an annex to serve the needs of Washington Heights. The three-story structure was sorely in need of renovation by that time, but it was solidly built and large enough for its purpose.

The Board of Education assembled a faculty of twelve under the direction of Frank M. Wheat, and admitted its first class of 350 students in 1917. The high school was truly unique, as three bungalows, heated by stoves, joined the original building to accommodate the area's rapidly expanding teenage population. The name was officially changed to George Washington High School three years later when the school was re-designated an independent regional high school. George Washington High had already become cramped for space within a few years of its birth, so the city added several more bungalows in 1923. A year later, George Washington High opened

15

its own annex in a block of stores on Dyckman Street, a second annex a few months later at P.S. 189 on Fort George Hill, and a third annex in 1924 at P.S. 98 opposite Isham Park. By then the faculty had soared to more than one hundred teachers, and the student body had metastasized nearly tenfold to three thousand over seven years. The city was exploding, as was Washington Heights right along with it.

By 1939, the old building and bungalows had been torn down and replaced by a more imposing structure further south on Audubon Avenue. Architect Philo B. Ruggles drew his inspiration from the Colonial era, in keeping with the school's historical link to George Washington, and also from the Greek and Roman periods. The final design contained elements of the White House, Independence Hall, and New York's City Hall. The four-story building was huge for its day, with a total frontage of 367 feet. The portico was tall and classic, supported by six Ionic columns. Huge urns and eagles surmounted the windowed pediment, cornice, and balustrade. An octagonal tower atop the building contained an observation room in the shape of a lantern.

Thirteen-year-old Alan Greenspan took his place alongside a large contingent of predominantly Jewish kids from the neighborhood, most of them serious about their studies. On their first day of school, they assembled in an auditorium large enough to seat fifteen hundred students. The school principal addressed the incoming student body from a high stage fitted out with a booming pipe organ. George Washington High had already established a reputation as one of the better high schools in the city, where students who applied themselves could get a grounding in the creative and performing arts, including music, journalism, and public speaking, as well as in history, math, science, and the technical trades.

Alan was torn among his loves for math, music, and sports, and he was determined to find time to pursue all three interests. Like most city kids, he liked to play handball, and George Washington High had two handball courts on the premises. There was a concert hall with the capacity to seat 154 students and parents, an equally large theater, and a huge library with a twenty-foot-high ceiling and towering stacks of books. The school had its own bank; a printing room for the school newspaper and magazine, *The Cherry Tree* and *The Hatchet*; and various laboratories equipped with facilities for the study of chemistry, physics, biology, botany, and zoology. There were six art studios on the premises, and a cafeteria large enough to accommodate more than a thousand students at a sitting. Along with the Bronx High School of Science, Brooklyn Tech, and Stuyvesant, George Washington High School was one of the top-tier high schools New York had to offer at the time, and blended the best architectural elements of the Greek, Roman, and U.S. Colonial eras.

Alan didn't know it then, but a fairly large percentage of his fellow students would go on to achieve fame of their own. Henry Kissinger, three years older, was two grades ahead of Alan. Singer and actor Harry Belafonte, a year younger, was there around the same time, and comedian George Carlin followed a decade later. As Dominicans and other Hispanics migrated to Washington Heights in future generations, the school graduated many athletes good enough to play professional baseball, among them Rod Carew. Even in Alan Greenspan's day, George Washington High School fielded pretty good baseball, football, and basketball teams.

Alan wanted to do it all. He was primarily interested in math, but he also tried out unsuccessfully for the baseball team and joined the school band as a clarinet and tenor saxophone player. Uncharacteristically for a city kid, at a time when the sport was largely the preserve of rich kids from the affluent suburbs, he learned to play tennis, thanks to Rose, who thought it would be good for his future advancement. Not too many teenagers raised in the concrete jungles of New York and other cities during the period could tell one end of a tennis racquet from the other.

The biggest disappointment during Alan's teenage years was his social life—or lack of one. There were dozens of girls he wanted to date, but none who seemed to be interested in him. Not even his reputation as a lead musician in the school band carried much currency with the female sex. The girls whom Alan liked most chased the jocks on the various sports teams, and he was too shy to approach the ones who might have responded favorably to him. He was reasonably tall for his age and skinny, gangly in appearance, all arms, legs, and sharp angles, like most teenage boys who attain their full height quickly before the rest of the body has a chance to catch up. His main diversion outside of school was going to see his beloved Dodgers play baseball at Ebbetts Field, practicing on his clarinet and sax, and doing large sums in his head. The Halperts traded in their Rockaway bungalow for a summer house in New Jersey, and Alan spent his weekends there trying to pick up girls with Wesley.

"As I recall, during the summers he always had more dates than me, which wasn't saying much," said Wesley, "and he tended to fall for girls who looked a bit like Rose."

The war overseas was a hot topic of conversation for Alan and his classmates, particularly when the true dimensions of Hitler's campaign to exterminate the Jews emerged. They listened to war news on radios crackling with static, followed the stories about Allied victories and defeats in the newspapers, and watched footage of battle scenes in movie theaters, which served as a precursor to televised news a few years later.

Most teenage boys have other things on their minds than politics and economics, but Alan was an exception. Thanks to his father and his views about President Roosevelt, Alan had taken an early interest in politics and was particularly intrigued by the relationship between the individual citizen and the government. Even at age sixteen he was something of a gut-level individualist, but after reading his father's book several times with its endorsement of an American welfare state, Alan was more confused than ever. He dismissed his own doubts with a shrug and embraced the notion that nothing is really provable. It was easy for an intelligent person to argue both sides of an issue with equal fervor and conviction, he thought, and the best debater always won out in the end.

He was particularly troubled when *Time* magazine chose Joseph Stalin as 1942's "Man of the Year" in its January 4, 1943, issue. Stories about the atrocities committed under Stalin, the millions murdered and millions more sent off to die slow deaths in slave labor camps, had already started to surface, although the full extent of his evil did not come out until after his death. However, intellectuals of the period were largely sympathetic to the so-called "noble experiment" of Communism and were loath to equate the horrors of Stalin with those perpetrated by Adolf Hitler. Even realists in the West regarded Stalin as the butcher we could trust and contain, who had no designs on territorial expansion, while Hitler was intent on spreading his poison across the entire globe.

Time justified its award with the statement, "Had German legions swept past steel-stubborn Stalingrad and liquidated Russia's power of attack, Hitler would have been not only man of the year, but he would have been undisputed master of Europe, looking for other continents to conquer." The magazine went on to say that "Stalin had the magnificent will to resist of the Russian people— who had as much claim to glory as the British people had when they withstood the blitz of 1940." Young Alan Greenspan had devoured every particle of information he could find about the war, and was convinced that Stalin could have done no better than fight Hitler to a stalemate without the help of the Allies. Eisenhower's occupation of North Africa was primarily responsible for diverting Hitler's attention and resources away from Russia, against the advice of his own generals, until it was too late to mount the most effective attack possible against Stalin's forces.

Alan believed the magazine's award was a serious blunder. Even then he saw Hitler and Stalin as different sides of the same coin, two destructive forces that had to be resisted by everyone who valued liberty. He argued endlessly with his schoolmates, many of whose opinions were shaped by their parents, about the twin totalitarian evils, as he saw them. He was particularly upset by *Time's* assertion that "there are reports in high circles that [Stalin] wants no new territories except at points needed to make Russia impregnable against invasion." Alan had heard stories from his grandfather about the persecution of the Jews under the Communists, about the confiscation of their businesses and their private and personal property, about the destruction of their synagogues and communities. He tried to convince his contemporaries that Stalin was as bloodthirsty as Hitler, but he could not make them understand.

Alan felt he was right, but how could he be absolutely sure? His father pulled him in one direction with his love for Roosevelt and his conduct of the war, and his grandfather pulled him in the opposite direction with his stern lectures on the Communists and their sympathizers in America—Roosevelt included. Alan was obviously highly intelligent, but he was frustrated with his own inability to reason things through. "How can one be absolutely sure of anything?" he often asked himself. "How can one prove what one assumes to be true?" In his teens he had already developed the habit of depersonalizing his thoughts, discussing what *one* thinks or does rather than what *I* think or do.

"How can one be absolutely sure of any situation?" he wondered. "And even if one is sure, how can one prove he is right?"

CHAPTER 3

Graduation from high school left Alan in a state of confusion about the direction his life should take. He was a whiz at math and statistics and intrigued about the possibility of pursuing a career in economics. On the other hand, he loved the sax and clarinet and believed he had enough talent for a professional career in music. He had taken lessons from one of the leading music teachers in the city at the time, Bill Sheiner, who held classes at the Bronx Musical Mart on 174th Street and Southern Boulevard. Stan Getz was one of Sheiner's protégés, among many others, who had gone on to become a jazz legend. Alan and Getz became good friends and spent many hours practicing together.

What would it be for Alan, economics or music? How could one be absolutely sure which way to turn? With Rose's encouragement, Alan decided on the musical route. Rose told him that if he was really serious about music, he should apply to The Juilliard School in Manhattan, which offered the best musical education in the country.

There was little question that Juilliard was the premier institution of its kind in 1943. Frank Damrosch founded the school as the

Institute of Musical Art in 1905, a time when the notion of a serious American music academy was considered fanciful at best. Damrosch was the godson of Franz Liszt and director of music education for New York City's public schools. Therefore, his idea of opening an American conservatory that would rival the best in Europe, with its centuries-old tradition of classical music, carried the day. Damrosch believed that gifted Americans should be able to get the training they needed in the United States, not have to travel abroad for it.

With the backing of financier James Loeb, Damrosch opened his school in the old, stolid Lenox Mansion on the corner of Fifth Avenue and 12th Street, just above Greenwich Village. The building was a three-story fortress that was built to withstand the blasts of time. He handpicked his faculty from the best the profession had to offer, mostly transplanted Europeans. Woodrow Wilson, then president of Princeton University, addressed the initial group of five hundred students at the opening ceremonies. The school was an immediate success and continued to grow in size and popularity.

In 1919, textile merchant Augustus Juilliard left $20 million for the advancement of music in America. This was the largest bequest ever made by a single individual and led to the creation of the Juilliard Graduate School in 1924. Juilliard was established in the Vanderbilt Guesthouse at 49 East 52nd Street in midtown Manhattan. Students who demonstrated sufficient talent could pursue their dreams without worrying about money: thanks to Juilliard's benevolence, all students accepted for admission received scholarships.

In 1926, the year of Alan's birth, Juilliard and the Institute of Musical Art initiated a gradual merger of their facilities that would evolve slowly over the next couple of decades. By 1931, Juilliard was bursting at the seams, and the school's trustees looked around for a new facility to house all the musical protégés on scholarships. Juilliard moved north to Claremont Avenue, just west of Broadway near Columbia University. By then it was known as the Juilliard School even though its name was not officially changed to The Juilliard School of Music until 1946.

For Alan, Juilliard was a fifteen-minute subway ride some seventy blocks south from his grandparents' apartment in Washington Heights. The Broadway line let him off at West 116th Street, just a block away from the school. He started attending classes in the summer of 1943 after his graduation from George Washington High School. Rose was delighted that he had qualified for a scholarship and took pride in the knowledge that her son had inherited his talent from her.

Once again Alan had a big decision to make. He loved both Baroque music and be-bop and had to choose between the two for a course of study. Alan, who was accepted as a clarinet major, opted on the side of modernity, primarily because he liked the smoky nightclub atmosphere and knew several musicians who played with the swing bands that were popular during the war. This was the age of Harry James, the Dorsey brothers, and Glen Miller and his Band of Renown, as well as be-bop groups that drew big crowds to the jazz joints down in the Village.

The mecca for jazz was the Village Vanguard on Seventh Avenue in the heart of Greenwich Village. Whenever he could scrounge up the price of admission, Alan took the subway downtown with a couple of classmates in the evenings after class. The Village Vanguard was the "Mecca of Hip," the "Carnegie Hall of Jazz," and Alan experienced an overpowering feeling of exhilaration each time he stepped down into the small, triangular, smoke-filled basement room that had been America's premier *boîte de nuit* for the past eight years. Numbers were exciting for Alan, but jazz transported him to a new dimension. It was the magic that stirred his soul.

Max Gordon, a bohemian Village intellectual with an ear for spotting musical talent, opened the doors to the dimly lighted, wedge-shaped netherworld in 1935. His dream was to create a dive where not only musicians but also struggling poets and actors could hop on stage and do their thing in front of an appreciative audience. He sponsored poetry readings hosted by a transcendental, pre-Beatnik Theosophist named Eli Siegel, who quickly became the patron saint of a counterculture group of self-labeled "Aesthetic Realists." Most of the early poets were little more than crackpots,

23

but there was talent among them. Max Bodenheim, Harry Kemp, and Joe Gould read their poems there almost nightly between jazz sets. Adolph Green, Betty Comden, and Judy Holliday got their starts at the Vanguard in 1938 with a skit that served as a prototype for *Saturday Night Live*.

It was jazz, however, that put the Village Vanguard on the map and drew aspiring musicians like Alan to the club. Alan was spellbound by the sounds of Leadbelly, Josh White, and aspiring folk and calypso singer Harry Belafonte, who was still a senior at George Washington High School in Alan's neighborhood. Everything about the Vanguard looked too small. The ceiling was low, clearing Alan's head by only a few inches when he stood up. The tables were slightly larger than checkerboards. He felt hemmed in on three sides by the darkness and the encroaching walls. How could this place be the apogee of the most exciting musical movement America had ever produced?

Alan had a good ear and understood immediately that the diminutive size and unusual shape of the joint lent the Vanguard an acoustical quality that was destined to become the standard for what intimate jazz should sound like. Alan and his fellow students enjoyed the palpable feeling of being at the epicenter of hipness, an affirmation that jazz equaled romance and they were right there at the heartbeat of an emerging, uniquely American art form. The Vanguard was open seven nights a week, with the featured group playing Tuesday through Sunday, and Monday set aside for new talent.

The musicians made up their own rules as they went along, experimenting with different riffs and different approaches from night to night. Alan was bewitched by the improvisations of Thelonious Monk and Kenny Clark on piano and drums. Some nights they were joined by Dizzy Gillespie, Charlie Parker, and Charlie Christian, who came down to play be-bop after a night's work in midtown Manhattan with Benny Goodman's big band. Monk, Gillespie, and Parker were in the process of establishing their reputation as the trinity of be-bop, the medium's preeminent innovators, and Alan was there at the beginning, absorbing the experimentation through osmosis as it were, wondering how he could put his own imprint on this riveting new sound. What could he do to make a difference?

Week after week new groups took the stage and pushed the music into altogether new dimensions. Art Blakey left the Fletcher Henderson band to hook up with the velvety smooth voice of Billy Eckstine. Other nights he joined forces with Parker, Monk, Christian, Gillespie, and Miles Davis, who was adding a different twist to be-bop that the critics were calling "hard bop." On any given night, you never knew who might drop into the Village Vanguard to sit in for a set or two with the featured act.

When Alan was not down in the Vanguard listening to be-bop, he could most likely be found in Birdland further uptown on Broadway, absorbing the music of Count Basie and a hypnotic new singer he was breaking in named Joe Williams. Alan may have looked out of place in this dark bohemian setting, something like a rabbi playing hooky from schul with his black and white attire and thick glasses. Spiritually, however, he had found his home away from home listening to these mesmerizing new sounds in the smoky underground darkness.

While music was at the center of Alan's life in 1943, his *raison d'être*, he had not abandoned his other major loves: math and economics. He continued to read the financial newspapers and was particularly challenged by the mathematical problems posed by mathematician David Hilbert. Hilbert had delivered perhaps the most influential speech ever given before the International Congress of Mathematicians in 1900. In it, he had outlined twenty-three major problems that should be studied during the twentieth century. Some were extremely broad, encompassing such arcane topics as the axiomatization of physics, but others were more mundane.

Alan was especially taken with Hilbert's philosophy of mathematics, which Alan believed was equally applicable to the world of music. When Hilbert died in 1943, Alan Greenspan may have been one of the only people working outside the disciplines of math and physics who took note of his passing. He felt a deep sense of loss, as though an elderly family member had permanently departed. He tried to discuss Hilbert's importance with his classmates at Juilliard, but no one could relate to what he was talking about.

Another icon of Alan's youth was nearing his end as the calendar turned the page to 1944. The health of Herbert Greenspan's hero, President Franklin D. Roosevelt, was deteriorating noticeably, despite the President's attempts to hide his frailty from the public. Alan had always had mixed feelings about FDR and was as torn between his conflicting emotions as he was between his loves for math and music. It was clear that the presidency was Roosevelt's life, and he was extremely reluctant to give it up.

Placed on a four-hour-a-day schedule by his doctors, Roosevelt began to spend less and less time on the country's business. He took long vacations in South Carolina, Warm Springs, the Catoctin Mountains of West Virginia, and Hyde Park, and also made lengthy journeys to Hawaii and Canada. He temporarily abandoned his policy toward Germany in favor of the so-called Morgenthau Plan, which proposed turning Germany's industrial heartland into a farm belt.

As the presidential campaign heated up in 1944, Roosevelt nearly destroyed Truman's chances as his running mate by wavering in the days just before the Democratic convention. FDR also negotiated an agreement with Churchill on sharing postwar development of nuclear weapons, but failed to let the State Department in on it. In perhaps his most duplicitous decision of all, FDR concealed the true nature of his illness and accepted a fourth term for the presidency knowing full well that he would never be able to survive it.

Alan was evolving into something of a political animal himself at this time, and he grew increasingly troubled by his father's devotion to economic and political policies that he himself had difficulty agreeing with. He began to question whether the creation of an American welfare state was really the best way to deal with the Depression. The more he studied the causes of the collapse, the more he believed that the curtailment of free trade (the Smoot-Hawley act imposed onerous tariffs on imports, triggering similar legislation in other countries) was at the root of the problem. And Alan continued to entertain doubts about the U.S. alliance with

Soviet Russia, regarding Communism as nothing less than the evil twin of Nazism. These concepts were still gestating within him. He had yet to fully formulate a comprehensive philosophy of his own, and he invariably took refuge in the notion that nothing can be known with certainty.

How can one be sure of anything?

Most of the time, at age eighteen, Alan Greenspan tilted toward the classical liberal, or libertarian, end of the political-economic spectrum, with its emphasis on individual freedom and self-reliance. Yet he had doubts about full-blown laissez-faire as well and studied the ideas of John Maynard Keynes, who believed in the use of tax and fiscal policy to influence the direction of the economy. Alan regarded himself as something of a Keynesian, although he distrusted labels of any sort. Logically, he could make a good case for free markets and laissez-faire. However, history taught him that free markets did not work perfectly at all times under all conditions. Did that give government the right to exercise power and interfere with the rhythm of the market, or was Adam Smith's "invisible hand" sufficient to correct the excesses of bull and bear cycles?

Alan could argue either side of the issue with equal fervor and conviction. Philosophically, he believed in individual liberty and limited government. The real world, however, constantly presented nasty surprises. What was the proper role of government in human affairs? How could any collective entity be sure its actions were proper and would not make a dire situation even worse?

Between classes, between practice sessions with his music, between trips to the Village Vanguard, Alan could be found voraciously reading books on economic theory. He devoured the entire lineup of classical liberal utilitarians such as Adam Smith, Jeremy Bentham, and others who had made the practical case for capitalism but failed to address the broad moral issues. He kept his foot in both worlds but was determined to make his mark as a musician. His soul ached for it. He had the talent to make it big, and he wasn't going to let anything get in the way of his dream.

CHAPTER 4

"I think I hired Alan in the early forties," said Leonard Garment, who was the manager of the Henry Jerome swing band in 1944, before leaving the group to become Richard Nixon's law partner. When the band was in New York, it played at Child's Paramount Restaurant below the Paramount Theater in Times Square.

"It was a huge plaster and marble bomb shelter of a place," said Garment, who played in the horn section. "Alan played the saxophone and the clarinet and did the books for the band. There were fourteen of us earning fifty-five dollars a week."

Henry Jerome and His Orchestra, as the group was officially known, was popular during the time Alan played with it, and he was with the band when it toured the country as World War II raged overseas. Competition within the orchestra was intense as a bevy of talented musicians elbowed one another for preeminence. Alan shared the spotlight with Johnny Mandel on trumpet and Gerry Mulligan on baritone sax, both of whom were destined to achieve superstar status of their own just a few years later. Mandel had started his own musical career at five, by his own reckoning, when his family discovered he had perfect pitch.

"My mother's brother wrote show tunes, he was very talented," said Mandel. "His name was George Rilling, George Roy professionally, and he worked mostly in England, although my family was all originally from Chicago."

Mandel began on the piano but found his true calling on the trumpet and, later, the trombone. "I never wanted to play an instrument that you plucked or struck," he recalled. "I wanted to play an instrument you could kiss."

Mandel started writing big band arrangements when he was only twelve, and by the time he was sixteen he was working in bands in Catskill Mountain resorts during summer vacations. "What drew me into music was the magic and the alchemy of combining this instrument with that instrument and getting these big clusters of different sounds. I was really interested in painting with the orchestra."

If Mandel was a big leaguer in the music game when he was still only a teenager, Alan recognized immediately that he was a minor league talent by comparison. After graduating from high school, Mandel worked with legendary violinist Joe Venuti, which led to other gigs for him. "This was during World War II, and all the good musicians were overseas, so I got into a lot of professional bands that I couldn't have gotten into otherwise. A lot of the people I came up with—Stan Getz, Al Cohn, Zoot Sims, Max Roach, Bud Powell, Dizzy Gillespie, Miles Davis—were out on the road when they were sixteen and seventeen years old. You can't learn this, you have to live it. We were very lucky because we had bands to play in, and it didn't matter how far you had to travel on bad roads every night, or how little sleep you got for weeks on end. That's how you learn."

Alan realized that his fellow musicians, roughly the same age as he was, were already seasoned veterans. He had a steep learning curve to surmount at age eighteen if he was going to be as good as people like Mercer and Mulligan.

"I was a *total* be-bopper," Mandel said. When he joined forces with Henry Jerome and His Orchestra, he shared the stage with Alan Greenspan and Leonard Garment. "Lenny was pretty good.

Alan is a wonderful guy, but probably the best thing he did in that band was the payroll."

"Alan was good," said Henry Jerome, who had attended George Washington High School a decade before Alan did, "although he wasn't primarily a jazz player. I hired him because he was an excellent musician, but I didn't use him as an improviser."

"The Henry Jerome band was assembled with a slightly lunatic orchestra at the instigation of myself and a couple of other younger players," said Garment. "Alan was part of that orchestra. He took care of the payroll, and he also helped me babysit the musicians and get them back on the bandstand. We dragged them back from Walgreen's drugstore, where they were indulging in less than altogether legitimate pharmaceuticals."

Walgreen's was located above Child's Restaurant, and the musicians used to go up there between sets to smoke grass in the telephone booths. The owner complained to Garment, and when he didn't have time to retrieve the potheads himself, he asked Alan to "get some of those guys down here. Tell them it's time to play and to stop smoking."

Alan saw the handwriting on the wall fairly quickly. Between sets, when he wasn't toting up the payroll and straightening out the books, he continued to read his economic tomes and stayed abreast of developments affecting the country. He checked out books on economics from public libraries on the road and found that he couldn't get enough of them.

"I found the stuff fascinating," Alan said.

It dawned on him that trying to keep up with the likes of Mercer, Mulligan, and some of the others in the band may have been a bit more than he was capable of. There are good, competent performers in every field of activity, and then there are the naturals—those who are so superior they comprise a different dimension of ability.

Alan could either continue in music as a competent clarinetist and saxophonist who did a great job of preparing the group's tax returns, or else he could move on to something he could really excel at. His biggest failing as a musician, as Henry Jerome noted, was that he could "read the sheets," but he couldn't improvise—that is, he could follow the themes on the page in front of him, but he was completely unable to add his own personality to the music. This was a fatal shortcoming for any musician aspiring to greatness. Alan knew after six months of touring with the band that he was a workmanlike musician who was really born to be an economist.

"I was a pretty good amateur musician, but I was average as a professional," he said. "And I was aware of that because you learn pretty quickly how good some professional musicians are. I realized it's innate. You either have it or you don't. So I decided that if that was as far as I could go, I was in the wrong profession."

The band traveled throughout most of the eastern part of the country in buses, trains, and borrowed cars and trucks. While on the road with the band one day, Alan checked a book out of the library that would change his life forever. *The Fountainhead* was a long novel written by a Russian-born writer named Ayn Rand. Alan had seen some reviews of the book when it was first published in May 1943, and he had made a mental note to read it at the time. The reviews had been mostly negative, he recalled, but the story line and theme of the novel piqued his interest. The months rolled by and Alan forgot about the book until, early in 1944, a friend told him he ought to check it out.

"I think you'd really enjoy it," Alan remembered him saying.

The Fountainhead was the romantic saga of an idealistic architect, Howard Roark, who refused to compromise on his plans for a housing project. Roark decides to blow up the building when bureaucrats alter his design in a way that destroys its integrity. The characters and plot, however, were only manifestations of Rand's underlying theme, which was a ringing defense of individual rights and, more broadly, laissez-faire capitalism. More important, as far as Alan was concerned, was that Rand's novel provided the first moral defense of the free-market system that Alan had seen.

Alan was familiar with all the utilitarian arguments—capitalism provides the greatest amount of good for the greatest number of people; capitalism is more efficient than state planning; and so on—but the pantheon of economic literature was sadly lacking in ethical discussions of capitalism. Until now, advocates of free enterprise had conceded the moral high ground to the left: communists, socialists, and welfare statists.

Alan was hooked from the beginning. Rand mesmerized him to such an extent that he had to be pulled back onto the bandstand, away from his book, when the break between sets was over. Leonard Garment kidded him about it and suggested that perhaps Alan was in the wrong line of work. Garment didn't know it yet, but he was preaching to the converted. Alan had already made up his mind to change professions. When the group returned to New York City, Alan went down to New York University in Greenwich Village and filled out an application to attend the School of Commerce in the fall.

Budding economist Alan Greenspan started classes at NYU in September 1944. NYU was a longer commute from Washington Heights than Juilliard was, adding an extra twenty minutes each way to his daily subway ride. He had saved a good part of his salary from his tour with the band, but he was still tight on money, as he had been all his life so far.

He economized by living at home and by dressing professionally but plainly. He owned one dark blue suit that was developing a brighter shine than he had on his shoes, a few white shirts, and a couple of nondescript blue ties. Food was merely a source of fuel for him, a necessity of life to keep the engine going. More often than not, he brought a sandwich from home and returned home for dinner in the evening when he didn't have evening classes. He drank little if any alcohol, and since his social life was virtually nonexistent, there was little outlay of cash for the pleasures of life. People who knew him at NYU say that he excelled academically but rarely made the grade socially. He was shy, quiet, and highly intellectual, and asking girls out for a date was never easy for him.

"He would constantly be ogling the coeds at New York University," said Robert Kavesh, a close friend and fellow student at NYU. "And it was tough because you had all these males descending from the armed forces, and very few women. And so we would wonder about whether we would ever be able to get a date. I don't think Alan ever burned up Washington Heights as a social butterfly. He worked hard at his economics, and when we got together on Mondays we would hum tunes from Mozart and Beethoven and try to stump each other."

Kavesh continued at NYU after Alan graduated, and ended up as the Marcus Nadler Professor of Economics and Finance at the Stern School of Business, the modern incarnation of the old School of Commerce.

"Alan had a long commute from Washington Heights and I had a long commute from Rockaway," said Kavesh. "We were there at NYU most of the day and sometimes stayed until late at night. We founded a classical music society there. Alan was a year ahead of me, so he was the first president and I succeeded him."

The end of World War II on September 2, 1945, with the formal surrender of Japan aboard the U.S. battleship *Missouri* in Tokyo Harbor, resulted in hordes of veterans descending on college campuses throughout the nation, their tuition largely funded by the G.I. Bill. Pandemonium reigned in the streets of New York City, and other towns and cities across the country, as thousands of young men in sailor suits and khakis danced in the streets with eager girls welcoming them back from the war. Alan took it all in enviously as he sat on a bench in Washington Square, eating his brown-bag lunch between classes. He had registered for the draft as the law required when he turned eighteen in March 1944, but a spot on his lung (a mistake, as it turned out) got him classified as 4F and he was never called to serve. He wondered what kind of a figure he would have cut in navy white or army tan, but he couldn't picture himself in uniform. Still, it was fun to speculate on whether a uniform would have put him in better standing with the opposite sex.

At the time, NYU was a bastion of economic conservatism. Austrian economist Ludwig von Mises taught there, as did Walter Spahr, the director of the National Committee to Return to the Gold Standard, and Alan was heavily influenced by both of them.

In the classroom, Alan found his true calling. He enjoyed his prerequisite economics classes, which prepared him for more advanced courses in statistics and econometrics. He was more influenced than he would admit later by the ideas of John Maynard Keynes, the most imposing economist of the time, who argued that free markets, left unattended, are essentially unreliable. Keynes believed that pessimism breeds more pessimism in a stagnating economy. When their personal fortunes take a turn for the worse, people respond by buying fewer goods and services, which leads to a further slump in an accelerating downward spiral. This state of affairs eventually brings on a recession or, worse, the kind of depression that millions, including Alan's family, suffered through when he was a boy. According to Keynes, the only way to reverse the trend is for the government to prime the pump, as it were, through increased spending. Keynes said it didn't really matter what the money was spent on; the government should pay men to dig holes and fill them back up if necessary. The main point was that people should get a paycheck, which would renew their confidence and get them to start buying things again.

Alan had a difficult time resolving his confidence in the efficacy of free markets on the one hand with the appeal of Keynesian interventionism on the other. Free markets would sooner or later correct whatever economic excesses had taken place, and the economy would regain its footing. The marketplace was best left alone. However, were there any circumstances under which the government should intervene in economic affairs, or was such intervention destined to make things worse than they already were?

How could one be sure?

"We would have long discussions," said Kavesh, "about what could be done and what couldn't be done to make sure that we moved ahead without inflation and with jobs for as many people as possible. Alan at that time was very much interested in the role of government in economic life, and I daresay, as I think back, he knew more economics than anyone I've ever met."

According to Kavesh, Alan gave careful consideration to Keynes's views in 1945. "He discovered this book called *The Economics of John Maynard Keynes* by Dudley P. Dillard, which he devoured like he did many other texts."

"Take a look at this and tell me what you think of it," Alan said to Kavesh.

"I agreed with Keynes, since I was a Roosevelt Democrat and still am. Alan never jumped up and down and said that he believed in strong government intervention in the economy, but he never complained at the time that government was too big and ought to be cut back. Keynes influenced everybody in those days, and Alan was pretty much of the opinion that extraordinary circumstances called for government action. We took a course together on business cycles given by a conservative economist who advocated a laissez-faire approach, and neither one of us was impressed with it"

Keynes was unique in that he was the only economist to have an economic system named after him. His personal life defied the usual stereotypes, since he was flamboyant to a fault. He went to Eton as a scholar, then moved on to King's College at Cambridge to study the classics as well as math. His first job was in the civil service, but he left when he found it far too tame for his exotic tastes, which ran to young boys and skinny ballerinas, one of whom he married briefly. He joined the Bloomsbury Group, which was made up of the leading intellectual lights of the day, including Virginia Woolf, E. M. Forster, and Bertrand Russell. Keynes speculated wildly but successfully as bursar of King's College, another anomaly for traditionally conservative economists, and turned the college's relatively modest account into a small fortune.

The core of his economic philosophy held that government should intervene in the economy to manage the level of demand. If the private sector was not prepared to spend freely to boost demand in the face of a slump, according to Keynes, then it was incumbent on government to step in and run a budget deficit if necessary. Then, when the economy took an upturn and the private sector was once again reinvesting in growth, government could trim its spending and pay down the debts it had accumulated during the downturn.

There was little question that Alan was impressed by Keynes's line of thinking, but he harbored his doubts as well. Alan was a student of history, and he knew that once government got into the habit of spending more money than it had, the trend was virtually

35

irreversible. Therein lay the flaw in Keynes's philosophy. Public spending on various projects creates new special-interest groups that inevitably regard government largesse as a natural right. Attempts to cut back later, even when the economy picks up, are usually greeted by an outcry from those who are loath to give up their newfound subsidies. Perhaps Keynes's ideas might be viable, Alan reasoned, if government had the discipline to cut expenditures and pay off debt when a new up cycle got under way. But where was the guarantee that would happen, and when had it been done in the past? Expanding government feeds on itself and keeps on growing until a catastrophe, such as runaway inflation, forces it to scale back.

It was not all work and no play for Alan at NYU. "He was an avid baseball fan and went to see the Dodgers play every chance he had," said Kavesh. "We also played tennis together once or twice a week. Alan was a lefty and developed a pretty tricky slice. All in all, it was a reasonably happy time for him. He had found his true calling, we had our music society, and then there were the sports. If he had any qualms about giving up the band, I never heard him express them. The biggest problem was the lack of females in our lives, but he's a very smart guy and he eventually figured out a way to attract them."

CHAPTER 5

In his defense of short-term solutions to major economic problems, John Maynard Keynes had famously said, "In the long run we are all dead." The long run for Keynes ended on April 21, 1946, six weeks after Alan's twentieth birthday. He was sixty-three when he died, and obituaries in the *New York Times* and other major newspapers were filled with details about Keynes's odd passions outside the field of economics. Alan was shocked by some of the revelations, since he was culturally conservative long before he adopted his conservative political and economic views.

The economic environment improved considerably in the years following World War II. According to Alan, the U.S. economy combined "the ultimate in both technology and productivity in virtually all fields of economic endeavor. The quintessential model of industrial power . . . was the array of vast, smoke-encased integrated steel mills in the Pittsburgh district and on the shores of Lake Michigan." Output was measured in the production of "big physical things. Virtually unimaginable . . . was the extent to which concepts and ideas would substitute for physical resources and human brawn in the production of goods and services." This was an age in which radios were still being powered by vacuum tubes, whereas a generation later, transistors would "deliver far higher quality with a mere fraction of the bulk." Fiber optics would replace "huge tonnages of copper wire, and advances in architectural and engineering design" would make possible "the construction of buildings with much greater floor space but significantly less physical material than the buildings erected just after World War II."

At age twenty, Alan lived in a world characterized largely by physical brawn. Human beings relied on brawn to move equipment from here to there, and steel mills depended on brawn to relocate coiled sheets from one part of a plant to another. Alan delighted in calculating how many units of brawn and energy were required to accomplish any given task. He came alive when faced with columns and rows of numbers, just as his soul had been stirred by the sequential beats of musical sounds emanating from instruments powered by wind. Math and music, numbers and beats—they were all of a piece, identical twins spawned by a magical and mysterious universe.

Alan put on some brawn of his own as he evolved from his teenage years into young manhood. His lanky body filled out, his chest expanded, and his shoulders grew wider from hours spent on the tennis and basketball courts, and from the pure physical pleasure of walking, walking, walking everywhere, uptown, midtown, downtown, and through the narrow, twisting cobblestone streets of Greenwich Village. He would never be strikingly handsome, but he was far more appealing to women as a well-built twenty-year-old than he was as a gawky teenager. He was always neatly, if not elegantly, dressed. His long dark hair was swept back off his face, revealing an intelligent forehead. His large, thick, dark-rimmed eyeglasses gave him the myopic look of a compulsive bookworm. A generation later he would have been called a bit nerdy, but women a couple of years older than he were beginning to find some manly appeal in his shy, unassuming demeanor.

Alan learned more than statistics and economics at NYU. As he studied relentlessly for his baccalaureate, he discovered that brainpower, when not wielded like a club, could be as seductive as a well-chiseled face and rippling muscles—and it made a longer-lasting impression on women. His tastes ran to slim, highly intelligent women who were interested in music, politics, and ideas in general. If they could tolerate a baseball game or two, so much the better. By the time Alan was in his senior year, he had begun to date fairly regularly, which put further demands on his already strained budget. The primary woman in his life, his mother Rose, beamed proudly at his graduation ceremony in May 1948 when Alan graduated summa cum laude with a bachelor's degree in economics.

Alan decided to go on for his master's degree at the same institution, but his cash reserves were all but depleted. It didn't take someone with Alan's gift for numbers to figure out that if he were going to continue his education and eat at the same time, he needed a job.

"The year was 1948," said Alan, "and I brought my newly minted degree to what was then called the National Industrial Conference Board to work with my old professor, then chief economist at the Conference Board, Martin Gainsbrugh. Although I had other offers of employment at higher pay, it was an easy call to go to work at a research operation with, perhaps, one of the best business-oriented libraries in the country. Much of my professional development I trace back to those early days rummaging through a remarkable array of documents, books, statistics—all available at a young economist's fingertips. What I learned during my five years at the Board proved invaluable in later life."

Alan held down a full-time job by day and a full schedule of courses at night, which left him little time for the socializing he had recently begun to enjoy. Still, his ambition came first, and he was clear about the priorities he needed to set to pursue a successful career in his chosen profession.

The Conference Board was founded as the National Industrial Conference Board in 1916, and by 1948 it had long been widely recognized as the premier economic research institution in the world. It linked various global corporations through a cornucopia of economic data that was not available in one place from any other source, and held conferences where executives could network with their peers, expand their business knowledge, and find joint solutions to common problems.

The catalysts for its creation were declining public confidence in business along with rising militancy in the labor unions, which swept the country during a business down cycle prior to America's entry into World War I. The Board's founders designed the organization to be more than just another trade association, of which there was hardly any shortage. They set it up as a not-for-profit, nonpartisan compiler of information that would be helpful in forecasting economic trends and solving problems facing industry. Over the years it developed several measures of the country's economic health, including the Consumer Confidence Index and the Indexes of Leading, Lagging, and Coincident Indicators. It steered clear of lobbying Congress about pending legislation, and released its findings to the media for public consumption. In the decades since its birth, the Conference Board has been able to maintain its reputation as an objective processor of myriad facts and figures.

What would have been a deadly dull job for others was a mystical experience for Alan. He felt as though he were attuned to the mysteries of the universe as he delved through reams of arcane data that, somewhere along the pipeline, got translated into a rational sequence of clues about the state of the nation's economic health. In came tidbits of information about the spending habits of households across the country, and out went measures of consumer optimism or pessimism that could affect stock prices six months down the road. Alan and his colleagues used these countless streams of information to forecast how many automobiles, homes, and major appliances their fellow countrymen were likely to buy in the months ahead, and how these purchases would affect overall economic growth.

In came more figures on employment, unemployment, personal income, industrial production, interest rates, money supply, and other areas, and out went predictions about turning points in the economy and whether the cycle would be up or down. In came data on the number of jobs advertised in the classified sections of regional newspapers, and out went forecasts of relative growth in the East, West, North, and South. If Alan's job didn't already exist, he would have had to create it for himself. He found himself in hermit heaven at the Conference Board, a world sealed off in one sense from earthly tribulations, yet plugged into mundane concerns in ways too complicated for most people to fathom.

"I have a mental picture of Alan poring over his data runs to evaluate whatever information came in, then flipping the pages looking up more numbers," said economist Pierre A. Rinfret. Pierre was a friend of Alan's at NYU and worked with him two decades later when they were both advisers to Richard Nixon. "Alan was a frequent speaker for the National Industrial Conference Board, as well as for the financial magazine, *The Institutional Investor*." Those who knew Alan at the time claimed that he found his deepest happiness in numbers. Economic statistics resonated in his mind like the motif of a symphony, and constituted fathomable truths where others saw only chaos.

Alan continued his grueling schedule for the next two years. Every day he commuted by subway from his grandparents' home in Washington Heights to his job at the Conference Board in midtown Manhattan. After work he took the subway down to Greenwich Village, where he grabbed a quick bite before attending his evening classes at NYU. Late at night he returned to Washington Heights, again by subway, only to repeat the same routine the following day. The long hours Alan spent riding the rails beneath the noisy city streets provided him with ample time to study for his master's degree. He had an hour in the morning and an hour on the ride home at night, plus an additional couple of hours while he was eating lunch and dinner. Only a young man driven by a nagging ambition to accomplish something extraordinary would have endured the hard work without much in the way of a social life. Not even the deafening clatter of pounding metal wheels thundering over iron rails diverted him from his books.

□ □ □

Alan received his master's in economics in 1950, an impressive achievement for someone holding down a demanding full-time job at the same time. He decided to switch to Columbia to work on his doctorate under Arthur Burns, who had already established his reputation as one of the leading economists in the country. Pierre Rinfret also switched from NYU and joined Alan at Columbia.

"I studied under Dr. Arthur Burns when I attended Columbia University in 1951 after I came back from my Fulbright scholarship in France," said Rinfret. "At that time he was undoubtedly the foremost business-cycle theorist in the world. He was president of the then prestigious National Bureau of Economic Research, which had done incredibly valuable work on business cycles for the previous thirty-five years. He was well known and went on to become chairman of the Council of Economic Advisors for President Eisenhower, Economic Advisor to Richard Nixon, chairman of the Federal Reserve Board, and finally ambassador to Germany. He was the mentor to Alan, who followed a similar path."

Alan and Arthur Burns, twenty-two years older than Alan, established an instantaneous rapport. Burns had already authored two books, *Production Trends in the United States Since 1870* and, more recently, *Measuring Business Cycles* (with W. C. Mitchell), which had found a wider following. Nobel Prize–winning economist Milton Friedman had studied under Burns at Rutgers University more than a decade earlier and had high praise for him as a professor of economics.

"Arthur Burns shaped my understanding of economic research, introduced me to the highest scientific standards, and became a guiding influence on my subsequent career," said Friedman. A couple of decades afterward, however, Friedman gave him a failing grade following Burns's unsuccessful tenure as chairman of the Federal Reserve.

Burns regarded himself as a proponent of free markets who eschewed government meddling in the economy, but he later attempted to steer a middle path between laissez-faire and Keynesian interventionism—not always successfully. German chancellor

Helmut Schmidt called Burns "the Pope of Economics," while union leader George Meany dubbed him a "national disaster."

In 1950, however, Burns was rigorous in his defense of unhampered capitalism, which made an enormous impression on Alan, who was still evolving philosophically. Burns had a visceral disdain for unscientific information, and he believed public policy should be approached from an analytical perspective. Other economists at the time relied to a great degree on so-called "anecdotal information"—perceptions gleaned from observing what was going on in the country—when making decisions about public policy. They liked to talk about the "tone and feel of the markets." Burns thought that any policy not grounded in solid, scientific evidence was akin to witchcraft. He constantly discussed the need for high standards of analysis, and poured his resources into the development of the "red book" (later called the beige book) as a macroeconomic forecasting model.

"When Burns talked about reliance on cold, hard numbers to Alan, he was preaching to the choir," said Robert Kavesh, who remained at NYU. "In my view, sometimes your heart has to overrule your head."

Alan became more than just another one of Arthur Burns's students; they became lifelong friends despite the gap of a generation in their ages. They grew so close over the years that when Burns moved to Washington, D.C. in 1970 to take over as Fed chairman from William McChesney Martin, Alan, who had established a successful consulting business by then, offered to hold the first mortgage on his house. As a young Ph.D. candidate in 1950, Alan idolized the older man and sought to emulate him in every way, even once briefly taking up the pipe, which Burns smoked incessantly. According to Rinfret, Burns liked to blow smoke at everybody, including members of the Congress when he was testifying before them on monetary policy as Fed chairman.

PART TWO

The Randian

CHAPTER 6

Ph.D. candidate Alan Greenspan continued to shoulder a full course load at Columbia while working at the National Industrial Conference Board, and the pressure finally began to wear him down. He dropped out of graduate school after a year to focus on his job. His attire was still nondescript and he had no major vices or indulgences, except a love for gleaming new automobiles and a largely unrequited passion for certain members of the opposite sex. In the summer of 1951, Alan treated himself to his first major extravagance: a new Chevrolet Styleline Deluxe four-door sedan.

The car was one of the hot new models of the year, and Alan reveled in its solid Maryland Black exterior with strips of glistening chrome trim running horizontally along each side and around the windows, and a chrome awning jutting over the windshield to deflect the sun. The interior was gray cloth with a matching gray leather dashboard. Alan committed the specifications to memory and would tell anyone who was interested that the vehicle's weight was 3,150 pounds, the wheelbase measured 115 inches, the maximum brake HP was 92, the SAE HP rating was 29.4, and the six-cylinder engine boasted a 216.5 c.i. The car was Chevrolet's top-selling model in 1951, with 380,270 sold out of a total Chevy production run of 1,250,803 cars. Alan particularly liked the automobile's three-speed manual transmission, which gave him the sensation of feeling the road in his fingertips as he zipped up the Henry Hudson Parkway on Sunday drives into Westchester County.

After buying his dream Chevy for $1,680 plus freight charges and taxes, Alan liberated himself further by moving out of his grandparents' home in Washington Heights and taking his own apartment in Forest Hills, Queens, across the East River from his job in Manhattan. His salary at the Conference Board was $4,000 a year, a comfortable amount of money for a young professional hoping to make his mark on the world. At age twenty-five, he had finally snipped the family umbilical cord, although he remained extremely close to his mother Rose and visited her at home almost every weekend.

Shortly after moving from Washington Heights to the top floor of a Queens duplex, Alan fell in love for the first time in his life. He was anything but well-rounded and sociable, and until this time his infrequent relationships with women had been mostly transient in nature. As much as Alan enjoyed the company of intelligent females, he was still maladroit and ill at ease in their presence. They had all lost interest in him after the first or second date. Then, suddenly, he was introduced to a young artist named Joan Mitchell on a blind date, and the whole world changed for him.

Joan was as shy and insecure as Alan, and most important of all, she took a real interest in him and his work. She was twenty-three years old at the time and struggling to find her own way as a creative artist. She was extremely attractive, highly intelligent, petite, bubbly, and blonde. She and Alan, who was fairly tall, dark, and somber as he observed the world through thick, dark-rimmed eyeglasses, presented an amusing study in physical contrasts whenever they went out together. Despite their differences in temperament and interests, however, they somehow managed to find common ground.

"Intelligent as he was even then," Joan said many years later, "he didn't immediately ask me out. He talked to me for about half an hour so that I would want to go out with him—which I did want to do, and that's how I met him. I chose a concert at Carnegie Hall. It was actually a Menotti concert, so the music was the first thing that brought us together."

Alan had learned painfully that he couldn't compete with other men on the basis of his looks and personality, that, rather, it was his intellect that set him apart. He would have to use his superior intelligence properly if he were going to be successful with the type of women he admired. The sheer force of his brainpower clearly struck a chord with Joan—in the beginning at least.

New York City was brimming with intellectual excitement in the early 1950s, and Alan and Joan spent much of their time together socializing in Greenwich Village with artists, writers, and musicians. He took her to his old hangout, the Village Vanguard, to listen to jazz. Neither one of them drank much alcohol, but they liked the atmosphere of the White Horse Tavern on Hudson Street, the famous watering hole of Welsh poet Dylan Thomas, who drank himself into an early grave. There was Figaro's Café on Bleecker Street, where they went for espresso and Italian pastries, and Arturo's on Houston Street, which boasted a jazz combo on weekends and served some of New York City's finest pizza.

One writer with whom Joan Mitchell was particularly taken was the Russian-born novelist and iconoclast Ayn Rand, whose controversial novel *The Fountainhead* Alan had read when he was playing with the Henry Jerome orchestra. Alan was startled to discover that Joan knew Rand personally and attended her Saturday night soirées with a tight-knit group of true believers.

By 1951, Rand had become more than just a mere novelist and political philosopher. On the strength of *The Fountainhead* and some earlier works, she assumed the role of the infallible leader of a growing political and philosophical cult that was already taking on the aspects of a secular religion. By championing selfishness, or "rational self-interest," as man's highest standard of morality, Rand claimed to have repudiated three thousand years of Judeo-Christian ethics and their emphasis on putting the needs of others before one's own. However, Jesuit philosopher James Sadowsky maintained that much of Rand's rational individualism was in harmony with the teachings of scholastic theologian Thomas Aquinas. In his epic work *Summa Theologica*, Aquinas stated that our primary responsibility is to self and family, and only secondarily are we obligated to relieve the suffering of others with our *superflua*, or discretionary wealth. But Rand chose to believe that she had created a new morality that stood Christianity on its head.

Rand's soirées got started largely at the instigation of Nathaniel Blumenthal, who later changed his name to Nathaniel Branden (an acronym of Ben Rand, or son of Rand). As a young, confused Canadian college student living in the United States, Branden had been swept away by Rand's torrid defense of unregulated capitalism and her denunciation of altruism as the epitome of evil. He wrote a fan letter to Rand, who was then living in Los Angeles, telling her that her philosophy of life was the answer to the questions he had been asking himself all his life. Rand had crystallized everything he intuitively believed into a rational, comprehensive, irrefutable system of logic.

Rand eventually invited Branden to visit her in Los Angeles, and she was immediately mesmerized by the rapier clarity of his mind— as well as by his tall, blond, strikingly handsome good looks. The forty-five-year-old Rand had precise ideas about what her heroes should look like, and Branden, who was twenty-five years younger than she, personified for her the image of the heroic individualist who let nothing stand in the way of achieving his goals. Rand and Branden forged a tight intellectual bond (which would eventually become much more intimate than that, with the consent of their respective mates). When Rand moved to New York City shortly afterward, she asked Branden and his future wife, Barbara Weidman, to visit her and her husband, Frank O'Connor, in their apartment in the Murray Hill section of Manhattan, at 36 East 36th Street.

Nathaniel and Barbara soon became fixtures in the Rand household. They spent countless evenings with Rand and her laconic husband, Frank, who bore a strong resemblance to actor Gary Cooper but had no other distinguishing characteristics. Rand expounded on her philosophy of life, politics, and economics, while her two ardent disciples sat figuratively and sometimes literally at her feet soaking up this outpouring of wisdom. Gradually, with Rand's blessing, Nathaniel and Barbara invited some friends to join them at Rand's apartment to meet the great woman in person. All of them had read *The Fountainhead* and declared themselves to be in fundamental agreement with the ideas set forth in the novel. Within a short period, Rand and Nathaniel formalized the gatherings by holding them weekly, on Saturday nights.

The circle grew from week to week, with Rand, and more frequently Nathaniel Branden, discussing the virtues of laissez-faire capitalism and the evils of altruism. Rand insisted on complete adherence to her views, and Nathaniel—to whom Rand assigned the role of Grand Inquisitor to ensure philosophical purity within her growing circle of admirers—was responsible for weeding out "deviationists" and excommunicating them from the group if they failed to accept the full party line. Ironically, no one at the time saw the inconsistency of a band of self-avowed individualists being asked to leave their independent thought processes at the door whenever they entered their idol's living room. As the Saturday night soirées became a constant in their lives, Rand and her acolytes jokingly referred to themselves as "the Collective," since the word embodied everything that was at variance with Ayn's credo, which she started to call Objectivism.

One of those invited to join the weekly gatherings was Barbara Branden's friend from Canada, Joan Mitchell. Joan and Barbara had grown up together in Winnipeg and remained close friends ever since. "Joan was part of the Collective for many years," Branden recalled.

Nathaniel Branden was not overly impressed with his wife's friend initially, but he tolerated Joan because Barbara was close to her. "[Joan] was a childhood friend of Barbara's, an aspiring painter and a student of art history," said Branden. "She was twenty-three years old, blonde, petite, nervously arrogant one moment, shyly reticent the next. Joan struck me as affected, mannered, overly concerned with her image. I wanted to like her not only because Barbara did but because she seemed enthusiastic about *The Fountainhead* and wanted to learn about Ayn's philosophy. I wanted to expand our circle and wanted to believe she was a promising convert."

Branden did soften his comments somewhat on further reflection, but not all that much. "I did grow fonder of Joan as she embraced our philosophy, but I remained concerned with the fact that a woman could simultaneously see herself as an advocate of reason, individualism, and independence, and yet have a morbid preoccupation with favorably impressing other people."

Barbara Branden's views of Joan, naturally, differed radically from her husband's. "Joan has been my closest friend since we were about twelve years old—with a few unhappy years of noncommunication after the fiasco of Nathaniel's and my break with Ayn Rand. I love and admire her deeply. She is an extremely gifted artist. Was she 'eager to please' as an artist in the days of the Collective? Not in the sense in which that expression is commonly used. She, like all of us in the Collective, was concerned to do work that was consistent with Objectivist esthetic principles; for an artist, that meant painting skyscrapers, etc., etc., which was not her first-hand choice of subject matter. Joan—like myself—found her own artistic voice in the years following our breaks with Ayn Rand."

Shortly after Alan and Joan began to date regularly, she invited him to one of Rand's Saturday night socials. Alan entered Rand's living room shyly, observing the stark décor the novelist favored and the majestic view of the Manhattan skyline that embodied, for Rand, the living genius of mankind on earth. More than anything, the Manhattan skyscraper was Rand's shrine, the altar at which she worshiped. Rand's apartment was cloudy with cigarette smoke, since the great woman was a heavy smoker and viewed with suspicion anyone who disdained tobacco. This was not Rand's only quirk. She abhorred facial hair and regarded anyone with a beard or mustache as inherently immoral, as though he harbored a dark secret he was trying to hide. The clean-shaven Alan Greenspan passed muster on that score, but his dour demeanor and reticence did not make a good first impression on her. According to Nathaniel Branden, Rand took a strong dislike to Alan initially.

"He was tall and solidly built," said Branden of Alan, "with black hair, dark horn-rim glasses, and a propensity for dark, funereal suits. He was somberness incarnate, looking chronically weary, resigned, and unhappy. He was twenty-six years old. Barbara, Ayn, Frank, and I once encountered him, with Joan, coming out of an elevator. 'He looks like an undertaker,' Ayn commented."

Alan presented problems for Rand philosophically as well as sartorially. As Nathaniel explained Alan's thinking at the time, "He was not a free enterpriser but a Keynesian, at least in some respects, believing that the economy could be managed constructively by governmental manipulation of the money supply. He was also a logical positivist, which meant that he was adamant about his inability to know anything with certainty. He announced that logic was empty, the senses were untrustworthy, and that degrees of probability are all that is possible. 'I *think* I exist,' he stated, 'but I can't be certain. In fact, I can't be certain that anything exists.'"

Branden, after discussing his impression of Alan's economic perspective with him directly, altered his views to some extent. "Greenspan in the early years was a Keynesian only in the sense that most economists were in those days," he said later. Barbara Branden had a kinder take on Alan from the beginning. "I have the greatest respect and admiration for him—and I dearly love his sense of humor," she said. "No, he never was a Keynesian, although, before he met Ayn, there were Keynesian elements in his view of economics."

From his own perspective, Alan had reservations of his own about the weekly gatherings at Rand's apartment. Naturally shy to begin with, he said little during the early meetings and mostly observed as first Rand, then Nathaniel Branden elaborated on the topic for the evening in excruciating detail. Alan plunged headlong into the heady world of second-handers (those who lived primarily off the achievements of others); whim-worshipers (those who believed that faith took precedence over reason as a source of knowledge); muscle mystics (those who ruled others by either physical or spiritual intimidation); floating concepts (the application of conceptual knowledge to something other than its source); America's persecuted minority (the U.S. industrialist); A is A (a thing is what it is); altruism (collectivism); collectivism (altruism); the Cult of Moral Grayness (the notion that there are degrees of good and evil); heroes and heroines (individualists); rational human beings (those who accepted Rand's ideas in full); and thugs, hoodlums, savages, weaklings, and degenerates (those who questioned Rand's ideas).

Alan was not convinced that Rand had all the answers to the questions he had been asking all his life. How can one be sure of anything? However, he admired her tremendously, as he did all brilliant and accomplished women. Alan attended the meetings with Joan sporadically at first. Then, early in 1952, after less than a year of courtship, he and Joan announced to Rand's gathering of eager young disciples that they had fallen in love and were going to be married. The entire Collective trooped up to the Pierre Hotel for the wedding ceremony to see Alan and Joan commit themselves to a lifetime of bliss. The wedding was small. Besides the Collective, only close family members of the bride and groom were in attendance—including Alan's father, Herbert, who continued to enter his life sporadically and disappear just as quickly. Occasionally he dropped in on Alan at work, more often than not to borrow some money. Joan found him cold and distant, and was happy to see him leave early, as soon as the ceremony concluded.

CHAPTER 7

Joan gave up her Manhattan apartment, and she and Alan set up housekeeping in Alan's Forest Hills apartment. However, their marriage was a disaster from the start. Once they legalized their relationship, they discovered that they had little in common outside their interest in Objectivism. Alan was an economic animal first and foremost; Joan had little interest in the subject except as it fit into Rand's overall philosophy.

"Saturday mornings he loved to wake up and study numbers," said Joan. "He loved being in control of all these numbers."

Joan had different ideas about how she wanted to live. She wanted to go exploring, but he preferred to spend the day playing tennis or golf, which he had recently taken up. Joan wanted to move to Manhattan, but Alan wanted to stay in Queens.

Alan could not tell a Picasso from a Rembrandt and found his attention wandering as he trudged dutifully through museums; Joan was frantically seeking her own vision as an artist and trying to do her own work instead of the work Rand expected her to do. Alan consumed food indifferently as a necessity of life; Joan regarded cooking as an art form and reveled in the subtle tastes and aromas of a gourmet feast. Finally—astonishingly to Joan—Alan declined to attend Rand's gatherings regularly and said there were elements of her credo he could not accept.

It did not take long for both of them to realize they had made a serious mistake by making a lifelong commitment so quickly. Alan was only twenty-five when they first met, and his hormones were raging. He had allowed his biological needs to cloud his judgment for the first time in his life. Joan was twenty-three and insecure. She was nowhere near ready to devote her life to a single partner while she was still groping after her own identity. In addition, she needed the support of her family-away-from-home in Rand's inner circle, dysfunctional as it was in many ways, and Alan was tugging her away from her lifeline.

"We had different ideas about how we intended to live," Joan said. "But I do want to say that there was never a harsh word between us."

"There is no mystery whatsoever about Joan's and Alan's marriage," said Barbara Branden. "They fell in love, married, and soon found that they were very different people who should not attempt to build a life together. They have remained good friends, and are so to this day."

"Alan had never had intimate relationships," said Nathaniel Branden, who later established a successful practice as a psychotherapist. "My feeling is that the personal realm probably invoked anxiety in him."

Alan and Joan discussed their problems at great length and mutually agreed to end their marriage. At the end of 1952, after ten months together that sometimes seemed like ten years living with a stranger, they went down to City Hall and had their union annulled.

"My marriage to Alan Greenspan was brief," said Joan. "We did and do maintain friendly relations. Regarding the annulment, we chose that method of ending the marriage because the grounds for divorce in New York State at the time would have required that we pretend there was a question of infidelity. There wasn't any such question and to say there was would have been distasteful to both of us."

No sooner had the annulment come through, than Alan's interest in Objectivism suddenly intensified. He, too, needed a family away from home, a support group to help him resolve some burning philosophical issues. When he failed to find a solid home base in his marriage, he turned back to the only group available to him. Early in 1953, he began to attend Rand's Saturday night soirées regularly, even though his ex-wife was a constant presence in the novelist's living room. At first, Joan was startled to see him there.

"I was not really able to interest him in Objectivism," she said. Suddenly "he started showing up at Ayn's, a strange turn of events."

There was no rancor between them, so Alan and Joan quickly grew accustomed to seeing each other once a week in Rand's apartment, even after Joan started dating the man to whom she would be married for the next four decades, Nathaniel Branden's cousin Allen Blumenthal. Their ability to maintain cordial relations despite their close proximity to each other is a reflection of their emotional detachment at the time, in a world dominated by cold, hard, Randian logic.

Ayn continued to have problems with Alan's philosophical underpinnings, but—uncharacteristically for her—she was willing to cut him some slack for a couple of reasons. First, he was obviously highly intelligent and willing to become a convert to Objectivism, if only someone could convince him. And second, he was an economist who worked in the world of business, which for Rand was the highest calling possible. All of Rand's other disciples were academics and intellectuals, people like her who operated in a theoretical universe and had no opportunity to apply Objectivist principles to real-life situations. She had long been disappointed in the failure of America's businessmen to rally around her cause. Now, for the first time, she had a living, breathing businessman in her midst, one who took a serious interest in her ideas.

"He impressed me as very intelligent, brilliant, and unhappy," Rand said of Alan. "He was groping for a frame of reference. He had no fundamental view of life."

With some misgivings, Rand's number-one apostle, Nathaniel Branden, took on the job of bringing Alan around. "I sensed the presence of a romantic buried deep in his psyche," Branden said. "I was convinced that he had a first-class brain, his philosophy notwithstanding. He seemed almost ashamed of that hidden side that drew me to him. He confessed once that when he responded emotionally to something heroic in a movie, he reproached himself for his impracticality."

Rand remained hopeful, but she harbored reservations that someone like Alan could be brought around. "How can you stand talking to him?" she asked Branden in her thick Russian accent.

"I'm going to bring him around intellectually," Branden replied confidently.

"Never! A logical positivist and a Keynesian?" said Rand. She would clearly have had higher hopes if Alan were a leper. "I'm not even certain it's moral to deal with him at all."

Branden kept at it for months, engaging Alan in lengthy discussions about the meaning of existence, the source of knowledge, the code of ethical behavior, the place of government in a truly free society, the efficacy of the marketplace, and other topics of vital interest to Rand and her acolytes. From time to time Rand checked on Alan's progress with Branden.

"How's the undertaker? Has he decided he exists yet?"

Nathaniel answered that Alan recognized only that "probability is all that is possible." Barbara Branden acknowledged her husband's role in Alan's philosophical development. According to her, he engaged Alan in some "very long and involved philosophical, metaphysical, epistemological, political, economic, and moral conversations" that eventually had a profound effect.

Earning his stripes as an Objectivist was not the most important item on Alan's agenda. His career came first and foremost, and at the end of 1953 he decided that he had gone about as far as he could go at the Conference Board. His work there had brought him to the attention of a successful Wall Street bond trader named William Townsend, and Townsend approached Alan with the idea of the two of them setting up shop together.

William Townsend was already sixty-five years old, more than old enough to assume the role of the father Alan had always wanted. Townsend and a partner named Dana Skinner had started a bond consulting business in 1929, the year of the crash that had crushed Herbert Greenspan and hordes of other stock market investors. Townsend and Skinner eschewed stocks and migrated instead to the fixed-income side of the business, managing to launch a successful career as bond traders in the midst of the Great Depression. By 1953 they had established an extensive network of contacts throughout the financial world and grown extremely wealthy in the process. The National Industrial Conference Board supplied them with much of the data they needed, and Townsend, who was look-ing for a new partner after Skinner passed away, was especially impressed with the quality of Alan's work there.

Even though Alan was champing at the bit to move on after five years at the Conference Board, he was reluctant at first to give up the security of a steady paycheck for the financial uncertainty of going into business for himself. He expressed his doubts about the risky venture to Nathaniel Branden.

"I don't know if I have the talent to make this thing work," Alan said.

"You're still in your twenties," Branden encouraged him. "How can you be worried about security now? Take the leap. You can do it. And if it doesn't work out, for any reason—so what? You'll do something else. Anyway, this is nonsense, because you're not going to fail—not with your brains. You just don't appreciate how good you are."

Alan decided to step out of character for once and take the risk. He looked up to Townsend as a professional trader who toiled in the same pastures where Alan's father had labored before his fall. The two men complemented each other perfectly. Townsend had the hands-on experience of nearly two decades of successful combat in the trenches of Wall Street, and Alan had the theoretical knowl-edge that Townsend needed to expand his operation. Instead of sharing the spoils with others, Townsend and Greenspan together could sell their combined expertise to Wall Street professionals and keep the profits for themselves. So armed, early in 1954 the two of them hung out their shingle as Townsend-Greenspan & Co., a consulting firm offering economic forecasts to large corporations and financial institutions. Their company consisted of three others besides the two principals—two researchers and a secretary—all of them crowded into tiny quarters at 52 Wall Street.

Once again, Alan found a mentor he could look up to, as he had first in Arthur Burns and more recently in Ayn Rand. As president of Townsend-Greenspan, with Alan claiming the title of vice president, Townsend instructed Alan in the things he had learned during twenty-five years in the bond market. Particularly helpful to Alan were Townsend's lessons on how inflation depresses bond prices, driving interest rates skyward, since bond prices and interest rates move in opposite directions. If investors expect inflation to climb, they demand higher rates of return from their investments in fixed-income securities. This was invaluable information for a young economist who would eventually make his mark as, first, an adviser to several presidents and, afterward, as chairman of the Federal Reserve, primarily responsible for holding inflation and, subsequently, long-term interest rates in check.

The two men built their consulting firm into an extremely successful forecasting shop, providing economic and interest rate forecasts to major banks, brokerage firms, and other financial institutions. Alan's share of the profits came to about six thousand dollars a year—decent money at the time. With Townsend's help, Alan acquired a detailed knowledge of how things worked as he crunched numbers from every sector of the economy. He found it exhilarating to study the minutest details about inventories, shipments of goods, delivery of services, manufacturing lead times, scrap metal prices, overtime in the labor force, and hundreds of other industry data. Somehow, he pulled it all together into a comprehensive whole that made sense only to him. He felt that he had his finger on the pulse of corporate America in a way that enabled him to forecast where economic growth, inflation, and the level of interest rates were likely to be six or nine months down the road.

Alan quickly learned that forecasting was anything but an infallible science. Townsend-Greenspan bought a state-of-the-art computer that filled an entire room. "We thought we could really pin down the business cycle" with that tool, Alan said, but the economy never cooperated the way you wanted it to. "It moved. It wigged when it should have wagged." He would learn over time that even with the advent of more sophisticated hardware and econometric models, "our ability to forecast has not improved. The crazy economy out there just doesn't stand still long enough for us to get a fix on it. It continually changes too rapidly for us to apply our techniques."

Despite the shortcomings of his profession, the services provided by Townsend-Greenspan were in great demand. Their clients demanded the best "guesstimates" available about the direction of the economy, and they were willing to pay dearly for them, accurate or not. With many clients, Alan and his partner gave their forecasts away in return for hefty brokerage commissions derived from trades directed to them.

"Some of their primary clients were Wall Street brokerage firms," said economist Pierre Rinfret. "They would give his research away to their clients in return for the clients giving them brokerage business. Greenspan would give speeches quite frequently for the Wall Street houses whenever they held financial forums."

William Townsend and Alan Greenspan enjoyed both an excellent professional and social relationship, and their partnership flourished from the beginning. Within a year, they hired an expanding force of promising business school graduates eager to learn the forecasting business and moved the company to larger offices on Wall Street. Alan was particularly partial to bright, attractive young women anxious to gain a foothold in the business world—a distinct minority in 1954—and he added many of them to Townsend-Greenspan's payroll as the firm began to prosper. He was beginning to learn that women genuinely liked him for his finer qualities: his mind, his natural shyness, his modesty, and his interest in bringing them along professionally at a time when typing skills were considered to be a woman's major asset in the business world.

A woman named Bess Kaplan joined the firm shortly after it opened and stayed until Alan shut it down three decades later. Alan took a particular interest in Kathryn Eickoff, an attractive blonde who graduated with a degree in economics from the University of Missouri. After hiring her, Alan dated her regularly for several years—something that could have gotten him in trouble for sexual harassment had it occurred in the politically correct 1990s.

"He was a very attractive person," Eickhoff said, "very confident and sure of himself. That sureness may not have been there earlier in his life. He certainly could carry on a fascinating conversation. My relationship with Alan was serious. But I don't think we ever got anywhere close to talking about marriage."

She stayed on with the firm long after they stopped dating, and Alan later hired her husband, Jim Smith, a fellow Objectivist who owned a jazz club in Greenwich Village.

Eickhoff was not the only employee whom Alan went out with. He carried on a lengthy romance with a stunning redhead named Marjorie Scheffler, who supported her children from an earlier marriage. As deprived of romance as he had been all his life, Alan made up for it during his tenure at Townsend-Greenspan.

"Alan projected a great deal of strength at this time," said Barbara Branden. "I don't mean physically, but morally and intellectually. He liked women, and women generally respond to that."

Finally, Alan had found a way to mix business with pleasure in a way he had only dreamed about before.

CHAPTER 8

"Townsend-Greenspan was pretty successful," said Robert Kavesh, Alan's old friend and classmate at NYU. "Alan had a small staff and quite a few attractive women working there. I remember Lucille Wu, Kathy Taylor, Karen Kornbluh, and many others."

Kornbluh designed economic forecasting models and advised the firm's clients on economic growth projections. She would later go on to become an adviser to Fortune 500 companies on international marketing and manufacturing strategies, and then senior economic adviser to Senator John Kerry, a Democrat from Massachusetts. Eventually she was appointed Senior Policy Adviser for the Federal Communications Commission and Assistant Bureau Chief of the International Bureau.

There were many others who achieved prominence on their own after cutting their forecasting teeth at Townsend-Greenspan. Perhaps chief among them was economist John B. Taylor, who had a rule of economics—the "Taylor Rule"—named after him. Taylor began his career at Townsend-Greenspan and was co-editor for international economics at the *American Economic Review*. He moved abroad as a research economist at the Bank of Japan and the Bank of Finland, then returned to the United States as a consultant to the Federal Reserve Board and the Congressional Budget Office. In later life, he was appointed senior staff economist on the President's Council of Economic Advisers during the Ford administration, and a decade and a half later he became a member of George Bush's Council of Economic Advisers.

Taylor authored several books and more than a hundred research papers on economics, specializing on the causes of business cycles, inflation, and monetary policy. His books on introductory economics and macroeconomics became bestsellers and were selected as required texts at universities throughout the world. In 1996 he served as senior economic policy adviser to Bob Dole during the latter's unsuccessful presidential campaign. Like his mentor Alan Greenspan, Taylor also worked for Democratic administrations—in Taylor's case, a brief stint with President Jimmy Carter in 1977 and a longer one under Gray Davis, governor of California.

Taylor credited Greenspan with his early development as an economist, but in a classic case of the student informing the instructor, Taylor would influence Greenspan's policies as Fed chairman more than three decades later. Taylor postulated the theory, which became codified in economic history as the Taylor Rule, that short-term interest rates should be raised in lockstep with the level of inflation. Forget the money supply, the relative strength of the dollar, and the latest consumer confidence readings that Alan and his cohorts had calculated at the Conference Board. Replace them instead with Taylor's simple rule: If inflation is one percentage point above the Fed's goal, short-term rates should be lifted 1.5 percentage points to keep inflation from accelerating. Conversely, if the economy's total output is one percentage point below full capacity during a recession, short-term rates should be lowered by half a percentage point. That's all that economists, and Federal Reserve chairmen, needed to know about keeping the economy on track with steady growth and low inflation, according to Taylor.

Alan and his fellow economists were appalled at first by the

Taylor Rule and never thought seriously about applying it to their own work. Many economic forecasters and central banks, including the U.S. Federal Reserve, are not happy about the idea that their deliberations can be distilled into a simple formula. "A central bank cannot be bound by a simple policy rule," said Otmar Issing of the European Central Bank. Alan dismissed Taylor, whom he admired for other reasons, with the statement that the Taylor Rule embodies "a forecast that the future will be like the past," which is rarely the case. Put into practice, the Taylor Rule would eliminate the need for econometric models such as those used by Alan, and would have driven Townsend-Greenspan into early bankruptcy.

Taylor, however, refused to back off during hours of heated debate with Alan. Taylor intended his rule to instruct Alan and others about what they *should* be doing; it turned out that the rule also described what they *actually* did. Decades later, when the economic history of the final decades of the twentieth century was written, Taylor would enjoy the last word. A graph of where a key short-term rate, the federal funds rate, would have been had the Federal Reserve followed the Taylor Rule showed it to be almost exactly where it actually was before and during Alan Greenspan's tenure at the helm of the Federal Reserve. Alan has always maintained that his digestion of thousands upon thousands of arcane economic numbers drove his forecasts and policy recommendations—which, of course, was a lot better for business. However, he behaved as though he were following Taylor's simple rule to the letter.

"It's amazing that such a simple rule with only two explanatory factors fits the data so very well," said Leonardo Liederman, the top researcher for the Bank of Israel.

But Alan refused to be convinced. "He preferred to devour all his numbers and make a lot of decisions based on cold, hard facts," said Robert Kavesh. "He didn't let his emotions move him."

On a personal level, however, Alan was making significant progress. "He had all those smart, attractive women working for him," said Kavesh, "and he was always a neat but never a classy dresser. His big extravagance was his car. He graduated from the Chevy and started to drive a Cadillac or Buick convertible most of the time. He always had an eye for the ladies and now they started to respond to him."

Kavesh noticed that Alan's entire approach to economics had changed drastically since he met Rand. "He was trying to sell me Ayn Rand's philosophy with no success," said Kavesh. "He had become a total free-market person who believed in pure, unadulterated laissez-faire."

Ayn Rand's circle of admirers continued to grow, and Alan occupied an increasingly important place at her side. Over time he abandoned his Keynesian slant on economics and his logical positivism and slowly, but never completely, accepted Randian Objectivism. Rand began to warm to him, as did many others in her circle.

"Alan became much warmer, more open, more available," said Barbara Branden. "I mean, Alan will never be Mr. Warmth, that's just not his personality and nature. But the dourness, the grimness, the solemnity that he had when we first met him practically disappeared, I think, because he accepted us and knew that all of us including Ayn and Frank accepted him. It was like a family, it really was. And he was part of that family."

However, others who refused to be named continued to have a harsher view of Alan. "It's simply that he is a very cold person," said one prominent member of the Collective. "It's very hard to know what's on his mind. Through those thick Coke-bottle glasses, you can't even tell that he's awake sometimes."

Alan hit his full stride socially shortly after joining Townsend in their consulting venture. "It was incredible how he always had a beautiful woman at his side," said Barbara Branden. "I think it was the attraction of his intellectual power and probably his reserve. You couldn't knock him over by batting your eyelashes at him. He certainly had a profound affect on women."

"He is very clever," his ex-wife Joan concurred. "He knows a lot about a million things, and he has a wonderful sense of humor. Alan is charming and always interesting."

Edith Efron, another Rand disciple who would author a couple of best-selling books after Rand excommunicated her from the group, recalled that Rand warmed noticeably toward Alan. "He was her special pet because he was older and in the business world. She didn't know anyone else very well who was a businessman. I think this was very important to her. She allowed him more intellectual liberty than she did other people."

Rand beamed when Alan finally acknowledged that he existed. "Guess who exists?" Nathaniel Branden asked Rand six months after Alan's annulment from Joan Mitchell.

"What?" said Rand, her dark eyes widening. "You've done it? The undertaker has decided he exists?"

"You'll have to stop calling Alan the undertaker now," said Branden. "He's really an unusual person. I think you're going to like him."

Rand was diligently at work on *Atlas Shrugged* during this period, putting in ten- and twelve-hour days, and sometimes longer, on the sweeping novel that would eventually become an even more controversial bestseller than *The Fountainhead*. *Atlas Shrugged* turned out to be her signature work of fiction, the distillation of her entire philosophy of life into novel form, with each character representing various aspects of her creed. With Rand there were no shades of gray, only black and white. People were either good or evil, heroes or villains, enlightened egoists or immoral altruists who used the physical power of the state, or the spiritual power of religion, to force their political agenda on others.

While Rand worked on the book, she invited various members of the Collective to read her work in progress and discuss it at the Saturday night gatherings. Now that Alan acknowledged that he existed, Rand admitted him into this privileged group that was starting to call itself the inner circle—somewhat akin to Christ's twelve apostles, representing the elite band of believers within a broader, more loosely knit assemblage of mere disciples. According to various members of the inner circle, Alan immediately fell in love with Rand's depiction of businessmen and industry. Rand responded to his appreciation of her new novel by calling him a "sleeping giant" who was starting to come alive.

Still, Alan continued to have difficulty expressing himself in anything but the most disengaged language. "On reading this," Alan said at one of the weekly meetings, "one tends to feel . . . exhilaration. The reader is really inspired here." Occasionally he would let his hair down emotionally and make a personal statement. "Ayn, this is *incredible*," Nathaniel Branden remembered Alan enthusing uncharacteristically. "No one has ever dramatized what industrial achievement actually means as you have. What you've written is a hymn to human intelligence. *This is fantastic*." Such outbursts from Alan were rare, however, and they visibly embarrassed him when they occurred.

Within a year after joining the group, Alan evolved into one of Rand's favorites. Rand appreciated Alan's maturity compared with the youthful idealism of the rest of her disciples. She valued his practicality, his hands-on experience in the world of finance and business. It was important to Rand that Alan admired her portrayal of that world in her fiction. Her other followers existed in a theoretical universe created by Rand, but Alan actually believed that her philosophy had practical value in the real world in which he worked.

One point of contention Rand had with Alan that she discussed with the others but never with him was Alan's friendship with Arthur Burns, who had become the chairman of the Council of Economic Advisers during the Eisenhower administration. Eisenhower was elected president in 1952 and he appointed Burns to the post shortly after his inauguration. Rand despised Eisenhower, whom she regarded as an intellectual lightweight, a man who had difficulty defending the capitalist system in a much-publicized debate with Marshal Zhukov of the Soviet Union. To Rand, Eisenhower embodied all that was wrong with Western morality, based as it was on a Judeo-Christian ethic. He epitomized the type of unprincipled conservative whom Rand loathed when he conceded the moral high ground to Zhukov, a passionate communist, on the grounds that Communism was more "idealistic" than capitalism.

Rand, who had escaped from Russia following the revolution, exploded. "Is that a sickening evasion or isn't it? That abysmal bastard could not answer Zhukov. A representative of the bloodiest dictatorship in history is boasting of his country's moral superiority—and the President of the United States, the greatest, noblest, freest country in the history of the world, does not know what to say. That's the intellectual paralysis produced by altruism. That's why, without a morality of rational self-interest, capitalism can't be defended."

Rand was troubled that Alan could find common ground with Eisenhower's chief economic adviser at the same time that he claimed to be in fundamental agreement with Objectivism. After his first year or so of faithfully attending Rand's Saturday night soirées, Alan's attendance became increasingly sporadic. There were social obligations outside of the Collective that put demands on his time, including affairs in Washington that he attended at Burns's invitation. Rand began to wonder whether "Alan might basically be a social climber." She worried about an opportunistic side to his nature that was only just emerging. Yet Alan always returned after an absence of a week or two, and Rand was always happy to welcome him back into the fold. Only Alan could take such liberties, such philosophical leaves of absence, and get away with it.

Rand allowed him an independence that was denied to the rest of her followers. Many of the others resented his special treatment, but they stood in awe of him as well. In the small Randian cocoon that proscribed the universe in which they lived, Alan was their only link to the real world outside Ayn Rand's living room—outside their own imaginations.

CHAPTER 9

Alan Greenspan's name first appeared in print in the fall of 1957, following the publication of *Atlas Shrugged*. Rand had put the final touches on her novel in March 1957, and it was published on October 10 of the same year to blistering reviews from both ends of the political spectrum. Liberals hated it because of its harsh critique of the welfare state, and conservatives abhorred the novel's denunciation of Christian ethics and defense of atheism. The quirky Rand managed to infuriate just about everyone.

Whittaker Chambers, a reformed communist turned conservative, excoriated the novel in William F. Buckley's *National Review*. He linked Rand with Nietsche, stating that Objectivism, if put into practice, would eventually lead to totalitarianism—the precise opposite of the severely limited government the author advocated. Chambers based his argument on the notion that unlimited individual freedom, divorced from Judeo-Christian moral restraint, would result in a dictatorship of the rich and powerful over the meek.

Rand was enraged, as were her disciples. Alan defended the novel publicly in a short letter that appeared in the *New York Times*

Book Review a few weeks after the publication's own hostile review by Granville Hicks.

> To the Editor:
>
> *Atlas Shrugged* is a celebration of life and happiness. Justice is unrelenting. Creative individuals and undeviating purpose and rationality achieve joy and fulfillment. Parasites who persistently avoid either purpose or reason perish as they should. Mr. Hicks suspiciously wonders "about a person who sustains such a mood through the writing of 1,168 pages and some fourteen years of work." This reader wonders about a person who finds unrelenting justice personally disturbing.
>
> Alan Greenspan, NY

The controversy surrounding *Atlas Shrugged* generated a series of articles about Rand and her growing band of uncompromising capitalists. Lewis Nichols, who wrote a column entitled "In and Out of Books" for the *New York Times*, profiled Rand and her followers who gathered on Saturday evenings in Rand's living room "for discussions of philosophy," and he identified Alan as a Rand devotee who worked as "an economic consultant." Nichols referred to the soirées as a "philosophy class," noting that some dissenters were beginning to regard Objectivism as a new religion with cult-like aspects.

Despite Alan's misgivings about some of Rand's teachings, and his continuing aloofness within the group, he remained fiercely loyal to Rand throughout the furor. On a personal level, he admired her intelligence and accomplishments and regarded her to some extent as a surrogate mother—an alternate matriarch away from home. Alan "was different from the rest of us," said Barbara Branden. And that "was very wise of him. He kept his private life to himself, which the rest of us did not do." Another Rand follower who asked to remain anonymous recalled that Alan "used to come late to everything and leave early. He had his own relationship with [Rand], which was dignified. And he kept somewhat aloof from everybody, which was a smart thing to do," considering the control Rand exerted over her followers later.

Another acolyte said "Alan Greenspan is incredibly terse," as though "everything he sends is a telegram and they're charging by the word. He's deliberately low-keyed and ponderous. On the other hand, he is a musician, so there obviously is a side of him that has passion and emotion, but I would say he's very guarded. He must be a wonderful poker player."

"Alan had no talent for and no interest in small talk," said Barbara Branden. "So if people around him were engaged in small talk they wouldn't get anything from him. I mean that he would simply stand there and have nothing to contribute. But if there was something interesting, then he was very social."

While Alan held himself somewhat apart from Rand's other disciples, he always maintained that he was in "fundamental agreement" with her credo. However, he always allowed himself some room to maneuver. On the subject of economics, for example, Alan labeled himself an "eclectic, free-market forecaster" who "generally agrees with Austrian economics" as developed by Ludwig von Mises, sanctioned by Rand as Objectivism's official economic theorist.

"When I met Ayn Rand," Alan said, "I was a free enterpriser in the Adam Smith sense—impressed with the theoretical structure and efficiency of markets. What she did was demonstrate to my satisfaction that capitalism is not only efficient and practical, but also moral."

There was a good reason for Alan to keep some distance between von Mises's philosophy and his own, since the Austrian economist claimed that economic forecasting was impossible. In other words, von Mises believed that Alan's profession was a sham.

Alan was one of the few early members of Rand's clique who was not excommunicated by the high priestess for independent thinking. Many readers were inspired enough by her books to write her letters that resulted in invitations to join her circle. Economist Murray Rothbard wrote to Rand at the end of 1957, claiming that he was "enchanted" by her views. After attending several Saturday night sessions, it was clear that he would never become one of her favorites. For one thing, he was short, fat, and nearsighted and resembled one of the villains in her novels more than he did one of her tall, square-jawed, clear-eyed heroes. Second, Rothbard's wife, Joey, was a devout Christian who refused to be swayed by Rand's arguments against the existence of a deity. Third, Rothbard was a free-market anarchist who believed in no government at all, as opposed to Rand's insistence on a federal government limited to defense, police-keeping, and judicial functions. Finally, Rothbard was as opinionated about his views as Rand was about hers, a trait that irritated the philosopher/novelist greatly, so she had him declared *persona non grata* at a kangaroo court presided over by Rand, the Brandens, and a few other high-ranking disciples.

Philosopher John Hospers, with whom Rand had developed a respectful relationship over a period of several years, was also shown the door. Rand had tolerated Hospers's disagreements with various aspects of Objectivism during a long correspondence in which she eventually hoped to win him over. She even consented to debate him in front of the others when he occasionally showed up at the Saturday night soirées. However, when Hospers took issue with a speech Rand gave at a meeting of the American Society for Esthetics, she expelled him permanently from her circle.

Writer Edith Efron was another one of Rand's acolytes to feel the great woman's wrath. Rand had put up with Edith, who was every bit as prickly and stubborn as Rand, because she used her great intelligence and incisive wit primarily to skewer Rand's political opponents. However, Rand overheard Efron making a biting comment about her one day to another member of the group, and excommunicated her on the spot. Efron laughed it off as she headed toward the door, saying she was tired of "dancing on glass" around the old girl anyway.

One by one they fell from grace for one infraction of Rand's rules or another one. Many closet homosexuals in the circle maintained a painful silence as their goddess denounced homosexuality as an "immoral and disgusting" perversion reflecting psychological "flaws, corruptions, errors, and unfortunate premises." Most of them, fallen-away Jews and Catholics and Protestants, were looking for a religion substitute, although they would not have used that term to identify Objectivism at the time. They needed to belong to a group that gave them a moral foundation to make up for the one they had abandoned. Voluntary exiles from the religion of their families, they lived in terror of being excommunicated from their adopted creed—and they suffered untold psychological damage in their efforts to fit in.

As Nathaniel Branden later described the mentality of the Collective, to remain in good standing with La Rand it became necessary to believe and state openly that "Ayn Rand is the greatest human being who has ever lived. *Atlas Shrugged* is the greatest human achievement in the history of the world. Ayn Rand, by virtue of her philosophical genius, is the supreme arbiter of any issue pertaining to what is rational, moral, or appropriate to man's life on earth."

Alan coped with this stultifying atmosphere by keeping his distance, both physically and emotionally. He disappeared from time to time, and he reentered the Randian atmosphere when he felt a need for philosophical support and social comfort. He was truly fond of Rand despite the woman's towering eccentricities and domineering nature, and he would remain among her staunchest allies years later when Rand's affair with her archangel, Nathaniel Branden, came to light—and Branden, too, was excommunicated from the world he had played no small role in creating.

"I think Alan was searching for a total philosophy that would put a foundation under his ideas," said his ex-wife, Joan Mitchell. "That's what Ayn did for him."

Townsend-Greenspan continued to flourish as the partners added an expanding number of companies to their client base. They owed much of their success to the vacuum they filled, as very few corporations had professional economists on their staff at that time.

Then, early in 1958, Alan's partner, close friend, and surrogate father, William Townsend, became ill. Townsend had been a heavy cigarette smoker all his life and was diagnosed with heart disease. Throughout the year he grew increasingly weaker until he was finally unable to come to work. He succumbed to a fatal heart attack at age seventy, and the thirty-two-year-old Alan suddenly found himself in charge of a successful consulting firm with a rapidly expanding client base. Alan proceeded to buy out Townsend's heirs and became sole owner of the enterprise.

His partner's passing was a sharp blow for Alan on both a personal and professional level. Outside the Collective, William Townsend, Arthur Burns, Robert Kavesh, and a few of the women he dated were the closest friends he had. Alan had taken up smoking himself a few years earlier, first because it was the thing to do in the 1950s, and second because Ayn Rand considered it a moral obligation to enjoy the fruits of the U.S. tobacco industry. Following Townsend's death, however, Alan tossed a half-smoked pack of cigarettes in the garbage and gave up the weed for good.

Alan quickly redoubled his efforts to run the operation on his own. He had learned the marketing side of the business from Townsend after several years of working with him, and he was able to hold onto most of his clients and add to the list over time. With Townsend gone, Alan turned his attention more and more toward Washington, D.C.—more specifically, to his friend in Washington, Arthur Burns. Burns had served as the president's chief economic adviser from 1953 through 1956, and he was a member of the U.S. Advisory Council on Social Security Financing during Ike's second term in office. Burns's influence in financial circles had grown during the decade, and he also developed a tight relationship with Eisenhower's vice president, Richard M. Nixon.

Burns was born in Austria on April 27, 1904. His family emigrated to the United States when Arthur was ten and settled in Bayonne, New Jersey. He received his degrees at Columbia University, then went on to teach economics at Rutgers, where, as a staunch advocate of unregulated markets, he had a great influence over the young Milton Friedman. Burns transferred back to Columbia, first as a visiting professor of economics in 1941 and finally as a full professor in 1944.

After leaving Columbia to accept the chairmanship of the Council of Economic Advisers in 1953, Burns departed considerably from his laissez-faire views and became a Keynesian in practice. Many of Burns's free-market colleagues began to regard him as a contradiction in terms. Burns, who had previously eschewed government meddling in the economy, suddenly became an advocate of stimulating consumer demand in an effort to keep the economy growing briskly. Those who knew Burns well said that as a professor he had been arrogant but courteous all the time, but as a political economist he was simply arrogant and ungracious.

Alan was one of Burns's old students and friends who disagreed with that assessment. Burns explained patiently to Alan during his frequent visits to Washington that governing in the real world is a lot different than theorizing in a classroom. In the classroom you get graded on your theoretical brilliance, but in the real world you are rewarded for what you manage to accomplish. According to Burns, politics was the art of governing in an imperfect environment. In an ideal society, the free market would work just fine. But in the heavily regulated marketplace that actually existed, with politicians attempting to exercise more and more power over the economy, the best one could do was to make sure free-market principles did not get completely trampled underfoot.

This may have been the single most memorable message that Alan received from his friendship with, and tutelage under, Arthur Burns. Many have noted that the parallels between the two men's lives were startling. Burns worked in the private sector before becoming an adviser to presidents and, ultimately, chairman of the Federal Reserve—precisely the pattern Alan's own life would follow during the ensuing decades.

Burns's great mistake later on, however, when Nixon appointed him Fed chairman, was to politicize the institution in an attempt to keep the economy strong during Nixon's campaign for reelection in 1972. The result was rampant inflation that Nixon, taking Burns's advice, attempted to fight through wage and price controls, which were a basic violation of free-market principles. The controls were tantamount to holding a lid on a pot ready to boil over, and they proved disastrous for the economy and, ultimately, for Burns's reputation. Alan was an avid student of history, and he avoided Burns's mistake when his own turn at the helm of the Fed came a decade and a half later. Alan's independence would sour his relationship with President George H. Bush, who lost his own reelection bid in 1992, but Alan was determined to make sure that his own place in history did not suffer the same fate as his mentor's.

CHAPTER 10

In 1958 Nathaniel Branden founded the Nathaniel Branden Institute (NBI) with Rand's official blessing. The institute was a response to Rand's growing army of fans who were clamoring for a systematic presentation of her ideas. Alan was an important part of the organization.

Branden put together a course of twenty lectures called *Basic Principles of Objectivism*, dealing with different aspects of Randian philosophy. The lectures included a broad range of topics, among them "Objectivity Versus Subjectivity," "What Is Reason?," "The Nature of Emotions," "Are the Arguments for the Existence of God Logically Defensible?," "The Nature and Meaning of Volition," "Why Self-Esteem Is Man's Deepest Psychological Need," "Social Metaphysics," "Foundation of the Objectivist Ethics," "The Importance of Passing Moral Judgments," "The Ethics of Altruism," "The Principles of a Proper Political System: Freedom Versus Compulsion," "The Psychology of Sex," "The Nature and Purpose of Art," and "The Economics of a Free Society," which was taught by Alan.

One might think that an organization devoted to such arcane topics would have elicited a collective yawn from the multitudes, but NBI played to a packed house from the start. Dozens of eager fans flocked to a now-defunct hotel in Manhattan in the West Thirties to listen to Alan, the Brandens, and other members of the Collective expound on their particular topics, followed by an Q&A session with the Grand Matriarch herself. Alan taught his course there once a week in the evening and made economic forecasts for his clients during the day.

Before too long, NBI moved its operation to a larger conference room before finally expanding to spacious quarters in the Empire State Building, the Holy Grail itself as far as Rand was concerned. Requests to hear the lectures came in from other cities across the United States, as well as from other countries, and NBI put them on tape and licensed others to present the course in far-flung regions. Incredibly, hundreds of budding Randians huddled around tape recorders to listen to sermons on epistemology, social metaphysics, and related topics in more than thirty cities from California to Alaska, from Europe to Australia. Alan's devotion to Rand deepened even more during this period as he rapidly evolved into an ardent champion of her cause.

Alan was not the only one involved in NBI who would move on to achieve greater prominence in the world. Martin Anderson, later an adviser to President Ronald Reagan, discovered Objectivism at this time. Robert Bleiberg, the editorial director of *Barron's* for many years, was sufficiently intrigued by Rand to participate in NBI's program. Others drawn to her during the late 1950s and throughout the following decade included best-selling novelist Ira Levin, author of *Rosemary's Baby*; television producer Ted Yates; attorneys Henry Mark Holzer and Erika Holzer; actress Kay Nolte Smith; businessman Wilfred Schwartz; and countless others.

With the series of lectures taking off so successfully, NBI launched a publication called *The Objectivist Newsletter*, which eventually grew up to become *The Objectivist* magazine. Alan turned from the lecture podium to the typewriter to put his ideas about free markets and the gold standard in print for the first time. Bleiberg reprinted some of Alan's work in *Barron's*, but he resisted the Collective's entreaties to align himself more closely with the group.

"It became evident to me that they were a cult," he said in his avuncular style, "or that there was a cult-like atmosphere about them. Also, her philosophy seemed to be missing a human dimension. It occurred to me that if you were going to get the government out of the welfare business—something we all believed should be done—you needed to at least talk about what the private sector and the churches could do to help people who were down on their luck."

Bleiberg was a born and bred New Yorker who spent his entire life working in the concrete canyons of the city's financial district. With his balding pate and unsmiling demeanor, he most resembled the crusty Paul Volcker, who served as Fed chairman before Alan took over in 1987. Bleiberg was just as devoted as Rand to the free market and individualism, which was the major reason he resisted being sucked into her pseudo-religious, suffocating orbit.

Alan's major contributions to the body of Objectivist literature during this period were his articles in defense of the gold standard, which he refused to repudiate years later in his role as the nation's central banker in charge of defending the value of the dollar. His language reflects the thoughts of a True Believer who had embraced the hard-core elements of Rand's ideology.

"An almost hysterical antagonism toward the gold standard is one issue which unites statists of all persuasions," Alan wrote in an article for the newsletter that was reprinted in one of Rand's nonfiction books. "They seem to sense, perhaps more clearly and subtly than many consistent defenders of *laissez-faire*, that gold and economic freedom are inseparable, that the gold standard is an instrument of *laissez-faire* and that each implies and requires the other."

Alan maintained that a free banking system based on gold is able to extend credit and thus to create bank notes (currency) and deposits, according to the production requirements of the economy. Even though the units of exchange (the dollar, the pound, the franc, etc.) differ from country to country, when all are defined in terms of gold the economies of the different countries act as one—so long as there are no restraints on trade or on the movement of capital.

Reserving some of his harshest language for the opposition, Alan wrote: "This is the shabby secret of the welfare statists' tirades against gold: Deficit spending is simply a scheme for the 'hidden' confiscation of wealth. Gold stands in the way of this insidious process. It stands as a protector of property rights. If one grasps this, one has no difficulty in understanding the statists' antagonism toward the gold standard."

These remarks provide a good insight into Alan's thought processes at the time. While he softened his language later in his role as a public figure, he has never backed away from his basic assertion that a nation's currency is essentially worthless unless it is backed by a commodity with intrinsic value such as gold. The U.S. dollar, for example, has value only because of the underlying strength of the American economy and the stability of the political system. Remove these shaky props, however, and the U.S. currency could plummet in value as Germany's did in the 1920s. A more secure support for paper money, according to Alan and other gold advocates, is a currency convertible into specific units of gold.

Alan's consulting business remained robust, but ironically enough for someone so committed to the efficacy of capitalism, he had little or no desire to accumulate personal wealth.

"Alan was never much of an investor," said Robert Kavesh. "He invested in Treasuries and sometimes in commodities, but I don't ever remember him buying much stock. Making money was never his primary concern."

Pierre Rinfret agreed with Kavesh. "When Alan entered public service," he said, "he had very few monetary assets, and what he did have was in conservative vehicles. He had little income and no pension that was publicly known. In other words, he was relatively poor, with little in the way of future income for retirement."

Alan lived comfortably on his income from his consulting business and understood the workings of capitalism as well or better than anyone else. However, it was the machinery and morality of the marketplace that fascinated him, not the manner in which personal fortunes could be made. Alan worked in a world of numbers and ideas. He had other passions as well and was equally at home at a musical concert or the ballpark, preferably in the company of an intelligent young woman. His major forms of exercise were walking and tennis, and it was on the tennis court that Alan developed a chronic physical ailment that would plague him for the rest of his life.

While tossing a tennis ball up to deliver one of his trademark left-hand serves one afternoon, Alan felt a sharp twitch in the small of his back. It was the first time in his life that he had experienced anything like it. The pain intensified over the following week and Alan visited a series of doctors, none of whom were able to help him. The best advice he received was to take a long, hot soak in the bathtub each morning before he left for work. Alan was accustomed to rising at five-thirty every morning to read the financial newspapers and a sheaf of economic reports. He liked to brief himself on what had transpired throughout the world before he stepped into his office each day. Ever a creature of habit, Alan altered his routine only to the extent that he read his reports soaking in the tub for a couple of hours instead of at his kitchen table. It was a discipline he adopted over the next four decades.

The presidential election of 1960 was a devastating blow for Alan and his fellow Objectivists. While the rest of the country was basking in the glow of "Camelot," romanticizing the image of the handsome new President and his beautiful young wife, Alan and his cohorts were convinced that the Brave New World of Fascism had taken root in America. Dorothy Kilgallen, a popular liberal columnist of the day, deified John F. Kennedy and his wife as "American Royalty," and called the family matriarch, Rose Kennedy, "the closest thing America has to a Queen Mother." As cloying as those hagiographic remarks were, the statement that convinced Rand and the others that dictatorship was just around the corner came from the mouth of JFK himself. "Ask not what your country can do for you," the new President said. "Ask what you can do for your country."

To Rand and her acolytes, that statement was the height of altruistic infamy. Never one to do things halfheartedly, Rand responded in her typical style by attacking the new administration with a verbal chainsaw. She delivered a speech entitled "The Fascist New Frontier" at the Ford Hall Forum in Boston, where she appeared once a year. The New Frontier was the name Kennedy gave to the future society he envisioned. Alan, the Brandens, Leonard Peikoff, and a dozen or so of her other disciples sat attentively up front applauding her blistering attack with gusto.

Rand refused to let the matter rest there. Until this time, she had maintained a warm relationship with her publisher at Random House, Bennett Cerf, despite their opposing political views. Cerf balked, however, when Rand wanted to include her speech as the lead essay in a nonfiction book she was writing, *For the New Intellectual*. According to Rand, Kennedy advocated sacrificing the individual to the "public interest." Had she denounced JFK as a socialist, which Cerf expected she would do, her essay would not have been an issue. But Rand maintained that John F. Kennedy was actually a Fascist of the same stripe as Mussolini and Hitler.

"I read the piece and absolutely hit the roof," Cerf wrote in his memoir, *At Random*. "I called her and said we were not going to publish any book that claimed Hitler and Jack Kennedy were alike . . . I said, 'You can say anything you want in a novel, but this is something I didn't foresee. All we ask is that you leave this one essay out.'"

Rand flew into a rage. She quickly found a new publisher at New American Library, and Cerf remained fond of her, notwithstanding their tempestuous parting. "I liked her and still do. I miss her," he wrote in his book. However, Rand, Alan, and the rest of the Collective grew more and more convinced that they were the only rational individualists left in a world controlled by fanatics who were hell-bent on subduing them with their altruistic fantasies. For centuries, organized religion had held the masses enslaved with visions of raging infernos. Kings and other dictators had trodden on the rights of man with the jackboot of the state.

In 1952, the country had finally elected a Republican president after a decade and a half of New Deal socialism, and he turned out to be an intellectual airhead who could not even hold his own against a dedicated Marxist-Leninist. And now the election of 1960 had been snatched away—stolen, really—by a fascistic American blueblood who was a philosophical cousin to Adolph Hitler and Benito Mussolini. Clearly, the darkest days were upon us. The American Republic was about to go the way of Rome, and only Ayn Rand, Alan Greenspan, Nathaniel and Barbara Branden, and a handful of rational atheists stood in the way of the Barbarian hordes.

CHAPTER 11

With Kennedy in the White House, Alan had a new mission. A return to a gold standard was still of paramount importance, but Alan viewed the government's enforcement of the antitrust laws as the central issue of the day. In an article he wrote for *The Objectivist Newsletter* in September 1961 called "Antitrust," Alan maintained that the primary culprit behind the creation of any monopoly is none other than the federal government itself.

Government creates the conditions for monopoly, according to Alan, "by setting up barriers to competition." Government builds roadblocks to entering the market by granting franchises, licenses, and subsidies that promote cartels. It sets price controls, output quotas, tariffs, minimum wage laws, and maximum hour laws, and sometimes mandates unionization. Going further, Alan maintained that prohibitions against "narcotics, prostitution, and gambling engender monopolistic control of black markets."

Rand, taking her cue from Alan, referred to big business as "America's persecuted minority," but Alan did not spare the private sector, either, in his withering remarks. He blamed many large corporations for lobbying the government for laws that would exempt them from the rigors of competition. Some businessmen attempted to gain economic privilege by lobbying the government for subsidies to build canals and railroads. Both Alan and Rand attacked the National Association of Manufacturers and the Chamber of Commerce for ushering in a "neofascistic, corporative form of statist collectivism." Rand described the country's economic environment as a "mongrel mixture of socialistic schemes, communistic influences, fascist controls," all of it "rolling in the direction of a fascist state."

Alan drew a distinction between "coercive and non-coercive" monopolies. Coercive monopolies depend on legally enforced closed entry to their industries, he claimed, while non-coercive monopolies can emerge in particular fields such as mining. Alan stated that "non-coercive monopolists were forced to price their goods in a free marketplace and compete with other mining concerns to sell their products, while coercive monopolists enjoyed price monopolies thanks to their insidious partnership with, and dependency on, the enforcement power of the government."

Following his attack on economic fascism in the United States, Alan trained his sights on Communism in Europe. Writing in the *Objectivist Newsletter* in January 1962, Alan compared free enterprise in West Germany with economic stagnation in the Soviet camp. "History rarely offers so controlled an experiment in rival economic systems as has been seen in Berlin during the last decade. In the late 1940s, when the rest of Western Europe was sinking under a morass of socialistic experiments, West Germany, including West Berlin, turned instead to free enterprise (at least predominantly). The results were dramatic: from a country defeated and devastated by war, it rose to become spectacularly prosperous. Meanwhile, East Germany and East Berlin barely emerged from the rubble."

Alan had more than economics on his mind during this period. Even when he was making economic forecasts or analyzing the political environment, music, sports, and beautiful young women were always on the periphery of his consciousness. He was romantically involved with women he hired, although only with one at a time, and he enjoyed socializing within the Collective. Rand, in fact, encouraged it on the grounds that people who were rational enough to be attracted to Objectivism were the likeliest soul mates for one another. Getting involved with someone who was not an Objectivist was grounds for suspicion that one's basic premises were unstable.

A young woman who had begun to attend the lectures at NBI caught Alan's eye. She was tall, slim, beautiful, and highly intelligent—the perfect combination of attributes for Alan. Her name was Leisha Gullison, and Alan started to date her shortly after their first meeting in 1966. He did not know it at the time—it would take several more years for the truth to come out—but Leisha's identical twin, Patrecia, another member of the Collective, was having an adulterous affair with Nathaniel Branden. Branden's relationship with Patrecia was only part of the story. Unknown to anyone except their mates, Rand and Branden had been conducting an affair of their own for the past decade despite their twenty-five-year age difference. Now, without telling either Rand or his wife, he was cheating on both of them with Patrecia. Alan and Leisha were both oblivious to everything that was going on until the entire deception erupted in a volcanic outpouring of emotion a few years later.

The intellectually incestuous nature of these interlocking romances defied all powers of logic. Nathaniel Branden had been sleeping with his spiritual mother with the mutual consent of their respective mates. They justified this arrangement on the grounds that the most rational person in the world, Ayn Rand, should be romantically involved with the world's second most rational person, Nathaniel Branden. The psychological damage this inflicted on Rand's husband and Branden's wife has been well documented in books and film.

Then Alan started to date the identical twin of the younger, more attractive woman Branden was romancing behind the backs of Rand and his own wife. Neither Alan nor Leisha was aware of any of this until after Rand excommunicated both Nathaniel and Barbara several years later in a turmoil of confusion that bewildered not only the Collective, but the legions of Rand's fans throughout the world. The entire circle around Rand was devastated by the episode, but the two people most seriously and intimately damaged were Rand's husband, Frank O'Connor, and Nathaniel's wife, Barbara. As Barbara wrote many years later in *The Passion of Ayn Rand*, "I did not see it—I did not fully believe the evidence of my senses—because it appeared to me impossible that Nathaniel would lie to me. He had been completely honest about his affair with Ayn. Why would he not be honest now?—especially when our marriage was in tatters, and there was little left to preserve . . .

"Nathaniel did not tell Ayn of his affair . . . He had accepted—he was even teaching in classes all over the country, as he had taught his clients and friends in therapy—Ayn's theory that romantic love is one's response to one's highest, most exalted values, and to choose a lesser value over a greater one is an act of spiritual and moral depravity. Now he was in love, not with Ayn Rand, not with the woman whom he believed exemplified what was best and noblest in the human spirit, but with a young girl who did not comprehend the great issues and purposes that he told himself were all that was important in life."

Frank O'Connor was plunged into a pit of mental and physical anguish, and Barbara Branden was emotionally scarred by the cumulative effects of fifteen years of squalid infidelities and denial. If Alan was shocked by any of the revelations that slowly emerged over time, it did not show on his face. Alan presented the same face to the world through victory and tribulation. His expression rarely changed—laconic, mostly unsmiling, somewhat hangdog, and increasingly jowly as the years rolled by. His primary loyalties were to his spiritual mother, Ayn Rand, and to his biological mother, Rose, whom he continued to call religiously at seven o'clock each morning as he stepped out of his tub and prepared to leave for work.

When the time came to choose up sides after the Rand–Branden fiasco finally came to a boil in 1968, there was no question on which side of the divide Alan would cast his lot. In a fit of fury and betrayal, Rand penned one of the most bizarre articles in literary history, and Alan dutifully added his name to it.

To Whom It May Concern

This is to inform my readers and all those interested in Objectivism that Nathaniel Branden and Barbara Branden are no longer associated with this magazine, with me or with my philosophy.

I have permanently broken all personal, professional and business association with them, and have withdrawn from them the permission to use my name in connection with their commercial, professional, intellectual or other activities.

I hereby withdraw my endorsement of them and of their future works and activities. I repudiate both of them, totally and permanently, as spokesmen for me or for Objectivism ...

FOR THE RECORD

We the undersigned, former Associate Lecturers at Nathaniel Branden Institute, wish the following to be on record: Because Nathaniel Branden and Barbara Branden, in a series of actions, have betrayed fundamental principles of Objectivism, we condemn and repudiate these two persons irrevocably, and have terminated all association with them and with the Nathaniel Branden Institute.

Allen Blumenthal
Alan Greenspan
Leonard Peikoff
Mary Ann (Rukavina) Sures

The document never mentioned the true nature of the split. Rand implied in the course of her diatribe that financial malfeasance had triggered her wrath. The affairs between Rand and Branden, and between Branden and Patrecia, only came to light piecemeal over the ensuing years. None of the signatories knew the true reason for Rand's invective. For Alan and the others, it was enough to know that the Brandens had done something to offend the most rational woman who ever lived.

PART THREE

The Adviser

CHAPTER 12

On a warm spring afternoon in 1966, Alan was walking along Broad Street not far from his office when he ran into Leonard Garment, his old friend from their days with the Henry Jerome orchestra, whom he had not seen in nearly twenty years. The two men recognized each other immediately and went to the Bankers Club to catch up over lunch.

At this time, Garment was a partner in Nixon, Mudge, Rose, Guthrie, Alexander and Mitchell, a law firm located at 20 Broad Street. One of Garment's legal partners was Richard M. Nixon, who had lost his run for governor of California in 1962, following his defeat in the 1960 presidential election, and had subsequently moved to a sprawling Fifth Avenue apartment in New York City. Alan and Garment brought each other up to date and planned to get together for lunch or dinner on a regular basis. One evening during dinner at Oscar's, a dark, expensive French restaurant in the financial district, Alan explained the intricacies of his consulting business, the commodities markets, and his views on politics.

Garment was suitably impressed, even though he didn't understand half of what Alan was talking about.

"Alan was impressively obscure," said Garment. "He spoke in well-formed unintelligible sentences. He was passionate about the federal budget, which he called 'the central nervous system' of American politics. He also had an odd theory about the link between music and numbers."

Garment, a conservative Democrat, was on a mission to rehabilitate Nixon politically and was in the process of recruiting bright young conservatives for a possible Nixon presidential campaign in 1968. He asked Alan if he wanted to meet his law partner.

Alan met Nixon for the first time a couple of weeks later. "They met, and I sat with them for an hour or so after lunch," said Garment. "It was mutuality at first sight. They understood that each had something to give to the other. Alan was interested in political economy and he tried to explain to me what he and Nixon were talking about. They had this wonderful conversation, after which Nixon said, 'Get him aboard.' Nixon was very interested. He made it clear to me that he wanted Greenspan to become involved. After the meeting Nixon said to me, 'That fellow is a whiz. I want to see more of him.'"

Garment had been successful in attracting other talented conservatives to the Nixon camp. Beginning in 1965, he had brought in speechwriters Pat Buchanan and William Safire, political consultant Roger Ailes, general functionary John Sears, economist Arthur Burns, and industrial management expert Martin Anderson, the Objectivist fellow traveler whom Alan had met in Ayn Rand's living room. Anderson, ten years younger than Alan, had made a big splash with his book *The Federal Bulldozer: a Critical Analysis of Urban Renewal 1949–62*, which was published in 1964, and he was an avid opponent of the military draft. He had agreed to join Nixon as his director of research.

Alan discovered that he had a gift for convincing people in power that he was essential to their cause. He found it easy to persuade Nixon and other politicians that they needed the numbers he had rattling around in his head. Alan had a way of making them believe he had "this black box that explained it all—inflation, unemployment, GDP," said a close friend of Alan.

Alan, however, was not as enamored of Nixon as Nixon was of him. Alan was a bit of a social prude, and he found Nixon's constant use of four-letter words offensive. He sized up Nixon accurately as a social misfit determined to prove that he was a regular guy, but who had difficulty playing the role.

"Barry Goldwater would roll up his sleeves, drink bourbon, and use rough language naturally because that's exactly who he was," said F. Clifton White, a longtime Republican political consultant. "Nixon would take off his jacket and try to talk like one of the boys, and he came off like a fish out of water because it was strictly a pose with him. Nixon never figured out who he truly was. He was a man for any and all occasions—tough guy, sycophant, moralist, utterer of profanities—any man you wanted him to be, condemned to lead the life of an actor because of his monumental insecurities."

Alan was impressed by Nixon's intelligence and said later that Nixon and Clinton were the two most intelligent presidents he had ever worked with, but he could not take to Nixon personally. Also, Alan sensed a current of anti-Semitism in Nixon that was barely hidden beneath the surface. Nixon never said anything overtly anti-Semitic in Alan's presence. It was more of an attitude that Alan sensed, a gut-level feeling that refused to go away. Alan's assessment proved accurate three decades later when 445 hours of tapes recorded by Nixon were released to the public. In them, Nixon repeatedly lashed out at Jews in general and called them "disloyal." He made exceptions for the Jews who worked for him, including Henry Kissinger, Leonard Garment, and William Safire, but he complained to his chief of staff, H. R. Haldeman, that "generally speaking you can't trust the bastards. They turn on you." He ordered Haldeman to put someone in charge of key agencies "who is not Jewish."

With a lot of pressure from Garment, Alan agreed against his better judgment to join Nixon's domestic policy team, based in a building on 57th Street and Park Avenue in New York City. He was primarily attracted by Nixon's verbal commitment to fight inflation, something Nixon never followed through on in his presidency.

Nixon expressed a devotion to maintaining the integrity of the dollar that resonated with Alan, who had learned from Arthur Burns about the devastating impact inflation had on the value of money. Maintaining the value of the dollar in the absence of a gold standard was a top priority for Alan, and he believed that Nixon, flawed though he was, would be a far better alternative than any Democrat who ran for president in 1968.

At a meeting of policy advisers on Montauk Point, the easternmost tip of land on the South Fork of Long Island, Alan heard Nixon unleash a stream of profanity that deeply troubled him. The language itself was bad enough, but the insight it provided into Nixon's schizophrenic personality bothered Alan even more. Buttoned down and conservative on the outside, Nixon seemed to possess the soul of a gutter fighter deep inside. Alan later recalled thinking that the word *weird* captured the essence of this saturnine man who wanted to be president more than anything in the world.

Alan was disturbed enough about Nixon's dual nature to discuss the matter with his old college friend and tennis adversary, Robert Kavesh. Kavesh was not surprised to hear that Alan was interested in working in politics, but he was dismayed that Alan had gravitated even further to the conservative end of the political spectrum. In Kavesh's view, Alan had completely abandoned his Keynesian perspective under the influence of Ayn Rand.

"I tried to dissuade him from getting involved with Nixon the best I could, but to no avail," said Kavesh. "Also, I knew he had never completed his doctoral program, a prerequisite for anyone who wanted a high-level job with any president."

"Don't you feel a sense of incompleteness?" Kavesh asked Alan during lunch one day.

"I do," said Alan.

"Why don't you go back to NYU, then? They'll evaluate your record at Columbia and make you take some courses all over again. But it'll be worth it if you're serious about working in Washington."

So Alan transferred his transcripts from Columbia University to his old alma mater and returned there to work part-time on his doctorate. He would continue to do so sporadically over the next ten years, finally earning the elusive degree when he was over fifty years old.

Alan was faced with a true dilemma as the campaign for the presidential election of 1968 got under way. Revolution was in the air as New Left demonstrations against the war in Vietnam drew larger and larger crowds. Civil rights riots broke out in New York, Los Angeles, and other major cities, and students took over campus buildings at Columbia University and NYU. Conservatives were in disarray in the aftermath of Barry Goldwater's disastrous run for president in 1964, and their candidate of choice in 1968 was California Governor Ronald Reagan. However, Reagan was tentative about making a serious push for the White House, and other viable contenders fell by the wayside for one reason or another. Conservative Republicans had always detested New York Governor Nelson Rockefeller, and Rockefeller stand-in George Romney of Michigan—never the sharpest knife in the draw—blew himself out of the water when he stated bizarrely that he had been "brainwashed" during a trip to Vietnam.

"Romney was endowed with a high energy level," said F. Clifton White. "His idea of a golf game was to play three balls at once, then run through eighteen holes with them for exercise. He was also a domineering man who liked to force his views on people, even to the point of intimidating them. George really did think Rockefeller was going to support him for the presidential nomination, and Rockefeller in his inimitable fashion did nothing to disabuse him of that delusion.

"In the end, Rocky double-crossed him royally. The only problem for Rockefeller, however, was that Romney self-destructed early—on February 28, 1968—before Rocky was ready to launch a full-fledged primary campaign of his own. He was secretly hoping that Romney would fall apart closer to the convention so that he could be *anointed* as the candidate, rather than have to earn it in the primaries."

That ensured that the Republican nomination would go essentially by default to the ultimate compromise candidate, Richard M.

Nixon, whose two recent electoral defeats weighed around his neck like a pregnant albatross. Nixon had established his reputation primarily as a fervid anti-communist rather than as a champion of free markets. Indeed, he ate and breathed foreign policy and paid scant attention at best to the intricacies of a capitalist economy, the subject that was of paramount importance to Alan.

"Many delegates who would have cast their lot with Reagan had he declared his intentions unequivocally were left with Nixon as their only viable choice," said White. "I remember a conversation I had with Strom Thurmond after he came out for Nixon. 'Senator, what are you doing? Ronald Reagan is your kind of candidate.'

"'If we don't get behind Nixon now, that fellow Rockefeller's gonna make it.'

"'That's not true, not true at all. I know most of these delegates and they'll swing over to Reagan.'

"'Well, you may be right, son, but we just can't take that chance and let Rockefeller slip in.'"

Alan would also have preferred Reagan to Nixon in 1968, but the California governor did not make a move until it was too late, and the Republican Party accepted the inevitable and rallied around Nixon. Alan agreed to work for Nixon part-time during the campaign as director of policy research, and he took a pied-à-terre at the Watergate apartment complex in Washington to be closer to the action. Alan produced a considerable amount of work on a broad range of issues, including housing, crime, welfare, and the military draft, which he and other libertarians opposed. Alan created a valuable mathematical model of the Electoral College, on which Nixon relied heavily in his campaign strategy.

Despite Alan's work on the campaign, Nixon was a disappointing candidate who turned what should have been an easy victory into a close race. On the ticket with him as his running mate was a little-known Mid-Atlantic governor named Spiro Agnew, who had been elected governor of Maryland in 1966. The reason why Nixon had plucked him from obscurity was a mystery to most observers, particularly since Maryland was not a critical state in electoral terms. However, those close to Nixon claimed that Nixon wanted to even the score after being humiliated by Eisenhower. He thought he was choosing a running mate who would not overshadow him, someone whom he could dominate, perhaps send off on some remote errand and forget about. The strategy backfired to a great degree when Agnew became the darling of conservatives, thanks to the one-line zingers about liberals—"nattering nabobs of negativism," "effete snobs"—written for him by Pat Buchanan and William Safire.

Agnew kept a relatively low profile during the campaign, but he was a hard man to ignore. Tall, strapping, dapper, smoothly handsome, and extremely articulate, he contrasted favorably with Nixon's dark, somewhat menacing, and almost flamboyantly awkward appearance. A moderate-to-liberal Republican as governor of Maryland, Agnew stole a lot of Nixon's thunder during the campaign by positioning himself to the right of Nixon and winning over conservatives who had never accepted Nixon as one of their own. Later on he would join Ronald Reagan and William F. Buckley on a short list of favorite speakers at conservative conferences around the country.

Alan was one of the few people working in the campaign who was not impressed by Agnew's act. He familiarized himself with Agnew's economic record as Maryland's governor, and what he saw troubled him. Agnew, according to Alan, was a high-tax, big-spending liberal who was opportunistically masquerading as a conservative because the occasion demanded it. Nixon, too, Alan felt, was less than wholeheartedly committed to trimming back the welfare state and reducing the tax burden. Alan shared his reservations with only a few close friends and associates, however, as he struggled in vain to influence the economic policies of the next President of the United States.

CHAPTER 13

Nixon ran a poor campaign and turned what should have been an easy victory over a demoralized Democratic Party and the buffoonish Hubert Humphrey into a narrow win. Alan continued to work part-time for Nixon during the transition period, heading up budget negotiations with Congress and working on a commission to study the military draft under former Secretary of Defense Thomas Gates Jr.

"Alan was adamantly opposed to the military draft, as I was," said Martin Anderson. "His views were exactly the same then as they are now."

Alan argued for abolition of the draft and a transition to an all-volunteer military. The role he played in this major policy area has been overlooked by most observers, but the Gates report gave Nixon the political cover he needed to end the draft a couple of years later. Nixon, however, was primarily interested in having Alan join his administration as an economics adviser.

"Nixon wanted Alan to come in after he took office," said Anderson. "He could have had a substantial appointment, even chairman of the Council of Economic Advisers."

Alan agonized over his decision and finally turned the offer down. Most people throw themselves into political campaigns with the hope of snagging a plum job if their candidate wins, but Alan was a rare exception. He felt no regrets when the role of key economic adviser to Nixon went to Paul W. McCracken, who took the oath of office on February 4, 1969.

"You've got to find a few more members," McCracken told Nixon after he was sworn in.

The Council of Economic Advisers is typically made up of the chairman and two members. The chairman is responsible for establishing economic positions, while the two members conduct research in various fields, represent the council at meetings, and provide general economic advice. With Alan dragging his feet, McCracken presided over a council of one at that point. Nixon asked Burns and Garment if they could suggest anyone else, and both men recommended Herbert Stein, who had made a name for himself after World War II by calling for a balanced budget.

As he stood on the sidelines, Alan grew increasingly concerned about the economic tone of the new administration. Not long after taking office, Nixon immediately began to worry about the effects the weak economy might have on the off-year congressional elections of 1970. His main concern was assembling a new electoral majority to keep Republicans in office, and Arthur Burns told Alan that Nixon was prepared to do anything in his power to make sure that happened. Toward that end, the President installed Burns as the new chairman of the Federal Reserve early in 1970.

According to Burns, Nixon expressed the hope that Burns would loosen up the money supply to boost the economy before the elections. Fed chairmen, said Nixon, "have a way of holding the money supply as hostage" in a confrontation with the administration. Burns explained that the Fed was an independent institution and could not play politics.

Nixon replied by pounding the table and saying, "When we get through, this Fed won't be independent if it's the only thing I do in this office."

Alan listened in horror as Burns, whom Alan had always

respected as a man of integrity, confided that he didn't see how he could stand up against Nixon in a showdown. The independence of the Fed was at stake, but Burns seemed to be saying that the only way to keep it independent was by politicizing it in a way that made it dependent on the President's political agenda—a blatant contradiction. Bending the Fed to his will was only one of Nixon's goals. Later that spring, Nixon expressed concern about the high price of meat and put pressure on chain stores to lower their prices before the election.

According to one of Nixon's aides, the President complained that chain stores were "primarily dominated by Jewish interests," and he threatened to launch an antitrust inquiry before market forces finally took over and brought meat prices down. Nixon bragged privately—before going public later—that not only are we "all Keynesians now," but "we are all interventionists" as well.

McCracken, and eventually Burns, were not the only previously free-market types who threw their principles to the wind. John Connally, a conservative Texas Democrat who served as Secretary of the Treasury, embodied the heart and soul of Nixon's unprincipled approach to economics. Having become more and more of an outsider in his own party, he found the welcome mat spread out for him in Nixon's drive to create a new majority. Friends inside the Nixon White House, including Martin Anderson, told Alan that Connally had no fixed principles. "I can play it round or I can play it flat," Connally told Nixon. "Just tell me how to play it."

One of the greatest economic sins committed by Nixon, in Alan's view, was his closing of the gold window at the instigation of Connally. Prior to Nixon's election, while the dollar was not fully convertible into gold, holders of the greenback were able to cash in a portion of their holdings for a fixed amount of gold. In an interesting footnote to political history, severing the final link to gold was strongly opposed by Paul Volcker, a hard-money Democrat who was then an undersecretary at the Treasury and Alan's predecessor as Fed chairman. Always aware of the political implications of any policy moves he made, Connally was the perfect aide for Nixon, who had no discernible economic principles of his own.

Alan was relieved that his decision not to jump on the Nixon bandwagon had kept him above the fray and, therefore, unsoiled by the mess that followed. As a result of Nixon's comprehensive, deliberate politicization of the economy, the country endured the worst economic downturn since the Great Depression. Alan was primarily discouraged that the economic misery took place on the watch of economists whom he admired, including Arthur Burns, Herbert Stein, Paul McCracken, Bill Simon, and even fellow Randian Martin Anderson. Only Milton Friedman, who would win a Nobel Prize half a decade later, came away unscathed.

By keeping himself independent of Nixon's official team of advisers, Friedman was able to use his weekly columns in *Newsweek* to show how Nixon's policies did not jibe with his free-market rhetoric. He documented numerous examples of the ways Nixon's economic advisers sacrificed free-market principles for political expediency. One by one, he ticked off their inconsistencies on a laundry list of issues, from closing the gold window, to their quasi-socialistic agricultural policy, and later on to a disastrous energy policy that resulted in skyrocketing oil prices and long lines at the gas pumps. Economists who had been entrusted with political power turned their backs on well-established concepts and bungled the job of putting their beliefs into practice, all in the interest of pleasing their political master.

"The zigs and zags of policy gave the appearance of ideological confusion," Herbert Stein admitted later. "Politics provided the direction for Nixon because politics was always the main point with him. He cared more about the symbolism than he did about the substance of his programs."

Resorting to price controls was the ultimate heresy for both Alan and Milton Friedman. "Attempting to enforce price and wage controls in a complex economy is not only immoral, it's economically disastrous," Alan said. "The institutions responsible for enforcing the controls lack the necessary knowledge to do so with any semblance of economic rationality. Powerful labor interests received exemptions from the controls, as did certain industries. Clearly, Nixon thought that the controls would be worthwhile politically, and he convinced otherwise sensible economists to buy his argument."

The mess Nixon created is always a possible outcome when the state has the power to intervene as Nixon did, Alan believed. "The apparatus of state intervention is always there for those willing to use it. Inevitably the instruments of intervention will be turned to political uses. This is even more likely in an era when politicians are permanently campaigning, so that their explicitly stated goal, like Nixon's, is to get themselves and their party reelected. Nixon's use of the instruments of power in pursuit of his own political goals brought on disastrous results—double-digit inflation and the worst recession since the 1930s, not to mention a legacy of interventionism that has continued to the present."

Alan was culturally as well as economically conservative, and he blamed Nixon for creating the atmosphere that resulted in hundreds of thousands of antiwar demonstrators converging on the nation's capital in 1970. Nixon had campaigned largely on a promise to end the war in Vietnam as quickly as possible, but once ensconced in office, he failed to follow through until he was up for reelection in 1972.

During one of the largest demonstrations of all during a warm spring weekend, Alan stayed at his apartment in Washington on a business trip. He walked slowly down 16th Street after breakfast on Sunday morning and was revolted by what he saw. The Washington Monument on the south, the Lincoln Memorial on the west, and the huge field off the southern wall of the White House on the north formed the triangular hub of the day's events. Alan was spellbound by the spectacle of thousands of marchers decked out in everything from flowery gowns to beads and blue jeans moving along the broad streets toward the meadow near the White House. The police stood by nonchalantly, billy clubs and tear gas launchers well displayed.

College kids smoked marijuana openly, and the air was heavy with its cloying aroma. Patrolmen turned their heads the other way, apparently under orders to avoid an unnecessary confrontation and to react only to violence should it break out. Alan—decked out in his usual dark suit, white shirt, and nondescript blue tie—remembered having his senses assaulted at one point, by a gang of Yippies and Underground Weathermen in beads and war paint that spelled FUCK NIXON! in capital letters on their foreheads. They circled around a squad of policemen chanting, "Off the pigs! Off the pigs!" while the cops chatted among themselves and pretended to ignore them.

The meadow was carpeted with people of every age and description, spread out over the sloping grass as far as the eye could see. The sun raged high above, pulsing red in the clear blue sky, making Alan's shirt stick to his skin under his navy blue suit. He walked south up a grassy stretch toward the Washington Monument. Thousands were lying about, eating on the lawn, frying their brains with pot, and strumming guitars. He wandered in disbelief for over an hour and headed slowly toward the Reflecting Pool in front of the Lincoln Memorial. There, dozens of demonstrators had divested themselves of shoes and clothing and splashed naked in the water. Platoons of cops stood in the shade along the grassy knoll to the sides, some looking on with a grin but most observing grimly behind the anonymity of their wraparound sunglasses.

The demonstrators in the pool, mostly kids, sat on the water jets and deflected the spouts toward the spectators around them. There were hefty female students from NYU, Hunter, Columbia, and other universities frolicking in the middle of the pool with their pendulous breasts flopping like punching bags. Scrawny college boys with huge erections and boils on their backs plowed through the water in a diligent search for receptive partners. After a while, the scene in the pool degenerated into a universal group grope. Egged on by the media, the kids jumped up and down splashing one another with water and yelling, "One, two, three, four! We don't want your fucking war!" Alan got tired of the madness and slumped back toward his apartment.

He was profoundly disturbed by the spectacle he saw and believed it could have been avoided. Alan considered himself to be an antiwar libertarian who viewed our adventure in Vietnam as completely misguided. He was something of a military isolationist who would have preferred to restrict our considerable power to the defense of the country's vital interests. Yet it was impossible for him to sympathize with the motivation and tactics of the demonstrators, most of whom were enemies of capitalism and openly sympathetic to the communists. Alan blamed Nixon for prolonging the conflict longer than he should have, and for exhibiting an almost visceral hostility toward all antiwar demonstrators, including middle-class families with sons risking their lives in jungles halfway around the world.

Despite his perpetually gloomy appearance, Alan was normally an upbeat individual with a generally optimistic outlook on life. On that steamy Sunday in Washington, D.C., however, Alan was more troubled than he could remember about the direction in which this Republican president was leading the country.

CHAPTER 14

A year before his first term in office expired, Nixon was deeply worried about the sluggish tone of the U.S. economy. All the polls had Nixon well ahead of his likely Democratic opponents, but he understood that people voted their pocketbooks first and foremost, and he was determined not to let the economy undermine his reelection bid in 1972. On January 1, 1972, he replaced Paul McCracken with Herbert Stein as chairman of the Council of Economic Advisers. Arthur Burns was midway through his own first term as Federal Reserve chairman and was already doing his bit to spark the economy with low interest rates, even at the risk of accelerating inflation.

To Alan, Stein was even less acceptable in the role than McCracken was. A pragmatist's pragmatist if there ever was one, Stein admitted that while he was theoretically in favor of free markets, he subscribed to no particular school of economic thought. He was often referred to as "a conservative's liberal and a liberal's conservative."

Before joining the Nixon team, Stein had worked for twenty-two years with the Committee for Economic Development, which came into existence after World War II to study economic issues. During the war, Stein had served as head of economic analysis at the War Production Board. His son Ben would enjoy his own time in the limelight a couple of decades later, first as an actor in the movie *Ferris Bueller's Day Off*, and then as the host of *Win Ben Stein's Money* on the Comedy Central channel.

Unlike most free-market economists, Stein was never a big advocate of tax cuts unless they were balanced with permanent reductions in federal spending. Stein believed that "government ought to establish spending programs and then set a level of taxes that would support the spending," Alan said. Stein reiterated this view many times to Alan, with whom he played tennis whenever Alan visited Washington. They also shared a mutual interest in music, since Stein worked his way through college playing saxophone on excursion boats and clubs in Detroit, where he grew up.

Alan agreed that tax revenues and expenditures should be in balance; he never went along with supply-siders Jude Wanniski, Arthur Laffer, Jack Kemp, and others who maintained that lower income tax brackets would generate more revenue for the government. Alan was opposed on principle to giving the government more money to waste, but he believed that Stein had gotten it backward. Taxes should be lowered to no more than a certain level of the nation's gross domestic product, a maximum of around 20 percent, and spending trimmed so that the budget was balanced, Alan argued. By saying that spending priorities should come first, Stein was opening the door to high taxes that would be a drag on economic growth.

The two men were never able to resolve their differences on economic policy, but they remained good friends nonetheless. Alan had always been a bit of a social climber, as his mentor Ayn Rand was quick to notice years earlier, and he had developed a taste for life close to the heartbeat of political power, thanks in large part to his association with Burns. Despite his reluctance to jump on board the Nixon bandwagon, he enjoyed his relationships with those inside the administration, and he was flattered by the President's desire to have him on his team.

So, while Alan remained friendly with Burns, Stein, and others who stretched their principles to accommodate Nixon's political agenda, he was not shy about expressing his reservations to them in his usually low-key fashion. During his presidential campaign in 1968, Nixon had promised to eliminate the 10 percent income surtax that helped finance the war in Vietnam. Once in office, however, Nixon "took the advice of his conservative Keynesian advisers, Herbert Stein and Paul McCracken," said supply-side economist Jude Wanniski, "and decided to maintain the surtax in order to balance the budget." Compounding this sin with a worse one, Nixon also raised the capital gains tax at the suggestion of Stein and McCracken.

"Stein was a lifelong proponent of high capital gains tax rates," said Wanniski. "This combination caused a further decline in the stock market as it anticipated the weak economy of the early nineteen-seventies."

Burns predicted that the economy would slow significantly in the middle of Nixon's campaign for reelection unless they took drastic action to prime the pump. When Nixon asked Burns what kind of swift remedy would work, Burns replied that it would take a major increase in the nation's money supply to avoid a recession. The Fed needed to continue lowering interest rates dramatically to keep the economy moving ahead.

"The Fed began creating liquidity by keeping interest rates artificially low to hit the administration's economic growth targets," said Wanniski. "Burns had the support of his close friend, Citicorp president Walter Wriston. The Fed dutifully began shoveling reserves into the banking system to get Nixon reelected."

Monetary growth nearly quadrupled over the course of a few months, all but guaranteeing an inflationary surge six or nine months afterward. Burns rejected more than twenty calls from Federal Reserve banks to stem the flow of money before it was too late. The reelection strategy worked like a charm, helped along by the inept campaign of Democratic presidential candidate George McGovern. However, the predictable result was skyrocketing inflation shortly after the election was over and Nixon was safely entrenched in the White House for another four years—or so he thought. Alan was stunned as he witnessed this economic carnage taking place under the watchful eyes of men whom he had respected. He had already voiced his objections to what they were doing. All he could do now was scratch his head in disbelief.

"The crisis deepened," said Wanniski, "with private citizens hedging by selling dollars."

To Alan's dismay, Stein and Burns compounded their disastrous policies further when they called for the "temporary" institution of wage and price controls, which they euphemistically referred to as an "incomes policy." They also raised the tariffs on imports by 10 percent to reduce the amount of goods entering U.S. shores from Japan. Stein defended himself during a game of tennis with Alan by saying that his economic strategy should be viewed as "mosaic that had to be understood as a whole." The problem was, the so-called mosaic was coming unglued at the seams of its own accord. Alan observed that it more closely resembled a mosaic spawned in the Kremlin by a central planning bureau than it did an economic plan designed by men who supposedly believed in the invisible hand of the marketplace.

With inflation spinning out of control and interest rates soaring, stock prices began to plummet. The U.S. stock market entered one of the most sickening, stomach-churning bear markets in history. Just when it seemed as though the worst was over and prices had found a bottom, the selling began all over again. The end was nowhere in sight. The slide continued through most of 1973 and into the next year. The broad market had slumped 40 percent from its bull market highs, but some individual stocks were down more than 80 percent. In some respects, the loss of wealth was almost as severe as the great stock market crash of 1929 that had financially destroyed Alan's father along with an army of investors.

The economy and miserable stock market were not the worst of Nixon's problems. The word *Watergate*, which took on a special meaning during the 1972 campaign, had quickly become a synonym for political chicanery throughout the world. The crisis refused to go away. Each day brought new revelations surrounding the Nixon-sponsored break-in at Democratic Party headquarters.

There were rumors of taped conversations and denials from the White House, followed by finger-pointing and a search for scapegoats. Heads began to roll, followed by calls for further resignations and full disclosure of the truth. Nixon tossed his key lieutenants to the lions, hoping that their flayed hides would satisfy the blood lust of his enemies. But it was not enough. It would never be enough, and Nixon knew it. As the days and weeks flew by in a whirling frenzy, Nixon retreated further into the bog of paranoia that was his private hell.

Alan, already deeply saddened about the direction the economy had taken, knew that the entire fiasco surrounding Watergate could have been avoided. "There was nothing in the Democratic headquarters that Nixon needed to know about to win reelection," said Nixon aide F. Clifton White. "I can't imagine what he and his advisers thought they would come up with. A sense of paranoia develops in many campaigns, particularly closely contested ones, where one side starts to believe that the opposition has all kinds of secrets that will tip the balance to its side. There is always a con man who shows up at campaign headquarters, usually looking for money or a job, who claims to have secret information that you can use against your opponent. I can't remember a campaign I've been in where that did not happen. But the 1972 campaign against George McGovern was anything but tight. Nixon didn't have to get involved in anything as spurious as that, and later he admitted as much to me.

"The only thing that makes any sense is that Dick was looking to protect his brother Don. Donald Nixon had never been particularly successful, and the little success he did have was connected to his brother's status as one of the country's leading politicians. Many of Dick's close associates had been concerned about Don and his activities for some time. I went down to the Dominican Republic to give a speech one time, and I ran into Donald. There was a rumor afoot that he was on Howard Hughes's payroll, working for a shadowy character . . . who was a key Hughes associate at the time, possibly hired to see what influence he could exert on the government's nuclear testing program. I doubt there was anything illegal in what he was doing, but it's possible that Dick may have been worried about Don's relationship to Howard Hughes and the effect it might have on the campaign if it got out. This was a fundamental weakness in Nixon—his insecurity, his concern about being personally embarrassed about something he had nothing to do with. It clouded his judgment at times."

Alan sensed the despair, and panic, that gripped Burns, Stein, Anderson, and other Nixon advisers with whom he was friendly as the noose drew tighter every day. They were all afraid of being sucked into the vortex of criminality that swirled around Nixon like some black tornado from hell.

"Things began to unravel quickly," said White. "The media were calling every day, and I spent most of my time on the phone trying to answer their questions as best I could." White was in his office one evening at about six o'clock when Jeb Magruder, John Mitchell's assistant, walked in.

"Do you have time for a drink, Clif?" Magruder asked.

"Sure."

They went out for a drink, and White could see that Magruder was troubled. "If you were running the show around here, what would you do about this Watergate flap?" Magruder asked.

"I'd find the guy responsible and fire him," White said.

"What level would that have to be to make it credible?"

"Well, I guess that would have to be about your level," White joked.

"I was afraid you'd say that," said Magruder. His face had turned ashen, and White was shocked when he realized that his intended joke had struck a raw nerve deep inside Magruder.

Magruder ignored White's advice and attempted to blame the entire affair on low-level functionaries to save his own skin. It was a tactic that backfired in the end. Quite possibly, if Magruder had admitted his responsibility from the beginning instead of engaging in a whitewash and attempting to cover up the truth, the Nixon presidency might have been saved. Then again, most objective observers felt that justice was best served with Nixon's resignation when it came. His was a presidency that did not deserve to last, many, including Alan, believed.

"Nixon let down his family, the Republican Party, and the nation," said White. "It bothered me then, and it still does, that he did not level with everyone and admit his culpability. I knew many people who had worked and sacrificed for Nixon since 1960 who were devastated in the aftermath of Watergate. Most appalling of all was the way Dick let his daughters defend him tearfully in public—only to tell them in the end what really took place. I knew those girls from the time they were babies, and they were crushed by the truth when it finally emerged.

"Pat Nixon, too, was deeply wounded by the whole sordid affair. She had been beaten up by the press for a long time. She was not enthusiastic about her husband's campaign for reelection in 1972, yet she went along as a dutiful wife—only to see her family torn apart by the disgrace. She had survived in the nasty world of politics since 1946, and she was tired of it all. Richard Nixon victimized many people because of Watergate, but he victimized no one more than his own wife and family."

CHAPTER 15

In the summer of 1974 Alan received a call he had been dreading. The caller was Arthur Burns and the tone of his voice was insistent. It was time for Alan to come in out of the cold, said Burns. It was not a request. Burns claimed that Alan had a moral obligation, a *duty*, to enter the fray as Nixon's chief economic adviser and try to breathe some life into the devastated economy. Prices were out of control and it was time for Alan to enter the political arena. He owed it to the country.

"Arthur not only asked him to go," said Judy Mackey, one of Alan's top lieutenants at Townsend-Greenspan. "He told him that it was his duty to go, that it was their last chance to fight inflation."

Randian that he was, Alan was a bit miffed at the notion that he had any moral obligation to clean up someone else's mess, but he was flattered as well. The country was in turmoil, the economy was moribund, and he was being tapped as the only one capable of resurrecting Lazarus from the tomb. As he had done so many times in the past, Alan turned to his old friend Robert Kavesh for advice. Over lunch in a Greenwich Village restaurant near NYU, Alan said,

"Richard Nixon wants me to join his Council of Economic Advisers as chairman. I think I have to do it."

Kavesh detested Nixon and everything he stood for. He was nearly apoplectic at the suggestion that his old Keynesian buddy was on the verge of joining the sinking Nixon presidency in an effort to keep it afloat. If Kavesh saw any irony in the idea that it was precisely Nixon's *Keynesian* approach to economic policy that had caused the problems in the first place, he failed to mention it. He tried to dissuade Alan from following this course by appealing to him on a personal, rather than ideological, level.

"Alan, you're going to go down to Washington," said Kavesh, fairly bouncing up and down in his chair. "You're going to appear before congressional committees. They're going to know your views about Ayn Rand and the place of government—the *limited* place of government—in economic life. These people are going to kill you!"

Alan liked to use others as a sounding board when he was faced with a critical decision. However, he had all but made up his mind to accept the job in Washington, even though it meant taking a whopping pay cut from the income he enjoyed in his lucrative consulting business. It was not an easy decision for him. He now resided in a posh apartment at 860 United Nations Plaza, thanks to a special deal he received on the price from one of his clients, Alcoa, which built the complex. He employed about a dozen people, mostly women, including his mother, Rose, who served on the board of directors. Townsend-Greenspan had recently moved to larger quarters at One New York Plaza near the Staten Island Ferry terminal, and Alan and his staff lunched regularly at Fraunces Tavern, a watering hole that dated back to the American Revolution. All in all, he enjoyed a good, successful life in New York that he was not anxious to give up.

Lately, however, he felt more and more that he belonged in government, helping to direct economic and political policy. Taking a contrary view, Alan looked forward to facing the greatest challenge of his life so far while others claimed that joining the Nixon administration at this time was tantamount to jumping aboard the sinking *Titanic*. The environment could hardly have been worse: the

Watergate hearings were in full swing; unemployment was soaring; inflation was at its highest level in three decades, partly fueled by the Arab oil embargo; and the collective morale in the nation's capital was at rock bottom.

Herb Stein resigned from his post in July, and Nixon nominated Alan to replace him as chairman. Congress was totally absorbed in Watergate and could not spare the time to stop what it was doing to conduct a hearing on Alan's nomination. Alan's fate hung in the balance for several long weeks while Congress deliberated over the President's role in the break-in.

Finally, on the very morning of Nixon's resignation, Alan left his Watergate apartment (ironically enough) and traipsed over to the Senate Banking Committee meeting on Capital Hill to testify about his suitability to be the nation's chief economic czar. Oddly, none of Alan's interrogators questioned his academic credentials, or lack of them, as he was still three years away from earning his doctorate in economics. The senators directed their inquiries instead to Alan's ideological leanings, and to his credit, Alan was totally straightforward about his beliefs.

He told the assemblage of august inquisitors that the institution of government was inherently immoral, and that high inflation was largely the result of excessive government spending that led to unbalanced budgets. "In the last ten or fifteen years," Alan told the members of the Banking Committee, "there has been an extraordinary buildup of special interests in our society who have ongoing commitments from the federal budget running in excess of the revenue-raising capacity of our tax system . . . I would expect that it may account for from eighty to ninety percent of the inflation in this country."

When questioned about his belief in a gold standard, Alan reiterated the views he had been expressing for a decade and a half in Objectivist literature and elsewhere. Alan remained cool and unruffled throughout the hearing, and when he returned home that evening and turned on his television set, he learned that the man who had sent his name up to the Senate for confirmation was no longer President of the United States. Nixon was gone, and Vice

President Gerald Ford had been sworn in as President. Stein, Burns, and a few other Nixon aides had asked Alan to temper his views during the Senate hearing, and they were now in despair over his performance. The Senate would never confirm anyone who expressed such radical views about the proper role of government in society.

Alan, too, believed that his chances of being confirmed ranged from zero to minimal. Senator William Proxmire had concluded Alan's hearing with an admonition that stated in part: "I have great, great difficulty with the fact that you are a free enterprise man who does not believe in antitrust, does not believe in consumer protection, does not believe in progressive income tax. The latter may be consistent with a laissez-faire position, but you seem to be opposed to many of the social programs that we have been able to achieve."

So be it, Alan thought. If he had to downplay his beliefs to get the job, it wasn't worth it. The country was not ready for him, and perhaps it would never be. He was born too late. Government control over the economy and other areas of life had grown to a point where it was all but irreversible. He would have to remain with his consulting business near Wall Street and earn more money than he ever thought possible. It did not carry the same panache as a high government sinecure, but it was not a bad consolation prize when you thought about it objectively.

Alan had gotten to know Gerry Ford during his frequent trips to Washington, but he expected the new President to withdraw his nomination and name his own replacement for Stein. Ford had been a long-time representative and Washington power broker whose approach to governing was anything but radical. Surely, he would want someone with more traditional views advising him on how to run the economy. What Alan did not know was that Ford was making his own quiet inquiries while the Senate considered Alan's nomination. Ford had asked one of his top aides, William Seidman, whether he should proceed with Alan's nomination.

"I thought he was a good conservative economist, which there weren't a lot of in those days," Seidman said about Alan. "He assured me that he was a pure economist and not a politician. It turned out that he was a better politician than any of us thought."

While Ford was checking with Seidman on Alan's suitability for the job, the FBI was investigating his private life. One of the people the agents called on was Alan's first wife, Joan Mitchell Blumenthal. "They were asking all sorts of vaguely personal questions about Alan," she said, "and I could tell they weren't getting what they wanted. They didn't seem satisfied. 'Oh, I get it,' I said. 'You want to know if Alan's homosexual.' They said, 'Well, his ex-wife usually knows these things, if anyone does.' 'Well, he's definitely not,' I said. 'There have been a lot of women since me.' And there have! It's just he would never carry on in public. He's incredibly discreet—the most discreet person I have ever known. I told them that if they were worried about whether he would divulge sensitive information, they had lost their minds."

Following Seidman's endorsement, Ford invited Alan in for a detailed discussion about the economy. "We spent about an hour together," said Ford, "and to be honest with you, I was very impressed with him. I could tell he was very thoughtful. I just took an instant liking to him. It turned out to be a good judgment." Ford decided to stick with Alan, and when his nomination was confirmed two weeks after the hearing, Alan became the second (and last) economist without a doctorate to head up the Council of Economic Advisers since its inception in 1946.

Alan left his business in the care of Bess Kaplan, Judith Mackey, Lucille Wu, and Kathryn Eickhoff, and placed his majority shares of ownership in the firm in a blind trust to avoid any potential conflict of interest. When Alan took his oath of office on September 4, 1974, Ayn Rand beamed brightly in the first row, somewhat amused at the irony of Alan, an avowed atheist, placing his right hand on the Talmud that was held by Alan's mother, Rose. A reporter asked Rand if Alan was selling out by going to work for the enemy, and Rand dismissed the suggestion with a shrug. "Alan is my disciple," the novelist said. "He's my man in Washington." Left unspoken was Rand's conviction that an Objectivist with Alan's integrity would *never* compromise his principles. Alan knew how to shrug, too.

On a personal level, Rand had taken a strong fancy to the new President of the United States. Gerry Ford was clearly the model of a true Randian hero—tall, blond, clear-eyed, ruggedly handsome, and well built. Ford invited Rand to have her photograph taken with him and Alan, and Rand prominently displayed the glossy print of the three of them smiling broadly on the piano in her apartment until her death in 1982.

Ford's number-one domestic priority was finding a way to reinvigorate the economy, and he turned to Alan and William Simon, his treasury secretary, for advice. Alan presented Ford with a couple of options. He would prefer a large tax cut, Alan said, but only if it were balanced by sufficient spending cuts to avert a widening of the federal budget deficit. That was the "conservative" option. "If you take the conservative one," said Alan, "you will be accused of being too tightfisted, but in the long run, if you are reelected, you will have good economic times in 1977, '78."

The second option would be smaller tax cuts combined with modest spending restraints. "On the other hand," Alan told the President, "if you take the more expansive choice, you may get some good times in 1976, but if you are reelected you will pay a penalty, because you will go through another economic downturn in 1977, '78."

"Well, what do you recommend?" asked Ford.

"I think it would be wise to take the more conservative one, even though you'll probably get some politically unattractive statistical data in September or October 1976, just before the election." Ford followed his advice.

Alan and Ford became good friends as well as political allies. "Greenspan has an unbeatable way of getting next to the guys in power and getting their attention, and he certainly did that with Ford," said Seidman. "So he became an adviser not only on economics, but on politics and everything else. In fact, I'm not sure he didn't spend as much time on politics as he did on economics." Alan shared a love of sports with Ford and began going to football games with the President. "Ford was . . . very impressed with him," said Seidman, "and Greenspan has about as good a bedside manner with people in power as anyone I've ever seen, one of the reasons being he's very smart. But he also speaks in ways that sound profound even if you don't understand what the hell he's talking about." Alan developed a good political sense and provided Ford with advice on how to sell his economic ideas to the public.

One area in which Alan did not have much experience, however, was in his dealings with the press. Shortly after going to work for Ford, Alan jokingly told a reporter that while many people were suffering because of the weak economy, no one was suffering more than stockbrokers. Predictably, the media blew this up as an example of his and, indirectly, the President's insensitivity to the plight of the working man, and Alan learned a valuable lesson in political diplomacy. He vowed to weigh his comments carefully in the future when he was speaking on the record.

Ford was not the only person Alan finessed in Washington. He found a valuable ally in Secretary of the Treasury William Simon. The two men had their differences, but they were largely in agreement on the need for cutbacks in both taxes and spending. Others within the administration were urging Ford to trim taxes and *increase* spending to reinvigorate the economy before the next election—classic Keynesian medicine—but both Alan and Simon believed that would be a disastrous course of action.

William E. Simon had become the sixty-third Secretary of the Treasury on May 8, 1974, and when Ford became President, he asked Simon to remain in this position. Simon had previously served as Deputy Treasury Secretary, a post he had held since January 22, 1973. Beginning in December 1973, Simon had administered the Federal Energy Administration at the height of the oil embargo, chaired the President's Oil Policy Committee, and was instrumental in revising the mandatory oil import program. He was a member of the President's Energy Resources Council, responsible for coordinating domestic and international energy policy.

The son of an insurance executive, Simon was born in Paterson, New Jersey, on November 27, 1927. He graduated from Newark Academy and, after doing a tour in the army received his B.A. from Lafayette College in Easton, Pennsylvania. Simon began his financial career with Union Securities in 1952, then transferred to

Weeden & Company as a vice president before becoming the senior partner in charge of the government and municipal bond departments at Salomon Brothers, where he was a member of the firm's executive committee.

After Simon replaced George Shultz as Treasury Secretary in May, he immediately shifted the focus of the administration's attention to the sagging economy. Ford created a new agency, the Economic Policy Board, in September 1974, just after Alan joined his administration. The President named Simon to oversee the Board and asked him and Seidman to coordinate policy with Alan. The Economic Policy Board was charged with the responsibility for all domestic and international policy-making decisions.

Together, Ford's three economic czars dealt with a broad range of issues, including domestic economic policy, international trade, taxes, the New York City financial crisis, oil, unemployment, inflation, and antitrust legislation. They met almost daily to monitor the direction of the economy and to analyze a plethora of data on trade, particularly grain exports; tax revenues; and unemployment. They then presented Ford with their consensus forecasts on a weekly basis. The overriding thrust of their joint effort was a coordinated assault against inflation. Alan went along reluctantly with Simon's public relations fiasco, the ill-fated "Whip Inflation Now," or WIN, slogan that was all but laughed out of town by the Democrats and the media. Behind it, however, was a serious program to rein in inflation and reinvigorate the economy.

Ford was worried about the high level of joblessness that accompanied the recession, and he was especially concerned about unemployment among the young and hard-hit demographic groups. To minimize the effects of the recession, Ford's economic team emphasized the need for tax reform to boost the weak economy and lessen the government's drain on it. At the suggestion of his advisers, Ford implemented a series of measures to simplify the tax code starting in 1975.

To combat high oil prices, which remained a persistent problem for unemployed and working-class Americans, Ford created the Committee on Energy with Simon as chairman. Alan and a group of cabinet members were called in to help design a national energy policy to alleviate the situation. A month later, Ford replaced the committee with the Energy Resources Council, led by Frank Zarb, who became the Federal Energy Administration director in December 1974 before moving to Wall Street in the late 1970s. Ford asked Alan to work closely with Zarb to formulate a viable energy program. Their primary goals were to lower oil prices, induce Americans to conserve energy, and get the auto industry to clean up emissions and design more fuel-efficient cars. Alan devised a system to monitor the nation's coal supply and help ward off a threatened coal miners' strike.

International economic issues remained front and center among Ford's, and consequently Alan's, panoply of worries. Alan and Simon provided the President with extensive files on U.S. trade relations with Canada, Egypt, France, Israel, Japan, Saudi Arabia, and the United Kingdom. The two men worked together on U.S. policy on various commodities, including grain, coffee, and tin. Alan had always been interested in the status of the world gold market and the right of U.S. citizens to own the precious metal, and he convinced the President to liberalize government regulations in that area. Alan also pushed for a controversial system of providing corporations with tax breaks in an effort to boost exports.

Alan and Simon worked together on U.S. policy concerning the role of the International Monetary Fund and the World Bank in averting international economic crises. They coordinated the administration's efforts to reform both institutions as well as the international monetary system, giving particular attention to floating exchange rates and changes in the international balance of payments.

As Ford turned his attention more and more to the 1976 presidential election, Alan and Simon worked hand in hand to create position papers comparing the strengths and weaknesses of the two major parties. They kept Ford apprised of the likely Democratic candidates' positions on critical issues, including the economy, unemployment, international trade, and other key issues. All in all, it was a busy time for Alan as he submerged himself in a whirlwind of diverse activities covering every conceivable aspect of politics and economics.

It was no great surprise to Alan when he came to realize that he thoroughly enjoyed the heady elixir of political power in the capital of the most powerful nation on earth. Not only was he connected to the inner workings of the country's economic and political rhythm—the motor of the world in many ways—he was largely responsible for helping to keep the vast dynamo in motion. Finally, he was fully committed to the political fate of a President he admired, and he loved every maddening, frustrating, and exhilarating minute of his new career.

CHAPTER 16

As Joan Mitchell Blumenthal had told the FBI, her first husband thoroughly enjoyed the company of intelligent and attractive women, and he dated more and more frequently during the years after their annulment. Alan usually had a different woman by his side whenever he went out on the town, but shortly after he went to work for Ford, he was more often than not seen in the company of a special new woman who had recently entered his life. Her name was Barbara Walters, and she exhibited all the characteristics that Alan admired most in women: She was bright, good looking, inquisitive, and extremely successful in her own right.

Walters was born in Boston in 1929. Her father was the legendary show business impresario Lou Walters, whose influence in the industry eased her onto the fast track for what would turn out to be a long career in television. When Alan met Barbara, she was working as the first female co-host for NBC's *Today Show* and was a member of the reporting team that had accompanied President Nixon on his trip to China in 1972 and, later, President Ford on his China visit in 1975. By the time she switched over to ABC in 1976, her fifteen-year stint on the *Today Show* was the longest for any woman on the program.

Alan and Barbara met at a party hosted by Vice President Nelson Rockefeller. They dated regularly during his two years in Washington working for Ford, and they continued to see each other after Alan returned to his consulting business in New York. Alan had a genius for maintaining cordial relations with most of the women he dated after their relationship ended, and Barbara was no exception.

"Alan was and is a wonderful friend," said Walters. "In his private business, most of the people in his office were women. We saw each other until I got married and we've continued to be friends."

She described Alan as "a very sweet and kind man who never raised his voice, was enormously patient, slightly absent-minded, and totally trustworthy." She continued, "He's not formidable in person. He's a lovely, soft-spoken, quiet man who laughs at himself. I've never heard him sharply cut anyone off. I don't think he has such a thing as a personal enemy."

Personal enemies were the last drawbacks anyone needed in Washington, D.C., and Alan quickly learned that the best places to cement friendships were on the White House tennis court and on the golf links. Tennis matches in the nation's capital, however, were just as cutthroat as the political animosities that divided one camp from the other. Alan had been playing tennis with Kavesh, Stein, and other friends for years, but he was somewhat taken aback by the level of ferocity employed by Seidman, Simon, and President Ford himself, who had played football in college and was a natural athlete.

For Alan, this was like jumping overnight from AA to major league baseball, and he was clearly out of his element. According to Seidman, Alan "didn't know which end of the racket to use, and he saw that tennis was quite a great thing among people in the administration." He immediately signed up for advanced lessons in tennis, and also hired a golf instructor when he realized that Ford was passionate about the game. If you wanted to have the President's ear to yourself for an extended period, the best opportunity was on the golf course with him. Ford was more than a bit amused by Alan's awkward left-hand strokes, but he was gracious about Alan's progress with the game.

"He isn't a bad golfer for someone who doesn't play very much," Ford said many years later.

As the 1976 presidential campaign season heated up, Ford's major problem—and consequently Alan's—was the still stagnant economy. Alan's forecast of "politically unattractive statistical data" if Ford chose Alan's conservative option turned out to be a serious understatement. The economy continued to gasp for air like a terminally ill patient on life-support systems. With that albatross hanging around his neck, along with the political fallout from Watergate, Ford faced an uphill battle as the summer rolled around. On top of it all, he confronted a serious challenge for the presidential nomination from California Governor Ronald Reagan.

The Republican National Convention opened in Kansas City on August 15, 1976. Ford and Reagan were the only two serious contenders for the presidential nomination, and this time around Reagan decided to mount a credible challenge to the incumbent President. Reagan miscalculated when he selected liberal Republican Congressman Richard Schweiker as his potential running mate and asked Ford to name a candidate of his own. Ford refused to take the bait and outmaneuvered the Reagan forces on several key platform amendments. The relative strength of the two camps was close, but Ford had the edge. Delegates committed to Ford tipped the balance against Reagan 1,187 to 1,070, with 1,130 votes needed to win.

With the nomination secured, Ford prepared himself for a bruising campaign against Jimmy Carter. The Republican Party was in shambles in the aftermath of Watergate, and the economy refused to cooperate with Ford's dreams of reelection. Other observers, however, attributed Ford's loss to his generally inept performance in the campaign.

"Simply put, Gerry Ford's campaign was a disaster from the start," said F. Clifton White, who had advised Ford during the campaign. "He had been a congressman before becoming President by accident, as it were, and he never stopped thinking of himself as a congressman. On the campaign trail he comported himself more like a man struggling to retain his seat in Congress than like an incumbent President. A case in point, which no one talks about any longer but which for me was the turning point in the election, occurred during the first debate between Gerry Ford and Jimmy Carter."

A fuse blew at some point during the debate, knocking out the power system. For nearly twenty painful minutes, two men who were running for the most powerful office in the world stood speechless at their respective podiums, with no one in charge of what was going on. "If you're the most powerful man on earth," said White, "you're supposed to act the part, not stand by helplessly while technicians fiddle with the electric system."

However, both candidates decided to play it safe and not do anything out of the ordinary that might tip the balance to the opposing candidate. The television cameras remained fixated on two silent men who poignantly demonstrated that neither one of them knew how to act like the President of the United States. According to White, "Whichever one moved first and acted as though he were trying to get to the bottom of the problem would have won the election in November. He would have soared in the polls the next day." But neither said a word for seventeen excruciating minutes.

"Since Ford was the incumbent President, he was the bigger loser of the two," said White. "He was the one who presumably was supposed to know how to handle the problem. But he failed to act."

Carter's victory over Ford in November was by a slim margin of 2 percent of the vote—40,828,929 to 39,148,940 votes—and White attributed the loss to Ford's amateurish performance in the debate. Ford himself disagreed with White's assessment and blamed his defeat on the economy. Afterward, he said that he had no regrets about opting for Alan's more conservative course of action, which had dogged his campaign throughout the summer and into the early fall.

"I have no regrets," Ford said. "My conscience has always been clear. It was one of those gambles. It didn't turn out politically, but it was good for the country. I happen to think that was the major reason we lost the election." Timing is everything in politics. By the end of November, less than a month after the election, the economy finally took a turn for the better. Ford and Alan remained good friends afterward and golfed together frequently over the years. Alan said later that of all the presidents he served, Gerry Ford was the one to whom he felt closest.

"I was lucky to have someone as capable, whom I had as much faith in, as Alan Greenspan to give me advice and counsel," said Ford. "I endorsed his view and apparently he had confidence in my decision-making. We had a superb working relationship." Scarcely a week went by that Ford failed to ask Alan about Rose's health—a gesture that touched Alan deeply.

Whatever the primary reason for Ford's loss to Carter, the simple fact for Alan was that he was suddenly out of a job. He found his consulting business in reasonably good shape when he returned to New York City in January 1977 and moved back to his apartment near the U.N. Like most people retiring from powerful government posts, Alan found himself in great demand on the lecture circuit and was a frequent guest speaker at corporate conferences around the country, commanding a minimum of $10,000 per speech to dispense words of wisdom to the already converted.

Alan was a regular on the well-traveled circuit between Washington and Wall Street, expert at the game of advising New York financiers about Washington politics and Washington politicians about financial deals pending on Wall Street. During this period he was invited to join the boards of J. P. Morgan and other high-ticket financial institutions. Alan extended his consulting business to the savings and loan industry, where he made more powerful friends, including S&L kingpin Charles Keating and Texas financier James Baker, a close associate of George Bush who later became Secretary of State and Treasury in the Reagan White House.

From this time onward, Alan was never far out of the public eye. He heightened his visibility, and cemented his ties with the Republican Party, by becoming a frequent critic of the Carter administration and its ruinous economic policies. Jimmy Carter had put the country "on a track of inflationary deficits," Alan said during a speech to the National Press Club in February 1978. If not reversed, the deficits "will lead this nation into an economic crisis."

He continued to promote a gold standard for the dollar, which he believed would be the best restraint on inflation. However, he added that a gold standard "presupposes that governments are willing to abide by the exchange rate impact on their domestic policies. If you have a number of countries who are unwilling to abide by fixed exchange rates then you can't impose a gold standard." Alan stated then and later, even after he had become chairman of the Federal Reserve, that a country with the discipline to maintain a genuine gold standard would have no need for a monetary policy administered by a central bank. In other words, such a system would have no need to hire Alan and others like him to ensure the integrity of the currency; the link to gold would do that by itself. He remained consistent in his view on the subject throughout his entire career inside and outside the Washington Beltway.

When Carter assumed office in January 1977, he had inherited an economy that was slowly emerging from a recession. During the campaign, he had severely criticized President Ford for his failures to control inflation and relieve unemployment, but several years into his own presidency, both inflation and unemployment were considerably worse than at the time of his inauguration. The annual inflation rate rose from 4.8% in 1976 to 6.8% in 1977, 9% in 1978, 11% in 1979, and hovered around 12% at the time of the 1980 election campaign. The dismal statistics provided Alan with ample ammunition with which to attack the Democratic administration in his role as a private economist.

CHAPTER 17

Although Carter had pledged to eliminate federal deficits, the deficit for fiscal year 1979 totaled $27.7 billion, and for 1980 it was nearly $59 billion. With approximately eight million people out of work, the unemployment rate had leveled off to a nationwide average of about 7.7 percent by the time of the election campaign, but it was considerably higher in some industrial states.

Alan pointed out that Carter had also precipitated a drastic erosion of the value of the U.S. dollar in international money markets, and many analysts blamed the decline on a large and persistent trade deficit, much of it a result of U.S. dependence on foreign oil. The President warned that Americans were wasting too much energy, that domestic supplies of oil and natural gas were running out, and that foreign supplies of petroleum were subject to embargoes by the oil-producing nations, principally by members of the Organization of Petroleum Exporting Countries (OPEC). In mid-1979, in the wake of widespread shortages of gasoline, Carter advanced a long-term program designed to solve the energy problem. He proposed a limit on imported oil; gradual price decontrol on domestically produced oil; a stringent program of conservation; and development of alternative sources of energy such as solar, nuclear, and geothermal power, oil and gas from shale and coal, and synthetic fuels. In what was probably his most significant domestic legislative accomplishment, he was able to get a significant portion of his energy program through Congress.

Alan and other free-market economists criticized Carter for proposing a socialistic health insurance bill, which the President failed to get passed by a Congress controlled by his own party. Carter also failed in his effort to reform the welfare system and impose controls on hospital costs. His efforts to gain congressional approval of his plans to consolidate natural resource agencies within the Department of the Interior and to expand economic development units in the Department of Housing and Urban Development likewise ended in failure. Of even greater importance, the Democratic Congress shot down Carter's halfhearted program to reform the cumbersome federal income tax system, a top priority for Alan and his colleagues on the Republican side of the aisle.

As the 1980 election approached, Carter found himself under increasing attack by both Republicans and the leaders of the Democratic Party. The critics argued that his performance suggested an ineptitude and lack of leadership that had permitted the nation to drift during his presidency. Many contended that his policies had caused the United States to become militarily inferior to the Soviet Union, while others argued that his faltering commitment to economic and social needs had betrayed longstanding policies of the Democratic party designed to the help the poor and disfranchised.

Polls taken in July 1980 gave Carter a paltry 21 percent approval rating among the electorate. This was the lowest rating any President, including Richard Nixon at the time of his resignation, had received since polling began in 1936. It was but the latest evidence of Carter's dwindling support, which was fading to invisibility. The numbers prompted Senator Edward Kennedy of Massachusetts to take on the incumbent President in the 1980 primary campaign for the Democratic presidential nomination.

Ted Kennedy's entry into the race seemed to be a reasonable

political move at the time, and much of the party establishment backed Kennedy in its desire to dump the out-of-touch former governor of Georgia, who had remained a Washington outsider since his inauguration. The odds were against Carter, who was perceived by the public to be ineffectual during his four years in office. He had been unable to get much of his legislative program through Congress. His relationships with the Democratic leadership of the House and Senate were cool and distant. His White House staff was composed of old Georgia friends, few of whom appeared knowledgeable about Washington politics. He was criticized for allowing the U.S. embassy personnel in Iran to be taken hostage and for not having found a way to secure their release. His initiatives in the Middle East peace process had foundered. The economy was in disarray. The country had suffered through long lines at the gas pumps, as well as fuel oil shortages and high prices. There was little to suggest that he could overcome these obstacles and get himself reelected.

Despite this incredible array of baggage, Carter won the nomination on the first ballot at the Democratic National Convention in New York in August, with 2,129 votes to Kennedy's 1,146. Carter had fashioned his winning margin with victories in twenty-four state primaries while Kennedy won only ten, largely due to the public's disillusionment about the Massachusetts senator's role in an aide's death at Chapaquiddick more than a decade earlier. Carter had garnered 51.2 percent of the primary votes compared with 37.6 percent for Kennedy, 2.9 percent for Governor Edmund G. Brown Jr. of California, and the balance for an array of lesser-known contenders. In addition, he had won most of the Democratic caucuses in states that used them instead of primaries.

However, Carter left the New York convention with a divided party and a low standing in the polls, trailing the Republican contender, Ronald Reagan, whose team of close advisers included Alan and most of the economists he had worked with during the Nixon-Ford years. Moderate Republicans were dismayed about the conservative cast of Reagan's inner circle, and their discontent spurred former Republican Congressman John Anderson of Illinois to run as an independent.

Carter's lack of widespread support continued throughout the summer and into the fall, and the results of the general election reflected what the polls had been showing. The Republican team of Ronald Reagan and George Bush swept into office in a landslide victory, with 42,797,153 votes for Reagan and 34,434,100 for Carter. Anderson pulled a surprisingly strong 7 percent of the popular vote, but he appeared to take as many away from Carter as he did from Reagan. More significantly, Reagan won with 489 electoral votes against only 49 for Carter and none for Anderson. No sooner had the votes been tallied when Reagan's phrase-makers started to trumpet the beginning of a new American Revolution—the Reagan Revolution—that was destined to alter the political and economic tone of the country throughout the decade.

Reagan appointed Alan to his Economic Advisory Board, which also included Murray Weidenbaum, Arthur Burns, Milton Friedman, George Shultz, William Simon, and Paul McCracken. The President tapped Alan's old colleague from their days at Rand's soirées, Martin Anderson, to fill the role of Assistant to the President for Policy Development. Together, members of the advisory board and Anderson asked Reagan to adopt a program of steep tax cuts synchronized with equally sharp reductions in federal spending. The top income tax rate at the time was 70 percent, and Alan and the others argued that it needed to be lowered dramatically to finally put an end to the long, steep economic decline that had prevailed through most of the 1970s.

Almost immediately, there ensued a battle for Reagan's soul. Alan, Milton Friedman, and the more traditional conservative economists manned one side of the barricade with their call for both tax and spending reductions. Arrayed against them on the other side was a new generation of "supply-siders," including Norman Ture, Craig Roberts, Steve Entin, Jack Kemp, William Roth, and University of Southern California economist Arthur Laffer. They argued that lower tax rates would lead to *higher* government revenues, which would enable the administration to maintain a high level of federal spending. Supply-side economics would give the country the best of all possible worlds, they believed: more guns and butter financed by *lower* taxes. George Bush had labeled the concept "voodoo economics" when he had challenged Reagan in the primaries, long before Reagan asked him to be his running mate.

The polls indicated that the American people desperately wanted a tax cut. An underground economy amounting to $700 billion in unreported, off-the-books income testified to that clearly enough, even if one distrusted the pollsters. The American people simply were not in a mood to listen to any talk about tax cuts being inflationary, not when their salary checks were being decimated by federal, state, and Social Security taxes before they had a chance to spend a nickel of their own money. Reagan tapped a popular chord when he advocated not only a tax cut, but a whopping 30 percent reduction in taxes spread out over three years.

However, despite his rhetoric about bloated government and the need to cut back on spending, Reagan was not convinced that it was politically feasible to gut the federal budget. The same polls that revealed the public wanted lower taxes also indicated that Americans would not accept a corresponding cutback in the government services on which they had become dependent. In the area of foreign policy, the prevailing view at the time was that the Russians had outpaced us in military hardware, and we needed to spend more on national defense. It was the old story all over again: everyone was in favor of lower taxes and spending cuts as long as someone else's subsidy was eliminated. Once in the White House, Reagan announced that he would simultaneously reduce taxes, build up our military strength, and balance the budget without cutting any of the meat, only the fat, from social services.

Alan, Anderson, Friedman, and the other traditionalists squared off for a battle with Kemp and the supply siders before Reagan's first hundred days got under way. They told Reagan that the budget had to be balanced before the government could initiate any substantial tax cuts. There was no way to do it without generating some pain for the first year or eighteen months of Reagan's first term. Conservatives from Robert Taft to Barry Goldwater had argued for decades that Americans would have to be willing to live without all the social welfare programs that had come into existence since the

1930s if they wanted a small government and low taxes. Alan and his cohorts concurred with that view and Reagan said he agreed with them philosophically. However, he also knew that it was bad politics. Sound economic advice made common sense but, realistically, the voting public would not be willing to pay the price for a more frugal government.

Reagan listened to Alan and the other members of the advisory board and said he would give serious consideration to their suggestions. As governor of California, however, he had never been as fiscally conservative as his rhetoric indicated, and he was not inclined to take on great political risk at the start of his first term as President. With Kemp and his colleagues providing the cover he needed, Reagan decided to jettison the baggage of the past and actively promote their message. Certainly, it was far more palatable to the American people, since it promised so much more. Supply-side economics maintained that Reagan could simultaneously fight inflation, end the recession, and reinvigorate the economy.

Reagan urged Kemp and Laffer to sell their credo to the public. Using a sideways bell curve designed by Laffer, the two men showed graphically how taxes, when reduced to an acceptable level, stimulate the economy to a degree that will increase government revenue. Laffer stated that rising taxes drove more and more people out of the legal marketplace into the underground economy, where they could hang onto the money they earned. With low taxes, workers have an incentive to work legitimately and invest their money in a way that stimulates the economy.

Alan and the traditionalists grew increasingly alarmed when they saw the direction Reagan was taking. The supply-side approach would increase the budget deficit and lead to higher inflation, they argued. Not at all, said Laffer and Kemp, not if the Federal Reserve controlled the rate of monetary growth. The supply-siders were monetarists who believed that a rapid expansion in the money supply, not budget deficits, was the cause of inflation. By keeping interest rates slightly higher than the level of inflation and restricting the amount of borrowing in the market, the supply of money would be lowered, putting a dampening effect on inflation, they said.

The message had great appeal, offering as it did a third way between traditional conservative and liberal opinion, and no one was better at communicating it than the Great Communicator himself. For decades, conservatives had been telling people that we had to balance the budget by giving up all the goodies people had gotten used to. We all had to tighten our belts a bit. Liberals, on the other hand, had been saying that when inflation gets too high, the government has to raise taxes and put a freeze on prices and wages to get it under control.

Now, suddenly, along came supply-side economics, which maintained that the old rules no longer applied. It was possible to have low taxes, a balanced budget, government programs to house the homeless and feed the poor, a strong military defense, and a robust economy with low inflation. Reagan's great genius was that he was able to make the public believe it. It was clear that the voters had not elected a conservative. Their new President was nothing less than a right-wing revolutionary who actually promised people more than the liberals did, but in a manner that was new and fresh and stripped of all the tired rhetoric of the past.

Reagan had said he would hit the ground running right after his inauguration, and he was as good as his word. In quick order, Reagan established the framework of the supply-side New Deal he now championed. On Inauguration Day, January 20, 1981, he imposed a moratorium on government hiring. Two days later he announced a cutback on government travel, froze new business regulations that were about to go into effect, and appointed a task force to eliminate other regulations already in existence. On January 29, the President denounced the Soviet Union's aggressive behavior in various parts of the world.

On February 18, President Reagan submitted to Congress step one of his economic program, calling initially for a three-year, 30 percent reduction in income taxes combined with only a cut in the *rate* of spending growth—not an actual spending cut in real dollar terms. On February 27 he drew the line on Soviet-Cuban interference in El Salvador. On March 11 he traveled to Canada to visit Prime Minister Pierre Trudeau. On March 26 Reagan established a new council to study additional waste and fraud in government as targets for future budget cuts. On April 6 the President scrapped thirty-four separate safety and environmental regulations in order to help the moribund automobile industry. On April 8 he created an advisory committee, which included Alan, to explore ways of restoring various decision-making powers to state and local governments. On April 11, after recuperating from an assassination attempt, he returned to the White House and stepped up his campaign to get the entire economic package enacted by Congress.

Reagan clearly established the pattern of his administration during his first three whirlwind months in office: tax cuts, a reduction in the growth rate of government spending to 4.7 percent a year from an average of 13.6 percent during the previous three years, a tougher foreign policy, deregulation, and decentralization. Alan and the other traditionalists grew increasingly uneasy about the final shape of Reagan's economic program. In their view, a 30 percent reduction in taxes should have been matched by an equal cut in government spending, not a mere cut in the growth rate. It was apparent that they had lost the first battle in the war with Kemp, Laffer, Ture, and the rest of the supply-side camp. The program Reagan delivered had Laffer's fingerprints all over it.

CHAPTER 18

In its final version, the 1981 tax law—and the one that followed in 1986—led to a more simplified tax code with fewer and lower income tax rates. Over this five-year period, Reagan succeeded in bringing the top marginal tax bracket down from 70 percent to 28 percent in stages. However, with federal spending scheduled to *rise* by more than 4 percent a year, Alan, Anderson, Burns, Friedman, Treasury Secretary Donald Regan, and budget director David Stockman were concerned enough about the potential budget deficit to request a special meeting with Reagan.

They "wanted to slow down the tax cut, delay it, stop it," said Anderson. "All these guys came in to meet with Reagan. They'd gather in the Roosevelt Room. Then Reagan would come in and wink at Arthur Burns, tap Friedman on the shoulder, laugh with Alan Greenspan, and talk a bit. They were his old friends."

They spoke their minds and Reagan listened intently, nodding at them periodically. After about thirty minutes the President would rise to his feet, indicating that the meeting was over. He would walk over, make eye contact with each one individually, shake his hand, and thank him for stopping by to share his thoughts.

"Then they'd all leave, and we'd go back and start all over again," said Anderson.

Alan and the others initially believed that Reagan would give careful consideration to their words, but over the ensuing months the tax cuts went into effect and Congress refused to make real cuts in spending. Reagan did a great job of blaming a recalcitrant Congress for the exploding budget, gesticulating forcefully during press conferences as he demanded a line-item budget veto like many governors had in their home states. However, Alan was never convinced that Reagan fought hard enough for spending restraints. Throughout his entire first term in office, Reagan enjoyed broad public support and could have bent Congress to his will if he truly wanted to. But his heart was not really in it. The supply-side philosophy provided him with an easy way out, and the affable President was only too eager to take it.

Alan regarded Reagan's method of governing as a victory of style over substance. He considered Reagan to be a "psychologically professional comedian, a professional raconteur" with an uncanny ability to convey ideas through amusing anecdotes. Overall, however, Alan believed the President possessed an "unsophisticated" grasp of economics. In that regard, at least, he thought Reagan suffered in comparison to Gerry Ford, with whom he continued to have a close relationship. Throughout his entire tenure with the Reagan administration, Alan would never get that close to Reagan on a personal level.

After overhauling the tax code, reforming the Social Security system was another major priority of the administration. In December 1981, Reagan formed the bipartisan National Commission on Social Security Reform and appointed Alan chairman.

The President delivered a message to the public on December 16 that stated, "In September I announced that I would appoint a bipartisan task force to work with the president and the Congress to reach two specific goals: propose realistic, long-term reforms to put

Social Security back on a sound financial footing and forge a work-ing bipartisan consensus so that the necessary reforms will be passed into law.

"Senate Majority Leader Baker, Speaker O'Neill, and I agreed we would each select five members for a new National Commission on Social Security. Today I am pleased and honored to announce the formation of the commission and that Alan Greenspan has agreed at my request to serve as Chairman of that commission.

"I am asking the commission to present its report to the Ameri-can people at the end of next year. I can think of no more impor-tant domestic problem requiring resolution than the future of our Social Security system."

With that mandate in mind, Alan and his commission took on the onerous task of transforming the most sacred entitlement pro-gram in U.S. history into a viable retirement plan. In addition to Alan, other members appointed by Reagan included Robert A. Beck, CEO of Prudential Insurance Company; Mary Falvey Fuller, a management consultant based in San Francisco; Alexander B. Trow-bridge, president of the National Association of Manufacturers; and Joe D. Waggoner Jr., former congressman and consultant to Bossier Bank and Trust Company.

Senate Majority Leader Howard Baker appointed Senator William Armstrong of Colorado; Senator Robert Dole of Kansas; Senator John Heinz of Pennsylvania; Senator Daniel Patrick Moyni-han of New York; and union leader Lane Kirkland, president of the AFL-CIO.

House Speaker Thomas P. ("Tip") O'Neill's appointees were Congressman William Archer of Texas; Congressman Barber Conable of New York; Congressman Claude D. Pepper of Florida; Visiting Scholar Robert M. Ball of the Center for the Study of Social Policy; and former congresswoman Martha E. Keys.

Treasury secretary James Baker invited this eclectic and ideo-logically diverse group to meet secretly in his house on Foxhall Road in Washington, D.C. to deliberate the fate of America's retirees. The bunker-like location successfully concealed their activities from the scrutiny of the media, which was champing at the bit for juicy details before they became available. The commission set about specifically to analyze the long-term financial condition of the Social Security trust fund; identify problems threatening its solvency; come up with solutions to ensure Social Security's financial integrity; and, finally, make appropriate recommendations to the President and the Congress. At his discretion, Alan set the agenda and called for meetings approximately once a month.

All in all, it was an unwieldy job, involving as it did fifteen men and women from diverse political and ideological backgrounds. Alan favored privatization of the system—allowing Americans to invest their Social Security taxes in private retirement accounts similar to IRAs—and various other members of the commission, including Republican Bill Archer, Democrat Daniel Patrick Moynihan, and those from private industry, advocated at least partial privatization. For a model of what they would like to accomplish they looked toward Chile, which had successfully privatized its own retirement system a year earlier with the help of Milton Friedman and other conservative economists from the University of Chicago. However, union leader Lane Kirkland and most of the Democrats except for Moynihan were adamantly opposed to any talk of privatization. Their solution from the start was the same one every administration since Roosevelt had put into practice: higher taxes combined with patchwork changes when needed to keep the system afloat for another couple of decades or so.

It was difficult to envision how the commission would ever be able to take this stew of conflicting views and reach a consensus. Economist Peter Ferrara, author of *Social Security: The Inherent Contradiction*, said at the time that "It was obvious that there would be a disaster as soon as the names of the members of the National Commission on Social Security Reform [sic] were announced. The Washington establishment was firmly in control." His remarks, as we shall see, turned out to be morbidly prophetic.

□ □ □

Alan continued to visit his mother regularly whenever he was in New York City, and he occasionally dropped in to see Ayn Rand at her apartment in the East Thirties. Rand's health had been deteriorating rapidly during the past couple of years, and she had grown depressed over the continuing hostility toward her ideas among intellectuals and the media. She had become more reclusive in her advancing years, abandoning fiction in favor of an occasional article in her newsletter, and venturing out in public only once a year to give a talk at the Ford Hall Forum in Boston.

Early in 1981, Rand had visited her internist, Dr. Murray Dworetzky, at his office in Manhattan. She had been smoking two packs of cigarettes a day for fifty years, and Dworetzky was troubled about her health.

"You've *got* to stop it," he told her. "It's terribly bad for you. It's dangerous."

"But *why*?" she demanded. "And don't tell me about statistics; I've explained why statistics aren't proof. You have to give me a *rational* explanation. *Why* should I stop smoking?"

A nurse entered the office and handed Dworetzky copies of Rand's chest X-rays. Dworetzky sighed and pointed to shadows on the film where none should have existed. "*That's* why," he said.

"What's wrong? What is it?"

"I'm . . . sorry. It looks like a malignancy in one lung."

Rand removed the cigarette she had burning in her long black filter with the gold dollar sign embossed along the side, snuffed it out in the ashtray on the doctor's desk, and put the filter back in her purse. It was the last cigarette she ever smoked, but it was already too late. The surgeries and treatment she received during the next few months did little to reverse the downward spiral. She grew weaker and frailer through January 1982 and had to be hospitalized with cardiopulmonary problems in February. The end was drawing near. Rand breathed her last on the morning of March 6, 1982—the very day of Alan's fifty-sixth birthday. His intellectual mentor had turned seventy-seven years of age a month earlier.

Leonard Peikoff, whom Rand had designated as both her intellectual and financial heir, was the first of many to call Alan with the news. Alan placed the receiver back on its cradle and covered his eyes with his hand. Ayn Rand, and his mother, Rose, had been the two most important women in his life for decades, and now one of them was gone.

The novelist was laid out at the Frank E. Campbell Funeral Home at Madison Avenue and 81st Street. On the Monday night following her death, hundreds of her admirers stood outside in the cold dressed in everything from blue jeans to mink coats, awaiting their turn to pay their respects. Between seven and nine o'clock, about eight hundred mourners passed somberly by her coffin. A six-foot-long floral arrangement in the shape of a dollar sign lay in the coffin beside her body. On her breast was a photograph of her husband, Frank, and on her finger was the simple gold wedding band she had worn since Frank placed it there in 1929. Among those passing through for a final look at the woman who had made such a powerful impact on their lives were Alan; Robert Bleiberg, editorial director of *Barron's*; many leaders of the Libertarian Party; professors from various colleges and universities ranging from Vassar to York University in Toronto; and, of course, the remaining members of her Collective.

Alan, along with two hundred of Rand's friends and disciples, attended the private burial ceremony in Valhalla, an hour north of New York City. The casket was lowered into her grave on top of a rolling hill as snowflakes blanketed the grass and soil. The deceased novelist descended slowly to her final resting place beside her husband, then Alan and the others filed past and each dropped a fresh flower on the casket. Two stones marked the joint gravesite, one reading FRANK O'CONNOR, 1897–1979, and the other AYN RAND O'CONNOR, 1905–1982.

For Alan, Rand's death marked the end of an era. He was not a religious or a superstitious man, but he could not stop wondering about the timing of her death. Was there any significance in her passing on the date of his birth? It was an irony that would continue to haunt him. The goddess of laissez-faire capitalism was gone. As the most prominent of her followers, Alan was aware of a special calling to carry her ideas forward to the best of his ability. However, he was not sure that would be at all possible in the world of Washington politics that he chose to inhabit.

President Ford congratulates Alan Greenspan at the White House on Sept. 4, 1974, after Greenspan was sworn in as chairman of the Council of Economic Advisers. Rose Goldsmith, Greenspan's mother, stands at right.

President Reagan congratulates Alan Greenspan after he was sworn in as the new chairman of the Federal Reserve Board during a ceremony at the White House in this Aug. 11, 1987, file photo.

143

Federal Reserve Board Chairman Alan Greenspan speaks before the House Banking Committee on Capitol Hill in Washington, D.C. on Jan. 24, 1989. Greenspan spoke about domestic economic issues.

Federal Reserve Chairman Alan Greenspan and his new bride, NBC television correspondent Andrea Mitchell check the rain as they walk out of The Inn at Little Washington, Virginia, after being married on Sunday, April 6, 1997. Walking with the couple is seven-year-old flower girl Lauren Hunt, who is Mitchell's goddaughter.

Newlyweds Greenspan and Andrea Mitchell wait in the receiving line at the White House on Tuesday, April 8, 1997, during a state dinner in honor of the Canadian prime minister.

Senate Banking Committee Chairman Sen. Alphonse D'Amato, right, talks with Greenspan on Capitol Hill on Wednesday, July 23, 1997, prior to Greenspan testifying on the state of the economy before the committee.

The Reverend Jesse Jackson, right, jokes with Greenspan following Greenspan's address during the first Rainbow/Push Coalition Wall Street Project Conference in New York on Jan. 16, 1998. The conference explored minorities' needs in America's marketplace.

Greenspan looks on as President Clinton speaks in the Oval Office of the White House on Tuesday, Jan. 4, 2000, where the President nominated Greenspan to serve a fourth term as Fed chairman.

Greenspan speaks with European Central Bank president Wim Duisenberg prior to a meeting of the Group of 20 finance ministers and bank governors in Montreal, Canada, on Wednesday, Oct. 25, 2000.

Greenspan and treasury secretary Robert Rubin appear before the Senate Banking Committee on Capitol Hill on Wednesday, June 17, 1998, to discuss the financial modernization bill recently passed by the House.

President-elect Bush says goodbye to Greenspan following their private meeting at the Madison Hotel in Washington on Monday, Dec. 18, 2000.

U.S. Secretary of the Treasury Paul O'Neill, left, Greenspan, and Italian finance minister Vincenzo Visco, right, talk as they and other Group of Seven (G7) finance ministers gather for a group photo at Blair House in Washington on Saturday, April 28, 2001.

CHAPTER 19

The members of the Social Security commission labored fruitlessly over a plan to reform the system but found it increasingly impossible to reach a consensus. Alan and his allies pressed for at least partial privatization, but the opposing faction was adamantly against the concept. They argued vehemently for higher taxes and increased benefits for more people, and it appeared that there was no way to end the impasse. The commission had instructions from Reagan to come up with a program he could put before Congress by the end of 1982, and halfway through the year the members were no closer to an agreement than when they began their deliberations. There was no way they could meet their deadline unless somebody blinked.

Clearly, it was not going to be the defenders of the status quo. Lane Kirkland and most of the Democrats had no incentive to cooperate with the current administration. If they were going to present Reagan with a program on time, it was going to be on their terms or not at all. Alan said later that he had no alternative but to go along with their demands for higher taxes, but others claimed

149

that he and his allies could have fought harder for real reforms. The program they cobbled together and gave to Reagan at the end of the year had no trace of Alan's imprint on it.

"Reagan was extremely disappointed," said F. Clifton White. "He had hoped for some element of privatization. He clearly expected that's what they would come up with in the final package."

"Social Security had become a mine field for the administration," said economist William A. Niskanen, another Reagan adviser, "but the funding problem would not go away. The outcome of the process was substantially determined by the initial personal choices. The outcomes of this process of drafting legislation by a commission served the political interests of the administration but were wholly inconsistent with the President's expressed policy objectives."

The substance of the final legislation was contrary to Reagan's objectives in several ways, according to Niskanen. Coverage was extended to new federal workers and employees of nonprofit organizations, and both state and local government workers were no longer allowed to opt out of the system. The new legislation committed general revenues to Social Security for the first time ever. Most damaging of all, 78 percent of the projected Social Security deficit was to be reduced by higher taxes, and the age for full retirement benefits was increased in stages from sixty-five to sixty-seven by 2022.

The commission "botched an opportunity to sort out these problems and indefinitely deferred their resolution," said Niskanen. "The Democrats' exploitation of the issue only compounded the problem."

The resulting legislation "roped even more taxpayers into the scam, and hiked taxes for everyone," said Ed Crane of the Cato Institute, a think tank based in Washington, D.C. It moved tax increases scheduled for the future into the present, raised self-employment taxes, taxed benefits for single people with incomes of $25,000 and couples with incomes over $32,000, expanded the program to new federal employees, and prohibited state and local government employees from leaving the system. The reform package delayed one cost-of-living increase, but this was more than outweighed by the onerous increases in Social Security taxes. Meanwhile, the forced inclusion of new payers "herded practically every worker into the Social Security leviathan in order to sustain its life," said Crane.

Reagan put as good a face on the so-called reforms as it was possible to do under the circumstances. Signing the new bill into law on April 20, 1983, Reagan called it a "monument to the spirit of compassion and commitment that unites us as a people."

One year after the reform passed, tax attorney Helen Rogers showed that working- and middle-class people were actually paying more in taxes to the federal government despite Reagan's income tax cuts. The original tax cuts "lowered rates in one place but vastly increased them elsewhere."

Following his personal defeat, Alan had little choice but to swallow his pride and defend the Frankenstein monster that had been spawned on his watch. It would take "a very adverse economic scenario to create major financial problems for the retirement-disability side of the Social Security system," he said in an interview published in the *Christian Science Monitor*. In other words, retirees' Social Security pensions were secure as a result of the new bill. Social Security had been "fixed" for at least seventy-five years through 2058, he claimed. Appearing on television on the *MacNeil/Lehrer Report* in 1983, Alan said accurately enough in his labored syntax that his commission was "really made up of a spectrum of individuals which come pretty much across the extremes of American politics from one end to the other." What he left out, however, was a description of the tensions and hostility that characterized the group's deliberations.

Alan knew as well as anyone, and better than most, that there was no real trust fund to finance Social Security's future obligations. His own projections indicated that privatization of Social Security was the only long-term solution that would lead to higher retirement income, greater economic growth, more personal freedom, and less government involvement in the financial lives of American citizens. But he had become a major player on the Washington scene, and he chose in this instance to keep these views to himself.

It was not Alan's finest hour.

□ □ □

Alan was less reticent, however, about reiterating his views on the gold standard. A gold-backed dollar and the overhaul of the antitrust laws, which he largely opposed, had long been his overriding ideological passions. In 1983 he further developed his proposal for a gold standard, saying "a gold standard with a freely fluctuating market price of gold is not only possible but desirable."

Alan based his argument on an article he published two years earlier on the Op-Ed page of the *Wall Street Journal*, stating that the transition to a gold standard would "not be difficult" and could "easily be monitored" by both investors and the government. He proposed that the U.S. Treasury issue five-year notes that paid interest in and were redeemable in gold when they matured. The new gold-backed notes would compete in the marketplace alongside traditional five-year notes that paid interest in and were redeemable in dollars. According to Alan, this would enable the government to measure the viability of a transition to gold by observing which notes investors preferred. Supply and demand in the free market would set price levels for each set of notes.

He reasoned that this type of competing system would act as a restraint on public spending. If the government continued to run up inflationary budget deficits, it would diminish the luster of the dollar and spur a rush to gold on the part of investors. If government reformed its profligate ways, and contained spending and, consequently, inflation, investors would have enough confidence in the integrity of the dollar to invest in it. Over time, the idea would spread internationally, leading to more stable foreign currencies and lower global inflation—and, most likely, less demand for gold.

It was an ingenious concept that was well received by other gold bugs and free-market economists. However, asking government— even a conservative Republican administration such as Reagan's— to voluntarily curtail its spending habit was like asking a glutton to voluntarily put a lock on the refrigerator and throw away the key. It made sound economic sense but required a superhuman act of will to put it into practice.

Gold was not the only thing on Alan's mind in the aftermath of the Social Security fiasco. Reagan dissolved the commission shortly after he received its recommendations, and Alan returned to his consulting business and his apartment in New York. He continued to date regularly and discreetly, but there was no special woman in his life at the time. During the past year or so, he had been attracted to one woman in particular, a correspondent from NBC who covered the Reagan White House on a variety of issues ranging from arms control to the budget and tax reform. She traveled extensively with Reagan to his summit meetings with Mikhail Gorbachev and other world leaders. Alan's path crossed the reporter's frequently in the course of her work for the network, but he made a point of not getting too cozy with members of the press out of fear of compromising his position in the administration.

Once back in New York working in the private sector, however, the old rules no longer applied. The correspondent who had caught Alan's eye was Andrea Mitchell, who had the same last name as his first and only wife. She was the model of the type of woman Alan favored: blonde, good-looking, and bright. Mitchell was twenty years younger than Alan. She was a physical fitness buff who worked out regularly at health clubs in Manhattan and on the road during her travels as a reporter. She had joined NBC News in 1978 as a correspondent based in Washington and was named the network's energy correspondent a year later, reporting on the lingering energy crisis and the nuclear incident at Three Mile Island.

Alan and Mitchell started to date shortly after his return to New York. Their first official night out together was in the winter of 1984. "It started snowing," Mitchell said. "I was being terribly independent and told him he didn't have to pick me up. I couldn't get a cab. I started trudging through the snow and it was a magical evening. It was the most romantic, lovely, interesting, fun date. We discovered that we loved music and that we loved baseball. The snow kept coming down and we went for a drive through Central Park, and we just had a great time. He's very romantic, very sentimental, very smart, and has the greatest sense of humor if you can ignore his puns. He's just a very special, private, shy man."

Their age difference never bothered her. "He's very boyish, he's athletic, and Alan's curiosity is such an important part of his makeup," she said. "He's wide open to possibilities."

Alan's personal life may have taken a turn for the better, but he discovered that his consulting business had suffered during his years at the center of politics in Washington, D.C. His long absences from the business over the years had put him pretty much in the position of an absentee landlord who returns one day to find a host of problems that need to be addressed. As a top player in the current administration, Alan was still very much in demand on the lecture circuit, but the type of forecasting he specialized in had attracted stiff competition from some of the top firms on Wall Street.

"Everyone thinks that Greenspan gave up a lucrative consulting business to go to work in the public sector," said economist Pierre Rinfret. "In actuality, his business had been losing clients steadily to the point where he hardly had any left by the middle of the nineteen eighties."

The truth was somewhere in between the popular conception of Alan as a wealthy Wall Street forecaster and Rinfret's grim assessment of Alan's fortunes. Making money had never been of paramount importance to him. He had enjoyed many lucrative years and always managed to live comfortably without giving too much thought to his personal net worth. However, there is no question that Alan experienced a financial pinch when he returned to New York after his work on the Social Security commission, and this may have played a role in the creation of the problem that plagued him shortly afterward.

CHAPTER 20

Nineteen-eighty-five did not start out well for Alan. For the first time in his life, he compromised himself in a way that nearly destroyed the reputation for unshakable integrity that he had fashioned throughout his joint career in private and public life. The man who was responsible for undermining him was savings and loan czar Charles Keating, who would go on to become a major symbol of the financial fraud and corruption that characterized the latter half of the 1980s.

Keating grew up in Cincinnati, Ohio, where he practiced law with his brother William, a former congressman and publisher of the *Enquirer*, before taking a job in the business world. After serving a stint as chairman of American Continental Corp., Keating moved to Phoenix, Arizona, and made his fortune in the S&L business. In 1982, Keating bought Lincoln Savings & Loan in Phoenix and embarked on a scheme to build golf courses and a hotel with $500-per-night rooms in manmade dunes alongside the fairways. Alan got involved with Keating indirectly two years later, when the New York law firm Paul Weiss, Rifkind, Wharton & Garrison hired Alan

to conduct a financial study of its client Lincoln, which Keating subsequently relocated to Irvine, California. Keating wanted bank regulators to exempt his S&L from a rule that limited the percentage of
depositors' money it could funnel into real estate development and
other risky investments, and he called upon Alan to intervene on his
behalf.

In his earlier incarnation as chairman of American Continental,
Keating had earned a less-than-stellar reputation as a big spender
who used corporate profits to underwrite his own lavish lifestyle as
well as inflated salaries for his cronies. Alan's consulting work for
the law firm uncovered these past indiscretions, yet in February
1985 Alan wrote a letter to the bank regulators stating that Keating
and his team of managers were "seasoned and expert in selecting
and making direct investments." He went on to praise Keating for
restoring "the association to a vibrant and healthy state, with a
strong net worth position." Alan concluded his letter with an offer
to meet with regulators "in Washington at the earliest possible
time" to give witness on Keating's behalf. Keating never did get the
exemption for Lincoln that he wanted, but he ignored the rules anyway and continued to roll the dice on high-risk investments.

Around the same time, Alan was also explaining to a Congressional committee that "a time bomb is ticking away in the financial
system . . . the whole thrift-institution system will undergo a massive crisis."

Despite Alan's defense of Keating at the same time he was
expressing concern about risky loans in the financial sector, the regulators exonerated Alan later when Keating was convicted on
charges of driving his S&L into bankruptcy by looting it of $3.4 bil-
lion. Keating was found guilty of racketeering, fraud, and conspiracy, and served more than four years of a twelve-year, six-month
sentence before a federal judge overturned his conviction on technical grounds. Alan was not the only prominent figure who was
caught up in Keating's web of intrigue. Arizona Senator John
McCain also grew too cozy with Keating and found his reputation
tarnished when the Senate Ethics Committee accused him of
wrongly intervening for Keating with bank regulators. McCain was

slapped on the wrist for "showing poor judgment," but no further action was ever taken against either him or Alan.

Alan felt humiliated when Keating was convicted and Lincoln had to be bailed out with $2 billion of taxpayers' money. "Of course I'm embarrassed by my failure to foresee what eventually transpired," he said. "I was wrong about Lincoln. I was wrong about what they would ultimately do and the problems they would ultimately create."

The episode left Alan shaken on both a personal and professional level. It is not clear whether the fee he earned from Lincoln's law firm influenced his testimony on behalf of Keating, but there is little question that Alan exposed himself to at least the appearance of duplicity. The incident was serious enough to threaten his standing in Washington and his ties to the administration. It is doubtful that Alan would have deliberately jeopardized his career for a consulting fee, however lucrative, and his need to go public with a confession only compounded his embarrassment. He vowed it would be the last time he would ever put himself in such a tenuous position.

Alan spent the next couple of years trying to expand his base of clients and dividing his time between New York City and Washington, D.C. He and Andrea Mitchell became regular fixtures at the major parties and social events in both cities. Before they met, they had traveled individually in complementary, overlapping circles—politics and journalism—and together they expanded each other's social horizons. Through Andrea, Alan became friendly with leading media figures such as Judy Woodruff and her husband, Alan Hunt, and through Alan, Andrea got closer to key Reagan advisers Jim Baker and Don Regan.

According to several White House insiders, Alan made a point of regularly massaging the people who mattered. "Alan kept up his contacts with congressmen in both parties when he would go to D.C.," said Judy Mackey, one of Alan's colleagues in his consulting business.

"He had one life, and that was it," said Martin Anderson. "I don't think I was in the White House once where I didn't see him sitting in the lobby or working the offices. I was absolutely astounded by his omnipresence . . . He was always huddling in the corner with someone."

Alan's socializing eventually paid off in a way he would never have thought possible when he was a young Objectivist attending Ayn Rand's Saturday night discussions. It seemed that his entire life so far had been a training ground for the next, and final, stage in his professional career. All those years of crunching the numbers, of forecasting economic trends for well-heeled clients, of stroking the egos of the rich and powerful, finally came to fruition. Alan had to restrain himself from gloating when he called his mother to tell her the news. A key job in Washington had suddenly become vacant, and Alan was next in line to assume the role of the most powerful banker in the world.

PART FOUR

The Chairman

CHAPTER 21

Most economists and political analysts consider the chairman of the Federal Reserve to be the second most powerful individual in the world after the U.S. President. A nation's central bank can make or break the incumbent political administration through its control of the country's money supply, which has a direct bearing on the strength or weakness of the economy. Since the U.S. economy is the most powerful on earth and often determines what happens in other countries, Fed policy has a major impact on the pace of economic growth, the level of unemployment, and the rate of inflation not only in the United States, but throughout the globe.

Toward the end of Jimmy Carter's first and only term in office, the economy resembled a train wreck. Inflation, unemployment, and interest rates hovered in the stratosphere, the economy was stagnant, and the stock market was gasping for breath. The housing market was all but dead, with mortgage rates running 16 or 17 percent; the automobile market was moribund, with the prime rate, which determines other borrowing costs, well above 20 percent; and jobs were scarce when they could be found at all. Various pundits cited something they called the pain index—the sum of the rates of unemployment and inflation—and discovered it was the highest in decades. In an attempt to fix this mess in 1979, Carter got rid of the hapless Fed chairman he had appointed only a year earlier, G. William Miller, and replaced him with the hard-money Democrat Paul Volcker, who was respected on Wall Street and in international financial markets.

Volcker's tough medicine eventually proved extremely success-ful, but the fruits of his efforts came too late to help Carter in the 1980 election. It wasn't until August 1982 that stocks awakened from their long slumber and embarked on what turned out to be the longest bull market in U.S. history. By early 1983 the effects of Reagan's first round of tax cuts finally kicked in and jump-started the economy. The long dark night of pain was over, and the good times had rolled in. Reagan appointed Volcker to a second term in 1983, but by 1987 the relationship between the curmudgeonly, unyielding Fed chairman and key members of the Reagan team were showing signs of strain. Volcker was famous for doing things *his* way, and he didn't appreciate receiving advice on how to conduct monetary policy from Don Regan and Jim Baker—or from anyone else, for that matter. Playing hard to get, Volcker indi-cated that he might be available for a third term if he were asked to stay on, but Reagan and company were in no mood to placate his ego.

Baker and Regan told Reagan that they would be happy to see Volcker go, but the big question was who should take his place. Treasury secretary Jim Baker's first choice was Alan, and he was supported by Don Regan, the former chief of Merrill Lynch who had served as treasury secretary before Baker.

"He was well regarded in the fields of markets and finance," said Baker, "well regarded in the business community and on Wall Street, and he was the one person whose name kept cropping up as being the only alternative to Paul Volcker who was acceptable to the mar-kets. So all those things combined, I think, led us toward the choice of Greenspan, and I don't remember a lot of debate about it within the administration. I think it was a rather general consensus."

Baker invited Alan to visit him at his home on Foxhall Road, where Alan and the other members of the Social Security commission had originally gathered to ensure their privacy from the media. Baker wanted an assurance that Alan would accept the job of Fed chairman if Reagan asked him to replace Volcker. Alan told Baker that he would definitely accept the chairmanship and would have no problem, in his view, with safeguarding the integrity of the currency. Alan was as taciturn as usual, but he struggled inwardly to contain his glee. *This* was the role he had been training for his entire life. Combating inflation was one of his major passions, and Alan could think of no other job that better suited him.

Alan had carefully observed Volcker from the sidelines during his tenure at the Fed. Grudgingly, Alan had to admit that Volcker had been a far more successful inflation fighter than Arthur Burns had been during his own two terms as Fed chairman. Volcker, in a series of well-calculated steps, brought inflation down from an average of 12 percent in 1979 to 4 percent by the summer of 1987, a remarkable achievement. The Fed had a clear mandate to keep inflation in check, and Alan truly believed that he was the person best qualified to continue, and possibly improve upon, Volcker's legacy.

To a great extent, the political establishment resented a great deal of what Volcker had accomplished. With the economy in tatters, Volcker had succeeded in wresting control of economic policy away from the politicians. He had strengthened the independence and integrity of the Fed at a time when it was in danger of becoming beholden to the political goals of the administration—and, indeed, it had become so under Burns. The Reagan administration was no different in that regard from those that had preceded it. They all wanted a Fed chairman they could count on to rev up the economy during the months before an election. Baker, Regan, and the President himself had grown impatient with Volcker's independence and preferred to have someone more cooperative in charge of the nation's money supply. With George Bush the likely Republican presidential candidate in 1988, Baker and other Bush allies in the administration regarded Alan as someone they could work with—someone who, perhaps, might be another Arthur Burns.

It was the worst political miscalculation they could have made, as they would learn later. Alan may have been unassuming in person, but he was a fanatic on the subject of inflation.

The Federal Reserve had come into existence in 1913, six years after the financial panic of 1907. Since the creation of the United States as a republic following the American Revolution, a debate had raged between the forces in favor of establishing a central bank and those opposed. Had Alan been alive at the time of Jefferson and Hamilton, he most surely would have been against the concept of a central bank and in favor of a gold-backed currency, as he has reiterated on many occasions throughout his life. In 1987, however, with the existence of central banks part of the financial landscape not only in the United States but throughout the developed world, Alan had little choice but to accept reality. As long as the Federal Reserve existed, he believed he might as well be the one in charge of it.

The foundation for a U.S. central bank was set in 1908 with the passage of the Aldrich-Vreeland Act, which created the National Monetary Commission, calling for a central bank and fifteen regional branches. During the next two years, Congress passed many plans and laws modifying the structure of the central bank, culminating in the Glass-Owen bill of November 1913. President Woodrow Wilson signed the Federal Reserve Act of 1913 into law on December 23.

The act was amended in 1922 following the bank's mishandling of the economy after World War I, which led to runaway inflation and a financial collapse in 1921. The act was again amended in 1935, midway through the decade-long depression of the 1930s. This new change greatly increased the autonomy of the Fed and removed the Secretary of the Treasury and the Comptroller of the Currency from their ex officio status as members of the Federal Reserve Board.

New amendments followed in short order, including the lengthening of membership on the Fed from ten to fourteen years to minimize the influence of party politics, and also increasing the Fed's power to determine interest rates and bank reserves through the actions of the Federal Open Market Committee (FOMC). The Humphrey-Hawkins Act of 1978 expanded the Fed's mandate to include "the pursuit of full employment," although every Fed chairman who has ever served has regarded the containment of inflation as the Fed's paramount duty. In reality, the dual mandate of fighting inflation while achieving full employment is impossible to pursue, since the two goals are mutually exclusive.

While Arthur Burns and others pursued policies that failed to achieve the Fed's primary goal, Volcker concentrated his attention on price stability, understanding that stable prices, in the long run, result in a sound economy with full employment opportunities. Alan could not have agreed more with Volcker's philosophy in that regard. He knew that the effectiveness of the Fed is closely related to the leadership abilities of its chairman, particularly his ability to refrain from bowing to political pressure. Before taking his oath of office, Alan reviewed the policies of the Fed chairmen who had preceded him in the job and evaluated their performances. He observed that when the Fed failed to pursue its primary goal of maintaining price stability, disaster followed.

According to his own assessment, Alan considered the chairmen who served in the Vietnam and postwar years to be weak and politically ambitious. He gave three of his predecessors top marks for performance: Marriner Eccles, who provided excellent monetary management in the turbulent depression and Word War II years; William McChesney Martin, who served during a long period of low inflation from 1951 to 1970; and Paul Volcker, his immediate predecessor. Volcker provided the muscle not only to bring inflation under control but, more significantly, to break the inflation psychology that gripped the nation throughout the 1970s.

Following are the grades Alan gave to the chairmen who preceded him:

Marriner Eccles (1934–48)	A++
Thomas McCabe (1948–51)	D

William McChesney Martin (1951–70)	A
Arthur Burns (1970–78)	F
G. William Miller (1978–79)	F––
Paul Volckner (1979–87)	A+
Alan Greenspan (1987–)	?

Alan hoped he would be able to grade himself an A or higher at the end of his own tour at the helm of the most powerful central bank on earth.

The way the system is presently set up, the Federal Reserve Board is the apex of the Federal Reserve System, which consists of twelve regional Federal Reserve Banks from which individuals can buy Treasury securities directly without going through a broker. The regional Federal Reserve Banks are located in New York, Boston, Philadelphia, Cleveland, Chicago, St. Louis, Atlanta, Richmond, Minneapolis, San Francisco, Dallas, and Kansas City.

Each regional bank has nine directors who serve for three years. The Federal Reserve Board is the Washington, D.C.–based center of the Federal Reserve System, and it is composed of seven governors appointed for fourteen years. The President of the United States, with the advice and consent of the Senate, appoints the chairman and vice chairman for four-year terms. They meet behind closed doors to determine Fed open market activities, such as buying and selling of currencies, domestic and foreign Treasury securities, and gold bullion—three of the Fed's primary weapons against inflation. The Fed also adjusts key short-term interest rates, such as the federal funds rate (the rate at which banks borrow from one another) and discount rate (the rate at which banks borrow from the Federal Reserve), which increase or restrict the level of borrowing in the economy. So, for example, by limiting people's ability to borrow money, the Fed slows the rate of economic growth and cuts back on inflation.

The FOMC usually holds eight to ten meetings a year in Washington to decide on monetary policy. If the economy is sluggish, the

Fed may want to lower short-term rates to stimulate demand. If inflation is a threat, the Fed will do the opposite and raise rates to slow economic growth. In attendance are the seven Federal Reserve Board governors, the president of the New York Federal Reserve Bank, and the presidents of four of the other Federal Reserve banks on a rotating basis.

The Marriner S. Eccles Federal Reserve Board Building was built in 1936 and named after one of Alan's favorite predecessors. It depicts the glory of ancient Rome with its towering colonnades and pristine white marble structure spread out over an entire block on Constitution Avenue between Twentieth and Twenty-first Streets. You enter the imposing building on C Street and find yourself in a vast open reception area dominated by Doric columns and a sweeping marble staircase. As you climb to the top of the stairs, you find yourself proceeding along a marble and tile corridor lined on both sides by the offices of the governors of the Federal Reserve Board. Finally, you step into a large, imposing conference room that is the heart and soul of the Fed's arcane operations. This is the room where Alan and his cohorts meet to determine the prices we pay for various goods and services, and the overall health of the economy.

Before Alan could preside over this august assembly, however, he had to pass muster at his confirmation hearings, scheduled for late July. While most observers expected his appointment as Fed chairman to be approved without much opposition, many senators were dismayed by the views Alan had expressed in the past on the gold standard and the nation's antitrust laws. Baker and Regan told Alan that there was likely to be some discussion about those issues, and he had best prepare himself for a heated debate before he faced his inquisitors.

CHAPTER 22

At a White House press conference in June 1987, when President Reagan formally announced his appointment to head the Fed, Alan said, "During the 1970s there was increasing fear that inflation was destined to ratchet ever upward with ultimately disastrous effects and consequences to economic growth and employment. Under Paul's chairmanship, inflation has been effectively subdued. It will be up to those of us who follow him to be certain that those very hard-won gains are not lost. Assuring that will be one of my primary goals."

Alan knew that Volcker would be a hard act to follow. It would be difficult filling his shoes both figuratively and literally: at six feet eight inches, Volcker was by far the most physically imposing Fed chairman in history. Many pundits were concerned that Alan was likely to favor less government intervention in the economy than Volcker did. Alan's views about the efficacy of free-market forces as a natural regulator of economic activity were widely known by this time. When he served as an adviser to Gerald Ford, Alan routinely excused himself from discussions of antitrust enforcement because of his philosophical opposition to the entire concept of antitrust laws. A number of journalists expressed their doubts about Alan's ability to distance himself from the administration, although they acknowledged that he did not have as strong a personal tie to Reagan as other advisers had.

Alan spent most of July boning up on the issues that were likely to be raised at his hearings later that month. The first session to officially confirm his appointment as chairman of the Board of Governors of the Federal Reserve System got under way. The senators favoring Alan's confirmation made the point that he was well prepared to handle the challenges of a sinking U.S. dollar, accelerating inflation, and staggering budget and trade deficits. They maintained that Alan was likely to pursue policies that would stabilize economic growth and benefit agriculture as well as the rest of the economy.

His critics were less enamored of his résumé. They claimed that he had failed to demonstrate that he could remain independent of the powerful corporations and political administrations he had served. The critics also cited Alan's views on antitrust legislation as a negative. The Sherman Antitrust Act of 1890 had been the country's fundamental antitrust statute for nearly a century, and Alan was on record as opposing it. This was a crucial consideration, since the Federal Reserve was the government agency with the greatest influence in denying and approving bank mergers. In addition, Alan supported the abandonment of the country's historical policy of separating banking and commerce, the reverse of Volcker's position.

Finally, the senators opposed to Alan's confirmation argued that agriculture in the United States was extremely vulnerable to an economic downturn, and Alan was likely to advocate a laissez-faire approach toward the industry. In his own defense, Alan stated that under his leadership, changes in monetary policy "certainly would not be on the basis of politics rather than economics," and he vowed to do everything in his power to assure the Fed's independence.

"If some person in the administration tried to muscle the decisions of the Federal Reserve System some time next year in advance of the election, what would be your response to that?" asked Michigan Democrat Donald Riegel.

"I certainly don't anticipate that happening," Alan answered, "but were it to happen, I obviously would reject it."

In the end, both Alan's backers and critics conceded that his qualifications were impressive and his record of public service distinguished. When it came time to cast their votes at 5:12 P.M. on August 3, they came down overwhelmingly in favor of confirmation. The final tally showed ninety-one yeas, two nays, and seven not voting.

It is worth noting that Senator Bill Bradley of New Jersey, who would bedevil Al Gore in his race for the White House in 2000, cast one of the nay votes.

Alan inherited a potentially explosive situation from his predecessor. When he assumed the chairmanship of the Fed, the unemployment rate stood at 6.3 percent, which was considered "full employment" at the time. Economists widely believed that an unemployment rate of 6 percent or lower, combined with economic growth of more than 2.5 percent, would act as a catalyst for accelerating inflation.

This had been the prevailing wisdom for decades, accepted as gospel by all but a handful of conservative economists. Most economists had long believed there was a link among economic growth, unemployment, and wage inflation. The relationship was known as the Phillips curve, named after British economist A. W. Phillips, who developed the concept of a country's "natural rate of unemployment." He stated that if the economy grows too strongly and unemployment falls below its natural rate, wages will start to rise, which in turn will trigger an increase in overall inflation, since wages are the most important component in the price index. Putting it another way, the economy has a speed limit beyond which it begins to overheat.

As 1987 got under way, Paul Volcker had grown increasingly concerned about the robust economy and the drop in the unemployment rate close to its perceived natural U.S. level of around 6 percent. In an effort to head off the possibility of accelerating inflation later in the year, Volcker and his cohorts at the Fed had embarked on a policy of monetary tightening by raising short-term interest rates. Meanwhile, the stock market continued to explode, ignoring the upward spiral in interest rates. Ordinarily, higher interest rates are harmful to the stock market, since they provide investors with more attractive returns on low-risk investment alternatives such as money market funds and bank CDs. Alan, who had bitter memories of his father's financial demise during the Depression, had distrusted stocks all his life and avoided them in his own portfolio as though they were tainted with smallpox. He watched in dismay as stocks continued their seemingly unstoppable launch into the stratosphere.

Despite the hikes in short-term rates, inflation started to follow the stock market skyward. After a rise of 1.9 percent in 1986, inflation climbed at an annualized rate of 3.6 percent during the first half of 1987, and it was clearly on an upward trajectory. While stocks were hitting precipitous heights, bonds were going the other way, falling at an astonishing speed. Because interest rates move inversely to bond prices, the yield on the bellwether thirty-year Treasury bond was zooming rapidly toward 10 percent. With all these countervailing forces in play, it was only a question of time before stocks ran into stiff headwinds and plummeted to earth.

When Alan took over as Fed chairman in August 1987, the Dow Jones Industrial Average was nearing the high point of a five-year-long bull market that had begun in August 1982 when the Dow hit rock bottom at 776.92. Alan faced a major decision on his first day on the job: Should he continue Volcker's policy of monetary tightening and risk a meltdown in the stock market, or should he ease off the monetary brakes and take the risk that inflation might spin totally out of control? For Alan the course was clear; he was an inflation fighter first and foremost. He tipped his hand about which way he was likely to tilt when he told reporters, "Basically, my own view is that the risk of snuffing out this expansion at this stage with mild tightening is extraordinarily small." The pattern of incremental increases in interest rates was going to continue.

Alan's decision was not altogether popular with some of his colleagues, but he received critical support from Gerald Corrigan, the powerful head of the New York Federal Reserve Bank. Corrigan was as much of a hawk on inflation as Alan was, and as director of the New York Fed he was first among equals among his fellow bank directors. Corrigan feared that without further rate hikes, inflation could tick up to 5 or 6 percent a year. "If we get to that point," he told Alan, "then we are looking at a situation that inevitably carries with it the risks of highly destabilizing consequences for the real economy here and around the world." The lessons of the past were clear, he warned. "If you wait to see that kind of problem staring you in the face, the costs of unwinding it are going to be exponentially greater than the costs of checking it in the first place."

Alan needed no further convincing. The widely followed Dow Industrials peaked at 2,746.65 on August 25, then suddenly ran out of gas and began a long, agonizing slide that continued through the rest of the summer. Bonds also continued to fall, driving long-term rates even higher to keep pace with the rising inflation numbers. The dollar was likewise weakening as overseas investors shunned the greenback in favor of the stronger Japanese yen and major European currencies. With Corrigan's support, Alan convinced his colleagues that quick Fed action was required to restrain inflation and breathe some life back into the bond and currency markets. The Fed under Alan inaugurated its own series of short-term rate increases, pushing the yield on the key Fed funds rate up to 7.25 percent just before Labor Day. Since the Fed funds and discount rates have an impact on the cost of borrowing money, consumers felt the pinch immediately through higher interest rates for mortgages and automobile loans.

Most Wall Street professionals regarded the rate hikes as necessary medicine for an overheated economy, and Regan, Baker, and other White House spokesmen publicly supported Alan's tight money policy. Behind the scenes, however, others were ringing alarm bells. Beryl Sprinkel, Reagan's chief economic adviser, who was normally an advocate of hard money, thought Alan was acting a bit precipitously. Assistant treasury secretary Michael Darby also expressed some doubts. Both men were disciples of Nobel Prize–winning economist Milton Friedman, dean of the Chicago monetarist school of economists, who believed that the total supply of money in the economy ultimately determines the level of prices for goods and services. As monetary aggregates were growing at less than 4 percent a year, they were worried that the Fed could trigger a recession by raising rates too quickly.

"I thought serious trouble was brewing," said Sprinkel, "and that it could lead to a very severe break in the market and probably a recession if it wasn't handled properly."

Privately, Sprinkel was miffed that Alan had succeeded Volcker at the Fed. He felt he should have been next in line for the post himself, but Jim Baker considered him an unpredictable loudmouth whose confrontational personality disqualified him from such a sensitive role. Darby, who was a Sprinkel ally in the administration, agreed with Sprinkel and abhorred Baker.

"There was concern," Darby said, "not only with myself but among a number of the administration and outside economists, that the Fed was tightening faster than we would want in terms of risking a recession and a potential financial crisis." He later blamed Alan's initial moves as Fed chairman for ushering in the coming crash in stock prices.

Economic figures released on October 2 added fuel to the financial fires. The latest data indicated that unemployment had dipped to 5.8 percent, below the 6 percent threshold that was supposed to be an augur of accelerating inflation. In addition, the federal budget deficit, which had been exploding in recent years, was growing worse. Reagan, as he had done repeatedly in the past, blamed the Democratic Congress for failing to go along with his spending cuts and said he would reluctantly sign a bill increasing the national debt limit to $2.8 trillion. In the process, he amended the Gramm-Rudman-Hollings balanced budget act of 1985, which was supposed to have put the federal government on a tight fiscal leash. Politicians are most adept at skirting whatever spending restraints are imposed on them, and the Reagan administration was no exception. Experts projected a federal budget deficit of $144 billion for fiscal year 1988, and were astonished when it actually soared above $200 billion.

The stock market continued its sickening slide, collapsing nearly five hundred points—close to 20 percent, the entry point into bear market territory—from its August peak. Investors were increasingly spooked by the impending economic crisis, and there was little in the way of good news on the horizon to bolster their spirits. In an effort to calm the roiling financial waters, Alan decided to appear on *This Week with David Brinkley*, a network television news show, on Sunday night, October 4. He had resolved to be more cautious in his public remarks ever since his comments about the pain endured by stockbrokers brought him so much grief during his tenure with the Ford administration, but once again he proved less than adept in his relations with the media.

Just a few days earlier, reporter Sam Donaldson had asked Alan, "Are you worried about speculation in the stock market? Do you think it's getting out of hand?"

"I don't think so, not yet," Alan had replied. Then he added as a joking aside, "I'm always worried about the stock market but . . . I worry about everything. It's part of the job."

The public had taken those comments as the joke Alan intended, so he was encouraged enough to say a bit more than he should have on the program with Brinkley. When the newscaster asked him about the specter of higher inflation, Alan stated that there were no signs that inflation was picking up, but "if everyone gets it into his head that inflation is inevitable, they will start taking actions that will create inflation."

This time his remarks backfired. Viewers interpreted them as meaning that the chairman of the Federal Reserve believed higher inflation was all but inevitable, and the following week investors resumed their selling in earnest. Over the week as a whole, the thirty-year Treasury bond collapsed, driving the yield above the psychologically important 10 percent mark, and the Dow dropped another 159 points. Alan was blamed for triggering the carnage and vowed that was the last time he would ever grant an interview to reporters. It was a promise he would keep throughout his tenure as Fed chairman.

One Wall Street analyst commented that Alan was "not establishing much credibility. He hasn't made a consistent view known."

Another mused that Alan "sounded more like a Fed watcher than the chairman of the Federal Reserve."

Economists overseas were no less critical of Alan's televised performance as they watched the selling in the U.S. financial markets spill over onto their own turf. Investors everywhere were hoping for some words of reassurance that the bottom was not about to fall out of the U.S. stock market. Alan was the most logical person to provide the comfort they craved, but he failed to recognize the full importance of the role he now occupied. The market continued to drift downward during the next few days, and only a handful of analysts were astute enough to recognize that the worst was yet to come.

CHAPTER 23

Alan sat quietly in his office at the Federal Reserve, staring at the two computers on his desk that continuously flashed tidbits of data on currency movements, commodities prices, labor costs, stock and bond market gyrations, and countless other minutiae that helped him form a consensus on monetary policy.

"When we intervene to affect interest rates," Alan said, "we are acting because we have a system of fiat money, and there is no automatic mechanism to constrain it."

Next to the computers sat a small television set tuned to CNN so Alan could remain connected to breaking news developments. Beside the television were stacks of foreign and domestic newspapers that Alan read voraciously before every board meeting. In the offices that lined the corridors beyond Alan's office, dozens of young economists recruited from the country's top business schools pored through reams of data that they dropped regularly into the in box in the chairman's office.

"I've spent all of my working life observing how the economy functions," said Alan. "I was at various times a specialist in virtually every major industry and generally knowledgeable about the remainder. When you go through every industry over your lifetime, you should know how the system works."

Information was Alan's oxygen; without it he was incapable of doing his job properly. "We have sources of information not available generally," Alan said. "Companies and member banks, for example, won't speak to their competitors, but they speak to us."

Alan was distressed. None of the news anywhere was the least bit encouraging. Wherever he looked he saw signs of pending gloom. Lines of concern deeply furrowed his brow, his jowls cascaded in folds down the sides of his neck, and his lips curled downward at the corners in an expression of grim resignation. He could almost see the coming disaster looming on the horizon. Alan tried to dismiss his premonition as just another example of his normally cautious nature, but this time was different. His sense of foreboding was almost palpable, like a gathering storm cloud crowding out the last trace of sun from the sky.

On Friday, October 16, the stock market suffered one of its worst tumbles in history, increasing Alan's fear that some unspeakable catastrophe was about to undermine the financial markets. The day got off to an ominous start when an Iranian gunboat attacked an oil tanker sporting an American flag just ninety minutes before the opening bell on Wall Street. The selling commenced immediately, and by late morning a major rout was under way. At one point the Dow was down 130 points before ending the day with a loss of more than one hundred points for the first time ever. Since the beginning of the month, the market had swooned 15 percent, for a cumulative decline of nearly 18 percent since its peak in August.

Beryl Sprinkel called a meeting with Baker, Alan, and the President in Reagan's quarters on the top floor of the White House. Baker reassured Reagan that there was nothing seriously wrong with the economy, that the stock market was merely responding to the continuous rise in interest rates, and Alan seconded his assessment. Sprinkel took a contrary view and used the occasion to disagree with both of them in no uncertain terms, maintaining that the Fed had gone too far with its rate hikes in an effort to prop up the sagging dollar. Baker, however, downplayed the incident afterward.

"The truth of the matter is Beryl was one of these guys who felt that you never did anything to coordinate economic policy. I mean, he was the foremost proponent of benign neglect . . . It wasn't his policy, he didn't know anything about it when we changed it, so he didn't like it."

The weekend was a tense one for everyone in the administration, and Alan spent most of it in front of his computers trying to divine hidden currents of meaning in the data that flowed across the screens. His worst fears were realized on Monday morning when the bottom fell out of stock markets overseas. The selling started in Japan and rolled westward across the time zones, toppling markets as they opened. The wave of panic hit continental Europe and London, and it seemed all but certain that the giant tsunami would inundate New York when stocks opened for trading at nine-thirty. By ten o'clock, the carnage was so severe that John Phelan, chairman of the New York Stock Exchange, called an impromptu meeting with the heads of major financial firms to decide whether they should take extraordinary measures to stanch the blood flow. Within an hour and a half of the opening bell, the Dow was off more than two hundred points and the yield on the thirty-year Treasury bond had jumped to 10.5 percent.

Greenspan took it all in from his ringside seat in front of his computers, trying to fathom in his own mind whether this was truly the end of the world as we know it, or merely a violent storm that would pass in time. He turned his office into a command post, fielding calls from financial leaders worried about the system's ability to cope with the heavy volume. Some buyers entered the market just before noon, picking up shares at what they hoped were bargain basement prices, and for the first time in weeks it appeared as though the market may have hit bottom. Alan was scheduled to fly to Dallas to deliver a speech the following morning to six thousand delegates attending the American Bankers Association convention, and he decided to leave Washington and keep the appointment.

While his plane was airborne, the selling commenced anew. Investors panicked when SEC chairman David Ruder stated publicly that he was thinking of closing the market early to stem the hemorrhaging. "There is some point," he said nervously, "and I don't know what that point is, that I would be interested in talking to the NYSE about a temporary, very temporary halt in trading."

Those who were previously determined to wait out the wreckage now feared that they would be completely wiped out if they delayed any longer. Phone lines were jammed at brokerage houses across the country when investors called in with orders to sell their stocks at any price. It was the old story all over again: people who loved a stock at fifty dollars a share couldn't wait to sell it at twenty, eighteen, fifteen, whatever price they could get for it. Logic said that if a stock was worth fifty, it was far more attractive at twenty or twenty-five, but greed had given way to fear and stocks at any price had suddenly become poison.

Alan stepped off the plane onto the runway at Dallas and found disaster waiting for him. Anxiously greeting his arrival was a phalanx of reporters and a dignitary from the Dallas Fed, who informed Alan that the stock market had closed down "five-oh-eight."

"That's a relief," Alan replied, believing the Dow had rallied back to a loss of only five points.

"You don't understand," the gentleman replied. "That's five *hundred* and eight points."

Alan performed a quick calculation in his head and was shocked to realize that the one-day loss amounted to nearly 23 percent—double the tragic decline posted on Black Tuesday in 1929, which drove his father over the edge into the financial abyss. Since August 25, the Dow had plummeted more than one thousand points to 1,738.74, a gut-wrenching wipeout by any measure. The S&P 500, Nasdaq Composite, and other major indices had all suffered comparable fates. Alan ignored the cacophony at the airport, with dozens of reporters hurling questions at him in unison, and bolted directly to his hotel, where he spent the next few hours on the telephone, gathering data from key financial people in banks and brokerage firms around the country. From his myriad conversations Alan arrived at a firm consensus: this was an extraordinary event calling for extraordinary measures. He needed to take the proper action, sooner rather than later.

"Anyone who knows anything about economic history," Alan said, "knows that when you get a five-hundred-point drop in the stock market, you will have a major problem in the economy. It wasn't a question of whether you would open up the taps or not open up the taps. It was merely how you would do it, not if."

Alan realized that he could not do it alone; he needed the support of his colleagues at the Fed. "Corrigan was crucial to the whole operation," Alan said, referring to the head of the New York Federal Reserve Bank. "To the extent that he was dealing with the larger banks that the Federal Reserve Bank of New York supervised, Corrigan was the key player as far as I was concerned. Without his skills, it would have been much more difficult for us."

At the White House, Reagan expressed full confidence that the Fed would do whatever was necessary to preserve the integrity of the U.S. and, by extension, international financial markets. The President "was the least uptight person that I saw around there at the time," said Sprinkel. "He was arguing that 'the market has overdone it, but it will come back.'" Sprinkel claimed that he urged Alan to "ease up. Put some money in the system."

That is essentially what Alan did the following day when he issued a statement designed to calm the waters before the market opened for trading on Tuesday. It read, "The Federal Reserve, consistent with its responsibilities as the nation's central bank, affirmed today its readiness to serve as a source of liquidity to support the economic and financial system."

The message to Wall Street professionals was unmistakable. The Fed would reverse its tight money policy of the past few months and supply liquidity—that is, it would pump as much money into the system as was needed to keep it afloat. Specifically, the Federal Reserve entered the marketplace and bought $2.2 billion worth of U.S. Treasury securities, supplying the markets with an immediate infusion of cash. It also lowered the rates at which banks borrow money from one another and from the Federal Reserve. Both short- and long-term rates headed downward instantly, reversing their upward spiral. The three-month Treasury bill yield slipped from 6.74 percent on October 13 to 5.27 percent on October 30, the Fed funds rate dropped by nearly two full percentage points, and the thirty-year Treasury bond yield declined a point and a half to 9 percent. Banks stepped up their lending to brokerage firms, ensuring that none would be threatened with insolvency by further sell orders from their clients.

This was precisely the right dose of medicine for the ailment, and Alan came through his first crisis as Fed chairman with flying colors. Investors were encouraged enough to enter the market and purchase stocks at bargain prices, and many corporations announced that they would buy back their own shares to arrest their price declines. Wall Street endured the worst impact of all and was forced to eliminate fifteen thousand employees from the payroll, but this time Alan was shrewd enough not to go on television and complain that stockbrokers had suffered more than anyone else during the crash. Indeed, the market regained its footing almost immediately, and by the end of December the Dow ended with a gain of 5 percent for the year.

In its assessment of the crisis and the Fed's role in ending it, *Forbes* complimented Alan on the actions taken by him and his cohorts. "Greenspan's finest hour," was how the widely respected financial magazine described his performance. "He got on the horn and told the banks they had to lend money to Wall Street. Then he dropped money market rates, and long-term rates fell sympathetically."

Jim Baker was equally lavish in his praise. "I don't think Alan Greenspan ever gets nervous," he said. "During the course of those meetings in my office the day after the market crashed, he was not extraordinarily nervous or fidgeting. He was taking catnaps in his office and cracking jokes. In the end, he did what he had to do to instill confidence in the markets."

When the dust finally settled, Alan took some time to reflect on the causes of the crash and the remedies, if any, that should be taken to avoid them in the future. Many analysts believed that so-called program, or computer, trading by large institutional investors was at least partly responsible. Arbitrageurs had programmed their computers to automatically place large buy or sell orders when discrepancies developed between stock prices and stock index futures, and there was little doubt that program trading increased volatility as the market swung sharply one way or the other. However, other stock markets that did not use program trading also crashed, and Alan concluded that these temporary swings were self-correcting and actually made the markets more efficient overall. The market had crashed in 1914, 1929, and 1962, long before computers, let alone computer trading, were even a figment of anyone's imagination. Most likely, other factors were of greater importance.

Others pointed their fingers at the sheer volume of trading activity, and the system's inability to process so many orders simultaneously. Many NYSE-listed stocks did not even open until late morning on Black Monday because the specialists could not locate enough buyers to accommodate so many sellers. The vast disparity between buyers and sellers only exacerbated the decline in prices. Huge supply combined with low demand was obviously a factor, but it failed to explain why so many investors felt a need to sell in the first place.

Economic reasons also came into play. The United States posted its largest trade deficit since 1960 in the third quarter of 1987, along with the largest budget shortfall in history. Investors might have been worried about the effect this would have on U.S. stocks relative to foreign equities. Here, again, other countries were enjoying trade and budget surpluses, and their stock markets fell out of bed as well. If deficits caused the U.S. crash, the surpluses presumably would have benefited international markets.

Alan believed the key problem was the one he had been most concerned about all along: accelerating inflation. Rising inflation means that people pay higher prices for goods and services. Higher prices erode the buying power of the dollar. Interest rates go up as investors demand higher rates of return on bonds to compensate for the rising cost of living. Since bonds and short-term investments are safer than stocks, investors sell stocks and buy fixed-income securities when they begin to offer attractive returns. There was no mystery in this at all. The marketplace is fundamentally rational, reflecting as it does the rational decisions of countless investors around the world.

To those who criticized Alan for creating a negative environment for stocks by raising interest rates, Alan replied that higher rates were a necessary response to budget deficits and rising inflation. In other words, cut back on spending, get your fiscal house in order, and the market will take care of itself.

CHAPTER 24

A

lan and Andrea Mitchell appeared on the Washington social scene together more and more frequently, and media pundits, ever on the lookout for a spicy story, began to speculate about the nature of their relationship. Since Andrea was a charter member of their group, as Barbara Walters had been before her, the notion of a professional newshound getting chummy with the chairman of the Fed was too delicious to ignore.

"Alan doesn't drink," Andrea said in response to a question about what the nation's top banker was really like. "He's very highly disciplined. He doesn't enjoy great food and wine. It's just not his thing. He's kind of old-fashioned and very simple."

Alan had learned his lessons well from past encounters with the media and chose to remain silent about his relationship with Andrea. However, he had little choice but to comment publicly about the role the Fed played during the October crash when he was called to testify before the Senate Banking Committee on February 24, 1988. Leading Democrats on the committee had all but accused the Fed of precipitating the stock market collapse by raising short-term interest rates too high. In his defense, Alan pointed out that rates were rising globally during the summer of 1987, and there was little the Fed could have done to reverse the trend.

"Even if that last surge in long-term rates had not occurred," Alan said, "the market would have topped out and come down anyway, and I find it difficult to perceive how actions of the Federal Reserve were material factors in the market."

While the crash had wiped out a trillion dollars' worth of stock market wealth from the more than three trillion that existed beforehand, the economy was still growing strongly and the world had averted a disaster. Alan politely reiterated that higher interest rates had been necessary to combat inflation caused by government spending—a suggestion that caused some members of the Congress to bristle with indignation. Among Alan's sternest critics was Texas Congressman Henry Gonzalez, who had been lashing out at "the tremendous power of the Fed" for years and had once filed a motion to impeach Alan's predecessor Paul Volcker.

Alan stood his ground in the face of the heated opposition, as Volcker had done before him, and refused to back off. Since the crash, he and other Fed members had grown increasingly concerned about the weakness of the dollar relative to major foreign currencies. In addition, the economy resumed its pattern of torrid growth, threatening to rekindle the embers of inflation that had begun to smolder a year earlier. It was clear to Alan, Corrigan, and other key Fed officials that they had merely won the most recent battle in the ongoing war against inflation, but had not yet put an end to the war itself. Now that stocks had stabilized and renewed their upward climb, it was "*déjà vu* all over again," as Yogi Berra was supposed to have said. Government spending was still out of control relative to receipts, the economy was red-hot, and the specter of inflation kept rearing its ugly face over the horizon.

Alan had little trouble convincing his colleagues that a new round of monetary tightening was necessary to contain the forces of inflation. However, he was faced with a potential political storm in that Vice President George Bush was seeking the Republican presidential

185

nomination in 1988 as Reagan's second term was coming to an end. Cynical Washington insiders predicted openly that Alan would most likely help Bush in his election bid by waiting until after the November election before taking any action on interest rates. Alan fumed at the suggestion that he would compromise the Fed's integrity to help Bush or anyone else. He remembered all too well the problems Arthur Burns had fomented when he subjugated the Fed's independence to Nixon's political agenda, and the subsequent damage it inflicted on Burns's reputation. He was determined to avoid the slightest hint of compromise.

"The idea that the Fed is not going to do anything to hurt Republican chances is wrong," said a Republican political consultant. "Greenspan is more likely to torpedo the Republicans just to prove his manhood."

Alan took his first preemptive strike against inflation in March, hiking short-term rates a quarter of a point. The move set alarm bells clanging within Bush's inner circle of advisers, and the clamor grew louder a couple of months later when Alan took one of the more astonishing actions of his life. A mere few weeks before the Republican convention, Alan boosted rates again by a full half of a percentage point, a substantial increase calculated to throttle the overheated economy. George Bush was personally dismayed by the move. Republicans who knew Bush well called him the "WASP Don Corleone," who valued loyalty to the Bush clan as the paramount virtue. While Reagan's heir apparent said nothing himself about Alan's treachery, his chief lieutenants lost no time in venting their outrage.

"I'm angry about it. I'm annoyed. I'm hurt," said Senator Al D'Amato of New York, a man who ran his own corner of Long Island like a feudal estate.

Assistant treasury secretary Michael Darby did not take Alan's move as personally as D'Amato did, but he was nevertheless put off by it. "The main players in the administration were all concerned that we were eliminating inflation in two years instead of four years," he said, "and the cost of that would be an unnecessary recession."

Richard Rahn, chief economist for the U.S. Chamber of Commerce, complained that Alan and his fellow inflation fighters were performing what amounted to "deep root canal surgery."

"They were tightening too much," added Beryl Sprinkel. "To try to throttle it that quickly could have led to a recession." He was correct in that assessment, although the recession would not arrive for another couple of years.

Alan had anticipated the criticism and was prepared when it came. "If you wait to see the whites of the eyes of inflation, then it's too late," he stated. The Fed needed to act preemptively, before the inflation genie was out of the bottle. If inflation got out of control, Alan argued, then the Fed would have been faced with the situation Volcker encountered in 1980 when he had to push interest rates into the stratosphere to restrain the onset of hyperinflation.

Bush went into the convention trailing Democratic nominee Michael Dukakis by seventeen percentage points, but he managed to pull off a crushing victory in November thanks, in large part, to Dukakis's inept campaign performance. When the diminutive Dukakis appeared in a Sherman tank with an oversized combat helmet all but covering his eyes and nose, looking for all the world like a little boy in his daddy's battle clothes, his own campaign manager, Susan Estrich, winced in pain and said, "There goes the election. Michael, how could you be so incredibly stupid?"

With Bush occupying the White House, relations between his administration and the Fed continued to worsen. Starting with Alan's first post-crash tightening move in March 1988, the Fed kept notching short-term rates higher in a series of incremental steps until the key Fed funds rate hit 10 percent in February 1989. Despite Alan's actions, annualized inflation also continued to rise, hitting a peak of 6 percent—a level that had prompted Richard Nixon to impose wage and price controls a generation earlier. Alan felt the heat from both the Bush camp and members of Congress, yet he refused to change course.

"The real danger you face in a period like that," he said, "is that you don't do enough. We were still dealing with an unstable inflationary environment, and it was very easy to make a mistake on the side of ease and find out that, all of a sudden, we had lost two percentage points of inflation on the upside."

Alan had some of his sharpest encounters with Nicholas Brady, who had replaced Jim Baker as Secretary of the Treasury on September 15, 1988. Brady had been a Bush loyalist for many years, a connection many people thought was his primary qualification for the job. Wall Street professionals considered him to be an intellectual lightweight at best, while less charitable observers often referred to him as that "nincompoop in the White House." Alan's opinion of Brady was hardly more flattering—an admission that embarrassed Alan later, since he had originally recommended Brady for the post.

Brady had added fuel to the inflationary fires with his public statements that the weakness of the dollar was of "no concern" to him, and that he was "opposed to higher interest rates" to combat inflation. The markets had interpreted his remarks to mean that the administration would continue to pursue a soft-dollar and an inflationary economic policy regardless of what the data indicated, and Brady's underlings at the Treasury were constantly engaged in damage control after the secretary's maladroit public utterances.

"The secretary really is in favor of the stability of the dollar," one of his spokesmen said. "He merely meant that he was not concerned about the volatility in the currency markets, since the markets go up and down."

Financial writers around the country had a field day with Brady's dim perceptions, joking that the treasury secretary's mantra was always the same: "Rates go up, rates go down, I don't really care." At a famous White House press conference following Bush's inauguration, a woman reporter decked out in a white sweater with a large red heart emblazoned across her chest raised her hand to ask a question. Brady unintentionally cracked up the audience when he called on her with the words, "Okay, the woman with the heart on."

Over the course of twelve months, from March 1988 through March 1989, Alan hiked short-term rates a total of six times to a peak of 10 percent. Bush grew increasingly annoyed, although he maintained publicly that he had a good relationship with Alan.

However, he was agitated enough about Fed policy to comment publicly about it for the first time since his election. The threat of inflation was a reflection of "adverse psychology," said the President. "I will just do my level best to send signals to the international markets that we're serious about the budget deficit and we're projecting it downward firmly. And I really believe that once that happens, the adverse psychology that is forcing interest rates up, in my view beyond where they ought to be, will turn around. Once the markets think we're definitely on track, that in itself will be enormously beneficial to world markets."

Nicholas Brady followed his boss's remarks with his own statement that interest rates should be going down, not up, further spooking the markets. Alan felt that Brady was undermining the Fed's efforts with comments like that, and their personal relationship soured considerably. Alan and Brady had been meeting for lunch to discuss their differences, but Brady flew into a snit over Alan's stubborn refusal to be a team player and laughably canceled their weekly engagement.

Despite Brady's inept performance, both camps had valid arguments. Monetary policy is not an exact science, and the Fed is always hard pressed to determine how high or low interest rates should be in any economic environment. If the Fed sets rates too low, it risks igniting the fires of inflation; too high and it risks slowing the economy too much and ushering in a recession. In the aftermath of Black Monday, there was little question that Alan was pushing the edge of the envelope with his rate hikes. Many Wall Street economists believed that Alan may have ratcheted up interest rates one time too many. Perhaps Alan's intransigence on this issue had something to do with his determination to keep his distance from Republican political goals, but he continued to maintain that the economic data justified his actions.

Whatever the case, the latest data indicated that the economy was beginning to slow significantly by the time interest rates peaked in February 1989. The official definition of a recession is two consecutive quarters of economic contraction, or "negative growth," as financial experts call it in their paradoxical fashion. The more mundane definition strikes closer to home for the average person: When *you're* out of work it's a recession and when *I'm* out of work it's a depression, the saying goes. Anxious to avoid the stigma of pushing the country into a recession so soon after he took over at the Fed, Alan reversed direction on a dime, as it were, and began undoing his work of the past eighteen months. Suddenly, it seemed, he could not drop rates fast enough to avoid the consequences of his own aggressive tightening policies.

Notwithstanding the key role he played in renewing confidence in the markets following the Crash of 1987, Alan had not yet reached his stride in the biggest financial job of his life.

CHAPTER 25

By the middle of 1990, the U.S. economy officially slipped into a recession. The Fed had been lowering short-term interest rates fast and furiously since they hit 10 percent in early 1989, and it had been using the other major weapon in its arsenal—buying government securities in the open market—in a frantic attempt to avert the inevitable. Alan's reversal of monetary policy, however, was not enough to undo the economic sluggishness engendered by his earlier rate increases.

With a recession taking hold a year and a half into his first term in office, Bush and his circle of advisers were quick to point their collective finger of blame at Alan as the immediate cause of the downturn. According to the administration, Alan failed to act quickly enough in the face of troubling economic indicators. Brady and Darby took the harshest line of all, with the treasury secretary stating that Alan had "ample room" to cut rates but failed to act in time, and Darby maintaining that Alan "cut it too close" and ignored his own monetary aggregates, thereby increasing the likelihood of a recession.

Others in the administration, including Michael Boskin, who had succeeded Sprinkel as chairman of the Council of Economic Advisers, were more charitable in their assessment of Alan's policy at the Fed. Boskin said that the "Fed's overall strategy of engineering a second round of disinflation" had been "essentially right," although he believed Alan should have "eased a bit sooner and a bit more rapidly." Boskin also admitted that other factors came into play, which the Fed could not possibly have foreseen. "The Fed didn't know that there was about to be a collapse of the Soviet Union and a dramatic acceleration of the defense slowdown." Neither could Alan have predicted that Saddam Hussein was going to invade Kuwait, triggering a war in the Middle East that would further drain U.S. economic resources.

Economists outside the administration debated publicly about whether the recession had been brought on primarily by the Fed's tightening mode or by the Gulf War. Some claimed the recession would have occurred in any event as a result of high interest rates, while others thought it would have been avoided if Desert Storm, along with the slowdown in military spending following the Soviet collapse, had not entered the picture. Alan himself was typically obscure in his own comments about the situation.

"It's not easy to tell," he said, "but what we do know is that the Gulf War very clearly had a shock effect, which in and of itself cannot explain what was a relatively mild recession by historical standards. But that's not the same thing as saying that if the Gulf War had not happened, we wouldn't have had a recession.

"My own impression . . . was that I thought we'd stopped tightening well in advance of the economy weakening, and in that period we did not see the type of deterioration which usually precedes a recession. So my inclination is to presume that, were it not for the Gulf War, we would not have had a recession. But if you asked me to prove it, I would not be able to do so."

In other words, the war may have been wholly or partly responsible for the recession; then again, maybe it wasn't. Alan had become a master at obfuscation, and he had been part of the Washington scene long enough to know that you should never take responsibility for anything that goes wrong. In reality, the administration in power needed a scapegoat to blame for the economic crunch, and Alan was the likeliest candidate. Trying to determine what might have happened if some event had or had not taken place was a speculative exercise at best. If Alan had been able to anticipate the external shocks to the economy, surely he would have begun cutting interest rates earlier than he did.

The Fed's monetary tools are only some of the factors that determine the strength or weakness of the economy. Taxes, government spending, and regulation of the private sector also have a massive impact on private economic activity.

"The direct negative impacts of specific regulations generally are confined to adding unnecessary costs, stifling innovation, and redistributing profits among producers or between producers and unionized workers in specific industries," admitted CEA chief Michael Boskin. "But a change in regulatory policy, unlike changes in monetary, fiscal, or trade policy, will generally not have sufficient short-run impact on the economy to cause a recession. That said, there is little question that wide swings in the supervision of financial institutions, from too lax in the late 1980s to too tight subsequently, contributed to the slow growth of the early 1990s."

Alan had pointed out many times that overregulation of industry adds hundreds of billions of dollars to the cost of doing business, dragging down productivity and innovation, and raising prices to consumers through a kind of giant covert tax. He agreed with Boskin that regulatory policy has a great impact on the efficiency and long-term growth of the economy. Most economists understand that wrong-headed government regulations can lead to worse consequences than might occur in a laissez-faire economy, which is self-correcting over time. The acceleration of new regulations in the 1970s was an undeniable cause of the slowdown in productivity growth, said Boskin.

"The government ought to deregulate where competition or its prospect is likely, and find ways to achieve necessary regulatory goals that are less costly to consumers and firms, and do not stifle innovation," he said.

In Alan's view, George Bush took office with a clear record of opposing costly and inflexible regulations, a record he established as vice president under Ronald Reagan. For example, the deregulation of interest rates and financial markets in general was a tremendous boon to investors and the economy, but Reagan's failure to tie deposit insurance to investment risk, at Bush's suggestion, gave the S&Ls carte blanche to invest in speculative real estate ventures. The S&L bandits knew that if their investments failed, the taxpayers would pick up the tab. As a result, the industry lost about a third of the value of its primary asset: long-term fixed-rate mortgages.

As President, however, Bush's record was mixed. Too much new regulation was added, and not enough effort was placed on deregulation and regulatory reform, which contributed significantly to the economic slowdown, according to Alan. He cited the Clean Air Act Amendments of 1990 and the Americans with Disabilities Act as major contributors to the recession. Both pieces of legislation imposed large costs on the private sector, notwithstanding Bush's good intentions in proposing them. Alan pointed out that the Clean Air Act Amendments were essentially a $50 billion central planning scheme whose benefits fell far short of their overall cost. While some legitimate environmental issues had to be addressed, Bush and the Congress ignored scientific studies indicating that the effects of acid rain, for example, were less severe than generally thought. Legislation such as this, Alan pointed out, helped to restrain economic growth.

Boskin had told the President that the bill was too costly and recommended vetoing it unless it could be implemented in a more flexible and less costly manner. In the end, however, the bill went through without Boskin's adjustments, which he said would have provided 90 to 95 percent of the environmental benefits for about 30 to 40 percent of the eventual costs.

As far as the Americans with Disabilities Act was concerned, the original bills floated on Capitol Hill were outrageously expensive, Alan had warned. Some members of Congress wanted every building in the United States retrofitted to give access to the disabled at a cost running into tens of billions of dollars. They also wanted every train car accessible to the disabled. Bush favored some sort of legislation to help the disabled, but with scaled-back costs. The bill Congress finally passed and Bush signed into law would have inflationary consequences, Alan warned, necessitating further vigilance on interest rates that would lead to an economic slowdown.

Many other factors came into play that shifted the burden of responsibility for the recession from the Fed to the administration, Alan maintained. Without mincing his words, he blamed much of the slowdown on bad legislation and claimed that no reasonable person could suggest that the Fed's actions to curtail inflation were the direct cause of the recession.

"The economy was expanding at a moderate pace," Alan said, "and underlying inflation pressures were probably beginning to ease as a result of our policy. This suggests that things were developing in line with our policy objectives, which were to achieve a slowing of inflation in the context of continued expansion of real activity."

He advised the administration to take a long-term view of Fed monetary policy. "The role of monetary policy is to provide the financial environment that is consistent with the nation's longer-run economic objectives . . . In the final analysis, I can only offer the assurance that the Federal Reserve will seek, as we have in the past, to foster economic stability and sustainable growth."

Further complicating Alan's job was the unreliability, at best, of the government's own economic data. Much of the figures disseminated by administration experts were downright erroneous, said Alan. For example, the government was wrong 25 percent of the time on the basic question of whether the economy was growing or shrinking at any moment. Most economists believed that government inflation figures were exaggerated by at least one to one-and-a-quarter percentage points a year. Worker productivity growth was being understated by as much as three-quarters of a percentage point, Alan said, and most of the time the Fed was forced to ignore government data in favor of its own private sources.

Interpreting the data correctly was crucial to establishing a viable monetary strategy. If economic growth adjusted for inflation is off by half a percentage point, Alan stated, it adds $200 billion to federal budget deficit estimates over five years. "A tenth-of-a-percentage-point error can have a profound impact on every household in the land," he added.

If the government's own inflation figures were more in line with reality, said Alan, "the correction would cut the government's Social Security bill by $48 billion a year, which would amount to about $100 a year per recipient. The reduction of at least $260 billion over six years could move Congress and the White House closer to a balanced budget agreement."

The figures were off largely because the way government collects its figures had not changed in decades, he noted. For example, 12 percent of the $3 billion annual statistics budget was spent on agricultural data, even though farming amounted to only 4 percent of the total economy. While services accounted for 75 percent of total employment and more than half of the country's economic output, less money was spent collecting information about that industry than about the antiquated mining industry. Boskin agreed with Alan that statistical agencies did not have the resources to provide accurate readings that would keep up with rapid changes in the economy.

"Some analysts also believe outdated methods of tracking seasonal and temporary employment also led to chronic overestimating of those who were involuntarily out of work," Boskin stated, adding ballast to Alan's views. So while the Bush administration publicly complained about Alan's handling of monetary policy, the President's own chief economist agreed that the primary responsibility for accelerating inflation lay at the doorstep of the federal government and the inefficient manner in which it ran the country.

CHAPTER 26

The economy worsened in the early months of 1991. Things that should have been going down, such as unemployment and bank failures, continued to go up, and things like housing starts and business activity that should have been going up were stagnant or declining.

Alan continued to lower short-term rates furiously. In all, he had reduced interest rates in a rapid series of steps by three percentage points since February 1989, yet the economy showed no signs of improvement. The Gulf War raged on, further exacerbating the problem, with investors uncertain about the cost, duration, and outcome of the conflict. Alan testified before the House Budget Committee on January 22, stating that "we expect that our actions to date will provide support to economic activity in the quarters ahead." Yet even after the war in the Middle East ended in victory for the U.S.-led forces, the economy refused to cooperate. Alan's relationship with the Bush White House and with Republicans in Congress deteriorated further. Senator D'Amato continued to play the role of Republican pit bull with his vitriolic attacks on the Fed under Alan's leadership.

The Fed's actions were "too little, too late," said the New York firebrand. "No one wants to tell you that because you're the big guru." D'Amato demonized Alan with the statement that he was "sick and tired of hearing the nonsense" that the recession was brought on by the Gulf War. "What inflation are you worried about? Do you need people to tell you that the real estate market isn't going to come back and needs a jump start? People are going to starve out there and you're worried about inflation." It was by far the worst public tongue-lashing Alan had ever received, and he had little recourse but to endure his humiliation stoically while the incensed senator flayed him alive.

The economic stagnation lingered into the following year, and Bush saw his public approval numbers melt away like snow in August as he geared up for reelection. Reluctantly, Bush had appointed Alan for another four-year term, feeling he had no other alternative because Alan enjoyed the confidence of movers and shakers on Wall Street. Incredibly, the Fed cut the key Fed funds rate to 3.75 percent on April 9, 1992, from its 1989 high of 10 percent, and *still* the economy failed to respond. Alan would eventually lower it to 3 percent—a drop of an astounding seven full percentage points in three years—before the November election. He knew it was simply a question of time before his policy of monetary stimulation finally kicked in, but as the summer wore on it became increasingly clear that the upturn would not come in time to salvage Bush's presidency.

In the midst of the campaign, Alan received the shock of his life one morning as he drove to work listening to the news on the radio. The announcer reported the death of painter Joan Mitchell, giving her age and list of accomplishments. Alan, who wouldn't have known an abstract expressionist painting from a Grandma Moses, immediately assumed that his first wife, who was about the same age, had died. Further confusing the matter was the announcer's statement that Joan Mitchell had been married to publisher Barney Rosset in the late 1940s, something Joan had never bothered to tell him. As soon as Alan got to his office, he dialed his ex-wife's number in Manhattan and was relieved to discover that she was still alive and well. Joan patiently reminded him that she was not that kind of artist. Alan had remained friendly with Joan and her second husband after their annulment and was truly distressed to learn of her ostensible demise.

The presidential campaign of 1992 was not going well for George Bush. What most pundits had believed would be an easy victory for the incumbent President, considering his soaring popularity after Desert Storm, turned out to be an unexpected dogfight against a charming, relatively unknown governor from Arkansas. The recession ground on into the early fall, and Bush's refusal to acknowledge how deeply it affected the average family made him look totally out of touch with middle-class America. The experts may have called it "a relatively mild recession by historical standards," but that definition was scant consolation to millions of Americans who had lost their jobs and had difficulty finding new ones. Real estate prices had fallen 30 or 40 percent since their peak in 1988 in many parts of the country, and the bottom was nowhere in sight. Average Americans were decidedly less wealthy than they had been a few years earlier, a grim economic fact that Bush seemed incapable of realizing.

Bush was bitter when the electorate removed him from the White House after one term in office, and his minions in the administration once again blamed Alan for tipping the economy into an unnecessary recession. This was the official line, but other Republicans had grown increasingly disheartened by Bush's entire campaign and blamed him directly for his defeat.

"When Bush got in he wanted to distance himself a little from Reagan," said conservative columnist and author Bill Rusher. "Unfortunately, he did it all too well. His campaign for reelection was dismal. His attempt to invoke family values was just plain laughable. He blared the term 'family values' into a microphone and paraded his grandchildren across the stage. But that's not what it's all about.

"Reagan understood that the social issues, which are real issues, are not like the economic issues on which you can often pass a bill in this session. Social issues deal with great fundamental beliefs as to

199

what America is about. American opinion moves slowly and the President's job is to be, in a sense, almost our spiritual leader—not to expect a bill to go sailing through Congress in this session, or even to demand that. Reagan pleaded for the great social issues. A lot of these ideas are going to take time to work their way through the system. Whoever understands that, and still stands for the social issues and for the economic issues and the libertarian issues, is going to be the one who will pull us together again."

Republican political consultant F. Clifton White was even more scathing in his critique of Bush's conduct in the campaign. "George Bush was a member of the generation that fought in World War II and lived through the Cold War, but his failure to articulate the great and important issues of the present time hastened his demise. He was on to something during Desert Storm when he talked about the New World Order; it was the germination of a grand theme. The problem is that George didn't have the foggiest idea of what the New World Order was. If he had possessed the vision, which he trivialized as 'the vision thing' in his reelection campaign, he could have used this theme to formulate a great concept of where the world was heading throughout the rest of the decade and beyond, and the role the United States would play in this evolving New World Order. Instead, he let the opportunity slip by. What could have been a spiritually and morally uplifting battle cry for his presidential campaign became nothing more than a public relations slogan penned by one of his speechwriters. Incredibly, George Bush followed up a decisive victory in the Middle East with a thoroughly inept and disgraceful campaign for the presidency."

Following the election, Alan sat in his office staring at the sign on the wall declaring "THE BUCK STARTS HERE," feeling like a fish out of water following the Republican rout at the polls. A new Democratic president whom Alan had never met now occupied the Oval Office. Alan had served Republican administrations all his life, and he had no idea what sort of relationship he would have with Bill Clinton and his staff. Alan's term in office would not end until Clinton would be running for reelection. While the Fed was independent from the three major branches of government, the chairman of the Federal Reserve had to coordinate monetary policy to some degree with the President and his financial advisers. If Alan had so much trouble getting along with the previous Republican administration, how in the world was he supposed to deal with a regime full of liberal Democrats whose philosophy of government differed widely from his own?

The Fed had already lowered key short-term interest rates to 3 percent, and Alan did not see how he could trim them further without triggering new worries about inflation and a weak dollar. The Democrats had traditionally been less concerned about inflation than Republicans had been and concentrated more on expensive, and ultimately inflationary, public programs to subsidize low-income workers. With a fairly conservative Republican like Al D'Amato snarling at him in public, liberal Democrats would be even more likely to demonize him and his fellow inflation fighters at the Fed. Alan sighed deeply and steeled himself for philosophical guerrilla warfare during the next four years. He had taken this job with the knowledge that people who worked inside the Beltway were self-serving demagogues for the most part, and maneuvering his way through political mine fields was par for the course. Political life is essentially "morally evil," Alan believed.

He was expecting the call from one of Clinton's acolytes when it came a few weeks after the election, inviting him to meet with Clinton, who would be taking his oath of office early the following year. Alan steeled himself for intellectual combat with the new President. Surely Clinton would try to convince him that social priorities took preference over the Fed's efforts to contain inflation and protect the dollar. Alan had been debating economic and political philosophy throughout his life, and he would have to find a way to convince this new regime that the integrity of the currency was the key to a healthy economy. He took some comfort in Clinton's likely selection of Texas Democrat Lloyd Bentsen as his treasury secretary. He knew Bentsen well and believed he could work with him. Bentsen was one of the most sensible Democrats in Washington when it came to economic issues, in Alan's view.

Alan's journey to Little Rock, Arkansas, on December 3 took five hours, since there was no direct flight to the Deep South capital, and Alan was out of sorts when his plane finally landed. Vice President–elect Al Gore greeted Alan at the governor's mansion, and the two men shook hands and spoke briefly before Alan's meeting with Clinton. Gore had always impressed Alan with his intelligence and command of details, and Alan believed Gore had a good grasp of economic reality despite his liberal political agenda. Bill Clinton remained a mystery, however. He had appeared from virtually nowhere to capture the presidency, and his underlying political and economic views were an open question at that moment.

The door to Clinton's office suddenly flew open, and Bill Clinton strode forth with a broad smile on his face and his right hand extended in greeting. Clinton was physically large and imposing. All the presidents whom Alan had served were tall men; Nixon, Ford, Reagan, and Bush all stood an inch or two above six feet. All except Nixon had been solidly built and physically fit. Clinton was not only tall; he was perhaps twenty pounds heavier than he should have been despite his much-publicized exercise regimen that included jogging and golf two or three times each week. Clinton shook Alan's hand firmly and ushered him into the governor's private office.

Clinton led the discussion expertly, touching on several unrelated subjects before getting down to the main subject. Obviously, future Fed policy was paramount on Clinton's mind, specifically the sluggish economy and the high level of long-term interest rates.

"What happened in the past was that presidents tended to get upset when whatever the Fed chairman was doing wasn't consistent with their purposes," said Robert Rubin, a Wall Street professional who would head the National Economic Council during Clinton's first two years in office. "This president had the good sense to recognize from the very beginning that by not trying, even verbally or rhetorically, to interfere with the activities of the Fed, he himself could gain credibility with respect to economic issues. And he was right."

To Alan's relief, Clinton did not try to change his mind about monetary policy. Clinton was looking to pick his brain about several aspects of monetary policy he did not fully understand and, ultimately, to see if he could make some sort of a deal. Clinton clearly wanted interest rates to come down and the economy to pick up steam, and he asked Alan what would be necessary for that to happen. This question gave Alan the opportunity to give the President-elect a brief course on Monetary Policy 101, something he had done many times before and enjoyed doing.

Contrary to popular belief, Alan expounded, the Federal Reserve controlled only short-term interest rates, not the rates on long-term bonds, which were set by millions of investors throughout the world who demanded a certain level of return for taking on risk in the current economic environment. In Alan's view, short-term rates, which were pegged to the discount and Fed funds rates, were about as low as they could possibly be at 3 percent. If the Fed lowered them further, it ran the risk of triggering a new round of inflation.

However, these were not as important as longer-term bond yields, which determine the interest rates at which consumers borrow money. For example, the thirty-year mortgage rate is closely linked to the ten-year Treasury yield, since the average mortgage is retired in seven to twelve years. Car loans and other borrowing costs also take their lead from the bond market. If the new administration wanted *those* rates to come down, Alan advised, it would have to make some progress in balancing the federal budget. If that were to happen, investors would be less wary of higher inflation and be willing to accept lower returns on their bond investments.

Lower long-term rates would serve as fuel for the economy. Corporations would be able to borrow money for their own needs less expensively, driving up corporate profits and, therefore, stock market prices. The federal government would benefit as well, since the cost of servicing its own huge debt load would decline. Lower debt service would help the government in its budget-balancing efforts, providing a double-edged bonus. In Alan's opinion, the single most important thing the new administration could do to rectify the dismal economic situation was to get its fiscal house in order.

Alan had been explaining the facts of economic reality to Republicans and Democrats all his life, with mixed results. The basic message was simple to grasp, but implementing it in the real world seemed to be impossible. The promise of government subsidies for one group or another was the easiest way to win elections, and getting reelected was the only thing politicians really cared about. Asking them to put themselves on a fiscal diet for the good of the country was like asking them to cut off their oxygen supply. Even conservative Republicans who professed to believe in limited government feathered the nests of their own constituents back home.

Alan was heartened that Clinton, who called himself a New Democrat, responded favorably to his message and did not try to deter the Fed from its primary role as inflation fighter. The two men seemed to hit it off well enough on a personal level. Their scheduled fifteen-minute meeting dragged on for nearly three hours, and Clinton extended it further by inviting Alan to lunch. However, Alan recognized a charmer when he saw one. Clinton was a consummate schmoozer, in Alan's view, and he had little hope that the new man in the White House would follow through on his advice, despite his apparent interest in the ideas Alan had presented.

C linton wanted a deal, but a deal was out of the question. The Fed was not supposed to make deals with any president, *could not* make a deal without jeopardizing its integrity—as Arthur Burns had discovered. Without saying it in so many words, Clinton made it obvious that he hoped the Fed would not start raising short-term interest rates again if the administration made a serious attempt to balance the budget. However, Alan knew it would take more than accounting gimmicks to satisfy investors. Too many administrations had resorted to smoke and mirrors as an alternative to real spending cuts in the past, and the result was an exploding budget deficit large enough to permanently sink the economy.

As someone who was still a self-described libertarian, Alan hoped that Clinton would attempt to balance the budget with a real reduction in expenditures rather than an increase in taxes. He was enough of a realist to know that a combination of tax hikes and spending cuts was probably inevitable, but he hoped the greater emphasis would be on a cutback in spending. Alan had never bought into the supply-side argument that lower taxes would result in increased revenues for the Treasury, but neither had he changed his view that high taxes were an abuse of government power and a deterrent to entrepreneurial creativity.

Following their meeting in Little Rock, Secretary of the Treasury Lloyd Bentsen called on Alan and reiterated Clinton's statement that the new administration was serious about reducing the deficit. Bentsen suggested that Clinton would most likely rely on a combination of tax increases and spending cuts to narrow the budget gap, and Alan made it clear he would have preferred greater reductions in expenditures to get the job done. However, it was not the job of the Fed chairman to dictate fiscal policy. How Clinton balanced the budget was strictly up to him and his advisers. As far as Alan was concerned, any progress on the budget front would probably be well received by investors and would allow the Fed to avoid lifting short-term interest rates.

"Greenspan can't give us a deal," Bentsen reported back to Clinton, "but he's prepared to be supportive if we come up with a package. I think we can work with him."

In February 1993, Bentsen and Rubin came up with a combination of tax hikes and spending cuts totaling $140 billion. This was the amount Alan thought would be needed to convince the financial markets that the new administration was serious about repairing the budget. "Greenspan believes that a major deficit reduction [above $130 billion]" would lower long-term interest rates sufficiently to counterbalance any economic slowing that would result from higher taxes, Rubin wrote in a memo to Clinton. Bentsen concurred that the figure was just about right. It represented significant progress in attacking a projected budget deficit of about $300 billion by the time Clinton would be up for reelection.

Bentsen resumed the weekly lunches with Alan that former treasury secretary Brady had abandoned in his snit with Alan about Fed policy a few years earlier. Both Bentsen and Alan were careful to avoid the appearance that a deal was in the works, and even that the Fed and the administration were coordinating their policies in any way. Robert Rubin denied emphatically that the administration had orchestrated any kind of an arrangement with Alan. "Not true," said

Robert Rubin. Clinton assumed that a significant budget package would give the Fed room to keep short-term rates low, but "it was an assumption as opposed to a deal."

Alan did not do himself any favors when he accepted an invitation to attend Clinton's State of the Union address on February 17, 1993, seated between Hillary Clinton and Tipper Gore. Alan argued that it would have been insulting for him to decline on the grounds that he did not like the President's seating arrangements, but others believed he had allowed himself to be co-opted by Clinton, who was anxious to give the impression that Alan endorsed his budget plan.

"What I worry about is even the unintentional perception of a lack of independence on the part of the Board," said former Fed governor John LaWare. "There is the possibility that anybody is going to conclude that the Board is an instrument of the Treasury or an instrument of the administration or, perhaps worse still, an instrument of Congress. I can't imagine to this day how Alan Greenspan got himself euchred into sitting in that box . . . I think that was a serious mistake."

LaWare's comments were kind compared with those of other critics. "I believe that Alan Greenspan is so dedicated to trying to get himself reappointed," said another former Fed official, "that he is willing to compromise some of his independence in order to do so."

The media had a grand time focusing their cameras repeatedly on Alan looking on sheepishly as Clinton proposed to sock the nation with the largest tax hike in history—a record $250 billion, including almost $30 billion in new Social Security taxes. It was a mind-numbing ideological setback for a man who still publicly advocated limits to government power. Once again, Alan's yen for the limelight at the center of public policy came into conflict with his political and economic philosophy, and his dignity suffered as a result, if only temporarily.

Alan compromised himself further two days later during his testimony before the Senate Banking Committee. "Leaving aside the specific details," he said of Clinton's economic package, "it is a serious proposal, its baseline economic assumptions are plausible, and it is a detailed program-by-program set of recommendations as distinct from general goals." Alan diplomatically left out any criticism of Clinton's whopping tax hike and concentrated solely on the administration's attempts to rein in spending, particularly soaring medical costs. Realizing that he might have gone a bit too far in his praise of Clinton's bill, Alan backpedaled a month later when he tried to put a bit more distance between the Fed and the White House.

On March 24, speaking before the Senate Finance Committee, Alan stated, "I commended [Clinton] for putting it on the table, because it's crucial to get the deficits down . . . but that's not the same thing as saying I endorse it . . . We at the Fed have a very distinct interest in bringing the deficit down because it's a corrosive force, but how that is done is a political issue."

Despite this caveat, Alan gave Clinton essentially what he wanted and cemented his relationship not only with the new president, but also with Bentsen, Rubin, and Clinton's other economic advisers. Bond yields declined almost instantly, as Alan had forecast they would, and the first glimmer of an economic upturn appeared faintly on the horizon. However, while the recession had officially ended, the economy was hardly out of the woods. Real estate prices continued to swoon all over the country, and it was strictly a buyer's market for anyone looking to purchase a home. Unemployment remained persistently high, and companies took three months or longer to sift through an avalanche of applicants for each new job offering. Alan had already reduced short-term rates as much as he dared to, so there was little left to do but wait for lower borrowing costs to work their way through the economy.

The upturn was slow and torturous and did not take place quickly enough to soothe the wrath of House Banking Committee Chairman Henry Gonzalez, who had been on a crusade to make the Fed more accountable to Congress. In October 1993, Gonzalez invited Alan to testify before his committee. During the course of his long interrogation, Gonzalez accused the Fed of being too secretive and asked Alan what records the Fed governors kept of their FOMC meetings. Alan stated under oath that the meetings were taped, but the tapes were erased afterward when a synopsis of each meeting was made.

Alan's words shocked not only Gonzalez, but Alan's fellow board members as well, who were unaware that their deliberations had been taped. Alan's statement that the Fed erased the tapes after each meeting was literally true but did not tell the whole story. While it was technically true that the tapes themselves were erased, verbatim transcripts of every meeting were filed in a cabinet in an office down the hall from Alan's. His response to Gonzalez's question was misleading at best, and Gonzalez's normal rancor against the Fed and its activities boiled over into fury. A week after the meeting, Alan lamely apologized to Gonzalez and his fellow committee members, saying he did indeed know about the transcripts but had simply forgotten about them.

One of Gonzalez's staff members described Alan's testimony as "a very conscious strategy to mislead." Even fellow free-market economist Anna Schwartz, wife of Alan's former colleague Milton Friedman, said, "It was not Alan Greenspan's finest hour . . . it reminded me of all the Fed people lined up before the House Committee saying that they had no idea they kept records."

Alan refused to say anything further on the subject, so it is worth speculating on his motive for giving the testimony he did. At his core, Alan was essentially a low-key intellectual elitist who distrusted anti-intellectual bureaucrats immensely. He particularly resented Gonzalez, whom he regarded as an apparatchik of the fuzzy-brained left who was only interested in demonizing the Fed to appease his welfare constituents at home. In Alan's view, Gonzalez came on like a Randian anti-hero who resented people of achievement. If people like Gonzalez ran the country, they would overburden the economy with astronomically high taxes. Alan simply did not think that Gonzalez and his ilk were serious thinkers who had any business poking their noses into the critical deliberations of the Federal Reserve. Therefore, he saw no reason to be forthright with him. Alan survived this encounter, as he did his earlier contretemps with Al D'Amato, whom he considered a Republican version of Gonzalez.

Alan further infuriated Gonzalez, and several of his colleagues on the Democratic side of the aisle, a few months later when he raised the Fed funds rate a quarter of a percentage point on February 4, 1994. Alan's prescription for reducing long-term interest rates had worked all too well, and the economy started to grow briskly in the fourth quarter of 1993, advancing at an annualized rate of more than 6 percent. Alan still subscribed to the old Phillips curve trade-off, which stated that growth above 2.5 percent combined with unemployment below 6 percent was likely to fuel accelerating inflation. In a preemptive strike against this eventuality, Alan and his fellow Fed members embarked on another round of short-term rate increases. Indeed, the inflation data reflected in the widely watched Consumer Price Index indicated that inflation was beginning to pick up.

Alan struck again in a series of rapid moves, boosting the fed funds rate a quarter of a point on March 22 and April 18, and a whopping half of a percentage point on May 17. The May hike in the Fed funds rate was accompanied by a half point rise in the discount rate as well. Both key short-term rates, which immediately affect the yields on short-term securities such as Treasury bills, now stood at 4.25 percent and 3.50 percent, respectively. When Alan notched both rates up another half a percentage point on August 16, congressional Democrats who stood to lose in the November off-year elections went ballistic.

"Every time the economy comes up out of the water to catch its breath," complained Senator Paul Sarbanes of Maryland, "you move in and push it right back down again."

"We're not against growth," Alan defended his policy. "Quite the contrary. That's the reason we're endeavoring to do this."

What Alan meant was that the Fed hoped to slow the economy to a more sustainable rate of growth that was compatible with an acceptable level of inflation. Too much growth in the economy, history showed, was a forerunner of rapidly accelerating inflation. President Clinton understood this argument, but he also had his eye on the November elections and was none too pleased with the timing of Alan's moves. Alan was chastened by his congressional critics, and he was well aware of the political implications of his tighter monetary policy. He had lived through precisely the same scenario with the Bush administration during the last presidential campaign.

Alan waited until after the November election before raising both the Fed funds and discount rates an alarming three-quarters of a percentage point each, but the delay was not enough to save the Democrats at the polls. The Republicans scored big gains, capturing both houses of Congress for the first time in decades. The so-called Gingrich Revolution was a *fait accompli*, and newspapers throughout the country were calling Clinton's presidency "irrelevant." The Senate and the House of Representatives would now be dictating policy, as outlined in the Republicans' Contract with America, to the crippled incumbent in the White House. Gonzalez, Sarbanes, and other congressional Democrats viewed Alan as the assassin who hammered the nails into Clinton's coffin lid with his relentless rate hikes.

However, as Mark Twain said after a serious accident, the obituary writers were premature in their reports of his death. Clinton and his fellow Democrats would rise again in the years ahead on the strength of something called the New Economy, the official beginning of which would take place a year before Clinton's reelection bid in 1996.

PART FIVE

The Boom

Alan was still not finished. He pushed rates skyward a half-point on February 1, 1995, before
deciding that the Fed's job was over for this cycle.
The Fed funds rate was now up to 6 percent, three percentage
points higher than a year earlier, and the discount rate was 5.25
percent. All in all, Alan had notched up short-term interest rates a
total of seven times in the past twelve months. Despite the harsh
criticism his policy had engendered, the series of tightening moves
achieved the desired effect of constraining inflation within
acceptable limits and moderating economic growth to a sustainable
pace. Once again, the economy hummed along like a well-tuned
car, and the prime beneficiaries of Alan's orchestrations would be
the very Democrats who had taken him to task in the summer
of 1994.

On February 23, Alan told Congress that he saw no need for further rate increases, and investors celebrated the news with a buying
spree that pushed the Dow Jones Industrial Average above 4,000 for
the first time in history. Until this time, there was still a question
about whether Clinton would reappoint Alan when his second term

expired. The President was fuming over the Democrats' shellacking at the polls the previous November, and many believed that Clinton would replace Alan with another Alan, Alan Blinder. However, former Princeton professor Blinder undermined his own credibility during a speech before his fellow bankers in Jackson Hole, Wyoming. He stated that in the short run, the Fed should settle for slightly higher inflation in order to add a few more jobs to the economy.

"Inflation is unworthy of the hysteria that attends it at the top of the Fed," Blinder said in an obvious swipe at Alan that did not go down well with the audience of mostly hawkish bankers.

Blinder may have thought he was earning himself some brownie points with Clinton and his team of economic advisers, but his pregnant attempt to position himself on the inside track for Alan's job backfired badly. Most economists in the United States and abroad regarded Blinder's comments as dangerous and portrayed Blinder himself as soft on inflation—about the worst criticism anyone could level against a prospective Fed chairman. Alan solidified his position at the helm of the Federal Reserve by default, as it were. With the economy once again gaining momentum and the stock market soaring to new highs daily, all speculation about Alan's early retirement dissolved virtually overnight.

Around the same time that Alan announced he was finished raising rates for the time being, he faced another economic crisis in the collapse of the Mexican peso. Philosophically, he would have preferred to adopt a laissez-faire attitude toward the situation, reasoning that the markets would correct whatever excesses had built up over time without leading to global chaos. Congressional Republicans argued against bailing out Mexico, since it would create what economists refer to as a "moral hazard"—that is, it would encourage other investors to act imprudently in the future, knowing that the government would come to their rescue. However, key figures on Wall Street and within the administration clamored for immediate action by the Fed. Mexico was our third-largest trading partner, and a lack of confidence there could spill over into the stock market and threaten banks that had loaned money to Mexico and other Latin American countries.

Alan opted on the side of caution, warning his critics to distinguish carefully between what he believed personally and how he acted as Fed chairman. With the help of Rubin, who had replaced Bentsen at Treasury, and undersecretary Lawrence Summers, Alan crafted an international rescue package that included a U.S. guarantee of $19 billion to help the Mexican government meet its credit obligations.

"[Greenspan's] view, which I think was right," Rubin said later, "was that what we did in Mexico had a moral hazard aspect to it that was unattractive. On the other hand, life is very often a choice between unattractive alternatives, and the question is which is the least unattractive. His view here, which was also Larry's and my view, was that the moral hazard aspect was a byproduct of doing something else so important—avoiding Mexico's going into default with possible contagion effects—that you simply had to accept the negative effect in order to get the greater good."

The greater good did not take long in coming. Stock and bond markets responded enthusiastically to the intervention, as investors were reassured that the financial institutions where they invested their money would not become victims of an escalating Latin American currency collapse.

Alan's long-term romance with Andrea Mitchell was growing more serious than ever, but all was not well with the other main woman in his life, his mother, Rose. By the summer of 1995, a few months shy of her ninety-third birthday, it was clear that the end was not far off. Alan had been calling her several times a week, and he visited her as frequently as he could when he was in New York. With her health deteriorating rapidly, Alan knew she would not last out the year. She died on August 6 in her apartment near Lincoln Center. Alan and Andrea attended the small graveside service in New Jersey with his immediate family and a few close friends, including his first wife and her husband. Alan was visibly shaken as he delivered a quiet eulogy at the side of her grave. He kept the news of Rose's passing a closely guarded secret, and it was not until a few years later that the public would learn that the mother of the Fed chairman had died. Alan himself did not yet know that his father, whom he had not seen in decades, had died in obscurity in Queens, New York, in October 1973.

Precisely a month before Rose's passing, Alan reversed the tight monetary policy he had been pursuing since the beginning of 1994. Stocks were still rising, but investors remained a bit jittery about the long-term outlook for the situation in Latin America. As a further insurance policy against renewed panic in the financial markets, Alan lowered the Fed funds rate a quarter of a percentage point to 5.75 percent on July 6. This commenced a series of further cuts that would eventually reduce the key short-term borrowing rate to 4.75 percent by the end of 1998. Investors got the message that the Fed was now in a loosening mode, with more available credit, and therefore easier borrowing terms, likely to speed the economy to an even stronger rate of growth. Corporate profits would benefit in this environment, and investors started buying stocks with renewed gusto, driving market valuations to levels never before seen in stock market history.

The stock market continued to boom throughout the year. After having passed 4,000 on the Dow earlier in 1995, equities soared past the next millennial barrier before the year was over. Investors did not know it yet, but the overall market had embarked on a five-year series of annual advances in excess of 20 percent—the longest streak of such gains ever recorded. Stock market valuations expanded to truly frightening levels for those who had lived through the savage bear markets of the past.

Historically, several primary measures had defined the level of stocks from oversold to overextended conditions. The most widely followed ones were the price-to-earnings ratio and dividend yield of stocks in the S&P 500 Index. In August 1982, at the depths of the bear market before the first Reagan rally built up steam, stocks had fallen to a price level around six times earnings, and the dividend yield was over 8 percent. This was an extremely oversold situation by all historical measures. When stocks had climbed in the past to a price/earnings level of fifteen or higher and a dividend yield below 2.5 percent, it had signaled a warning that the bull market was running out of gas. By the end of 1995, the market's overall price/ earnings ratio was in the high teens and the dividend yield was well below 2 percent. Many pundits compared the environment to that of 1929 and forecast a crash on the order of the one that precipitated the Great Depression of the 1930s.

Alan is an avid student of history as well as an economist, and he kept a wary eye on the indicators that crossed the screens of his computers each day. Traditionalist that he also is, Alan was deeply troubled by what he saw. In every bull market, new generations of analysts who have never lived through a bear market start claiming that "this time is different," the old rules no longer apply in the current economic environment, and the good times are going to roll on indefinitely. They had said as much in the heady days just before the crash of 1987, and now they were saying it again. Freshly scrubbed MBAs in their mid-twenties with no historical perspective, who were suddenly earning high six-figure incomes, refused to acknowledge the lessons of the past. "This time is different." Alan had heard it all too many times before, and he wasn't buying any of it. He began to worry that a major stock market crash lay just around the bend.

Pundits started talking about a stock market "bubble" building up that would burst at some point and leave the economy in ruins. The Japanese stock market had tumbled more than 50 percent from its own stratospheric perch a few years earlier, and Alan feared that a similar fate was in store for U.S. equities. He was tempted to take dramatic action to prevent a new collapse from happening, but he realized that any effort to restrain the dynamic bull market could backfire.

"There is a fundamental problem with market intervention to prick a bubble," Alan said. "It presumes that you know more than the market. There is also a problem of timing. You might prick it too soon, in which case it comes back, and you may just make it larger next time. There is also the very interesting question as to whether the central bank is intervening appropriately in the market. This raises some fascinating questions about what our authority is and who makes the judgment that there actually is a bubble."

Bubble or not, stocks continued to defy the law of gravity through the end of 1995 and into the new year. Stock prices shot straight up through the winter and into the spring before leveling off to pause for breath. Despite his misgivings, Alan helped fuel the rally with two more rate cuts—the first just before Christmas 1995 and the second at the end of January 1996—to further stabilize the situation in Latin America. While the strong advance in equities was troublesome to Alan, subtle changes were taking place below the surface of the economy that augured well for its long-term health. The changes were hard to fathom in the beginning, but they were centered in a couple of systemic developments that included the collapse of the communist empire and the subsequent explosion of free enterprise throughout the globe.

Alan was not yet convinced that these changes were real, but he began to entertain the notion that perhaps something *was* different this time around. Perhaps the old rules really did no longer apply, or no longer applied as well as they once did.

CHAPTER 29

With the economy and stock market booming, President Clinton reappointed Alan as Fed chairman before Clinton's successful bid for reelection got under way. In October 1996, the Bond Market Association's Public Securities Association (PSA) division presented Alan with its Distinguished Public Service Award at the organization's annual awards dinner at the Pierre Hotel in New York City. The organization gave the award each year to the individual who had the most significant impact on interest rate markets during the past year. New York Federal Reserve Bank president William McDonough introduced Alan, and PSA's chairwoman Elaine La Roche presented the award to him.

"As Fed chairman and chief architect of the nation's monetary policy for the past nine years," La Roche said, "Alan Greenspan has received widespread acclaim for his global leadership in managing monetary policy and reducing inflation. On the occasion of its twentieth anniversary year, PSA is delighted to recognize Mr. Greenspan for his role in guiding the nation toward sustained, non-inflationary economic growth, and his dedication to service, by honoring him with our most prestigious award."

On December 6, Alan returned to a major issue that had occupied so much of his attention when he worked in the Reagan administration during the early 1980s. Speaking at the Abraham Lincoln Award Ceremony of the Union League of Philadelphia, Alan said, "Today, I would like to address an issue that almost certainly will be at the forefront of American concerns over the next decade: our largest federal entitlement program, Social Security.

"It is becoming conventional wisdom that the Social Security system, as currently constructed, will not be fully viable after the so-called baby boom generation starts to retire in about fifteen years. The most recent report by the Social Security trustees projected that the trust funds of the system will grow over approximately the next fifteen years. However, beginning in the year 2012, the annual expected costs of Social Security are projected to exceed annual earmarked tax receipts, and the consequent deficits are projected to deplete the trust funds by the year 2029."

Alan stated that raising taxes further would be an impediment to economic growth. He was also opposed to having the Treasury invest part of the funds in the stock market, on the grounds that such a mass infusion of tax receipts into equities would amount to a subsidy of individual corporations. For a long-term solution, Alan recommended complete or partial privatization of the system by permitting Americans to direct at least some of their Social Security taxes into private retirement plans.

"Perhaps the strongest argument for privatization is that replacing the current unfunded system, which apparently discourages saving, with a fully funded system . . . could boost domestic saving. But, in any event, we must remember that it is *because* privatization plans might increase savings that makes them potentially viable, not their particular form of financing."

These were the strongest public comments Alan had made to date in favor of privatizing Social Security, but the news was overshadowed by another speech he gave the night before. Addressing a conservative think tank, the American Enterprise Institute for Public Policy Research, Alan expressed his concern that stock valuations might be too high. Musing out loud, he asked the audience, "How do we know when irrational exuberance has unduly escalated asset values, which then become subject to unexpected and prolonged contractions as they have in Japan over the past decade?"

His comments sent stock markets plunging from 2 to 4 percent around the globe. From Asia to Europe to New York, investors interpreted his rhetorical question as a signal that the Fed might start raising interest rates again to dampen investors' enthusiasm for stocks. Various Fed officials quickly reassured the media that the Fed was not in a tightening mode, and that Alan's remarks were merely an expression of his own personal concern. Others were surprised that a rhetorical question planted in a speech about the philosophy of central banking, delivered in the evening to a small group of free-market enthusiasts, could have had such a devastating impact on world markets. However, there is little doubt that Alan understood the influence his words would have on financial markets, and he was hoping to talk stock prices down.

The larger question was whether the Federal Reserve had any business trying to influence stock prices in the first place. It is worth noting that the Dow Jones Industrial Average was only at 6,300 when Alan asked his provocative question, and after a one-day nosedive of more than 2 percent, stocks blithely resumed their steady climb. The Dow would soar past the 8,000 mark before the next year was over, as investors cast all worries about "irrational exuberance" to the winds. It is an old Wall Street adage that "the market doesn't lie." Rationality, or the lack of it, is reflected in reality. If stocks were heading to levels that made Alan nervous, perhaps there were good reasons for it.

J. Bradford DeLong, professor of economics at Berkeley and co-editor of the *Journal of Economic Perspectives*, speculated that "the information technology phenomenon is ushering in a generation-long boom of rapid growth and rising profits. Past rule-of-thumb valuations based on earnings growth assume that economic and profit growth will continue in the future at roughly the same pace at which they have proceeded in the past. But because we are on the threshold of the post-industrial transformation, there is no good reason to think that economic growth, earnings growth, and stock price growth will be not be faster in the future than in the past."

He went on to say, "In the past, demand for stocks was limited by fear of risk. Investors could look over at the bond market, see the returns available to them if they invested in bonds or in the money market, and think: 'Investing in stocks seems to be much more risky than investing in bonds. I'm not going to run that risk unless I think stocks are very attractively priced and offer relatively high dividend yields.' Thus demand for stocks was fairly low. But, the inflation of the 1970s taught investors the brutal lesson that there is no safety in bonds. Your investment can vanish if interest rates rise, or if inflation devalues the purchasing power of your bond portfolio's principle. Investors today know that there is no safety in bonds, and they have less fear of the business cycle and other risks associated with stocks. Hence, demand for stocks today is higher than in the past."

Finally, "corporations have learned better how to avoid paying taxes," said DeLong. "Some companies have pushed up their debt-equity ratios and changed payments to investors that used to be called dividends into bond interest. Dividends are paid out of earnings after taxes, while debt interest is a cost paid out of pretax operating cash flow. The net effect is to shift some of this cash flow away from the government to private investors."

After analyzing these theories and weighing them against concerns expressed by Alan and others that stock prices were too high, DeLong concluded that the bullish arguments for the stock market were correct to a great degree. The extraordinarily high stock market valuations in historical terms may have been justified by a new set of economic conditions.

DeLong was not alone in this view. A study sponsored by McGraw-Hill at the time concluded that "productivity increases in service industries may actually be higher than current measures show," and "thus the rise in stock price indexes" may be valid. "U.S. productivity growth—and national output—is being understated about three-quarters of a percentage point."

In addition to economic signs pointing to greater U.S. productivity, the Congressional Advisory Commission on the Consumer Price Index believed that inflation was overstated because of the government's reliance on obsolete data: "What might appear as a small bias in the consumer price index (CPI)—which overstates changes in the cost of living by roughly 1.1 percentage points per year—carries enormous implications when extended over time. Over a dozen years, the cumulative additional national debt from over-indexing the budget would amount to $1 trillion."

The commission recommended that the Bureau of Labor Statistics should replace its outdated inflation index with a new one that took current consumer buying patterns into account. If this were done, it would save federal taxpayers $64.4 billion a year, the federal budget would be reduced by $148 billion annually by 2006, and the nation's outstanding debt could be cut $691 billion in the same period. Taking all of this into consideration, the economy was actually better off than it appeared on the surface, and stock prices merely reflected this new reality.

Despite his misgivings, Alan was slowly—and reluctantly—beginning to accept this emerging view about a rapidly evolving New Economy. "He is very open to the possibility that we have entered a new economic age," said Judy Shelton, a scholar who frequently consulted with Alan on economic matters. "He really believes in the organic nature of the market economy."

Economist Lawrence Chimerine agreed that Alan should stop fretting about outmoded stock valuations. "Most measures of market valuation indicate that the market is not grossly overvalued," he said, "particularly in view of the relatively low inflation and low-interest-rate environment that now exists. There is no evidence that the increase in stock prices has resulted in a big increase in consumer spending. Rather, it seems to be closely correlated with an increase in the personal savings rate. A growing number of families are using their savings to invest in retirement funds for the long term."

Chimerine also criticized Alan for taking measures during the past to curb wage inflation. "Chairman Greenspan's concern that wages are accelerating too rapidly—and that this will ultimately cause upward pressure on prices—is also unfounded. Real wages have been more or less stagnant since the mid-1970s. This clearly suggests that structural changes have been holding down wages. These changes include new labor-saving technologies, declining union influence, a rise in job-loss fears, and increased competition from low-wage countries. The modest pickup in wages Greenspan is concerned about is actually healthy in that it is permitting many families to finally experience at least a slight increase in their living standards, while not representing a threat to inflation. Greenspan should relax and enjoy it."

Members of the Senate Committee on Banking were annoyed that the Fed had extended its mandate to an area that was none of its concern. They worried that Alan might begin a new round of interest rate hikes to derail the stock market just as more and more Americans were beginning to enjoy the wealth effect of rising stock prices. During Alan's semiannual report to the committee, Jim Bunning, a Republican senator from Kentucky, called Alan's position on the stock market "misguided" and said it could "become more of a threat to our economy than inflation will ever be."

Alan's old nemesis, Senator Paul Sarbanes of Maryland, chastised Alan for his lack of concern about ordinary people. He described a visit he made to a job-training center in Baltimore during which he talked to a troubled young man who had just gotten his first job. "This young fellow, he's far removed from the wealth effect. He's barely struggling to get into a job situation. Now, what's going to happen here?"

Conservative Texas Republican senator Phil Gramm continued the senatorial pile-on with his own attack. "I think people hear what you are saying and conclude that you believe that equities are overvalued. I would guess that equity values are not only *not* overvalued but may still be undervalued."

Alan gulped audibly a few times. When he tried to defend himself, Bunning cut him off. "If we get prime interest rates at double digits, we are going to stop this economy in its tracks. I don't want to see that happen on your watch, and I surely don't want to see it happen on my watch."

Alan's shoulders sagged as it suddenly dawned on him that some of the most powerful politicians in the country, representing both major parties, were having a field day ganging up on him. "I appreciate that, Senator," he said in resignation. "I have the same view."

CHAPTER 30

On Christmas Day 1996, Alan and Andrea Mitchell returned to her renovated three-bedroom townhouse in the Palisades section of Washington, D.C., which Andrea had bought more than twenty years earlier. As they sat in the den, Alan turned to her and asked quietly, "Do you want a big wedding or a small wedding?"

Andrea was confused at first, then shocked when she finally understood what he was asking her. After twelve years of courtship, Alan was proposing.

"I was surprised when I heard," said their mutual friend, reporter Judy Woodruff. "I thought they had settled into a very nice routine, but I never necessarily thought that he'd move on to the next step."

Her husband, Al Hunt, Washington correspondent for the *Wall Street Journal*, concurred. "We were quite surprised, ecstatic. I thought central bankers didn't change a lot."

Andrea accepted immediately and said later that the long romance had never bothered her. "I knew he was committed to me," she said, "and that we planned to spend the rest of our lives together."

Although their age difference never concerned her, like all couples, they had other differences that threatened to get in the way from time to time. Andrea had been raised in a religious environment, while Alan had never abandoned the atheism that had been part of his philosophical makeup since his days with Ayn Rand. Andrea was willing to overlook this, however, since Alan had his own strong moral code and, according to Andrea, was one of the most ethical men she had ever met.

"One thing that's so refreshing about Alan," she said, "is that he is up front with people. He doesn't do things behind people's backs."

Alan also lacked Andrea's passion for elegant food, preferring simple fare like broiled fish and boiled vegetables to the delicate sauces Andrea and her housekeeper liked to prepare in her gourmet kitchen. "I've forgotten how to cook the good stuff," she said. "He's not a fancy eater."

On a personal level, Andrea said, "He is so supportive of me intellectually and emotionally. He's so interested in what I do, what I think. He shares his ideas with me. He is the least patronizing, least condescending person I know." Andrea's parents approved of the match, since "they know he's been so wonderful to me."

For twelve years, they had spent virtually all of their free time together or in the company of a handful of close friends like Hunt and Woodruff; World Bank president James D. Wolfensohn and his wife, Elaine; newsman Jim Lehrer and his wife, Kate; and former CIA director William Webster. Their evenings at home were normally quiet affairs, spent listening to classical music or jazz, occasionally watching a Baltimore Orioles game on television, and reading mystery novels for relaxation.

"It's very lonely when we have to travel and we're not together," Andrea said. When they went on vacation, more often than not they traveled to California, where they spent a week or so at John Gardiner's tennis camp in Carmel.

"I like playing against him," she said, "when he's not hitting his sneaky left-hand slices."

Alan and Andrea were members of the Chevy Chase Country Club, and Alan usually teamed up with William Webster in the annual seniors tennis competition, or played a round of golf with Securities and Exchange Commission chairman Arthur Levitt.

Alan continued his early-morning routine of taking to the bathtub for a two-hour soak to catch up on the never-ending slew of economic data that was delivered to his home each day. "My intelligence quota is twenty points higher at six A.M. than at six P.M.," he joked. While he was devouring the stack of literature piled high in the in box attached to the side of the tub, Andrea usually went for a long outdoor run when the weather was good, or to the gym for a brisk workout.

They set their wedding date for April 6, 1997, a month to the day following Alan's seventy-first birthday. It was a cool spring day with a light drizzle in the air. Andrea brightened the occasion with a knee-length, cream-colored Oscar de la Renta dress and a matching pillbox hat perched atop her frosted blonde hair. Alan, on the other hand, looked like a banker on his way to work. He wore one of his trademark dark suits, starched white shirt with a little "AG" monogrammed on the chest, and an eminently forgettable blue-striped tie.

Seventy-five guests attended the wedding. In addition to their inner circle of friends, David Brinkley, Henry Kissinger, Katharine Graham, Senator John Warner of Virginia, and Alan's close companion from his pre-Andrea days, Barbara Walters, were among the guests. They boarded chartered buses near the White House and were chauffeured about an hour away to the Inn at Little Washington in the Virginia countryside for the ceremony, which was conducted by Supreme Court Justice Ruth Bader Ginsburg. Andrea's seven-year-old goddaughter, Lauren Hunt, served as their flower girl.

"Neither of us forgot our lines," Andrea joked afterward.

"I married her for rain or for shine." Alan tried his own hand at humor with mixed results.

The bride and groom honeymooned in Venice after a meeting for central bankers that Alan attended in Basel, Switzerland. Alan wielded the power in their household, but Andrea was the primary breadwinner, with a high-six-figure income as one of NBC's star reporters. At the time of their wedding, Alan's salary as Fed chairman was $133,500, and his net worth totaled an estimated two million dollars—not a fortune for someone regarded as the most powerful financial figure in the world.

When asked about her husband's relatively meager circumstances, Andrea reiterated that "money does not motivate him. He couldn't care less. I drag him kicking and screaming to buy a new suit. He just doesn't care about money."

Power, and the proximity to people of power, was the primary aphrodisiac in his life. When he was not playing golf or tennis at his country club, he could be found at Jack Kent Cooke's private box at RFK Stadium, at a Gridiron Club dinner, or at any one of Washington's major social events. Arthur Levitt, who had observed Alan up close for several years, remarked, "I think he's very comfortable in this power environment. Yes, I think he loves this. His political instincts are superb."

Regarding the job he was doing at the Fed, Nobel Prize–winning economist Robert M. Solow gave him the highest grades. "Alan has done an excellent job as Fed chairman," he said. "But he's also been lucky. The economy has been well behaved in part for reasons that have nothing to do with the Fed. The Fed has been very skillful, and a substantial part of that skillfulness is his canniness and his flexibility. Two years ago most economists, including Greenspan, believed that when the unemployment rate got down near six percent, you've got to slow the economy down. We have learned that we can run the economy at five percent unemployment, and that's because of Alan's flexibility."

In other words, Alan's growing acceptance of the evolving New Economy had a lot to do with the success of the policies he implemented as Fed chairman.

In the late summer of 1997, a few months after his wedding, a black Mercury Grand Marquis sedan pulled up in front of Alan's home in northwest Washington, as it did every morning, and whisked him to Fed headquarters across town in Foggy Bottom. The chauffeur-driven vehicle was one of the perks of his position.

The news that morning out of Asia was not encouraging. Asian currencies and stock markets had plummeted overnight, and

Malaysia's firebrand leader, Prime Minister Mahathir Mohamad, blamed everyone from greedy speculators to a global Jewish conspiracy for his nation's problems. Mohamad specifically cited hedge fund manager George Soros for speculating on his nation's currency, and Jews in general, who allegedly had an "agenda" against Malaysia's twenty-one million Muslims. The corrupt regimes of Thailand and Indonesia spouted similar stories in the wake of their own countries' financial collapse, and the disease had spread throughout the emerging markets and threatened to overwhelm Europe and the United States as well. After a decade in which the sizzling "tiger" economies of Southeast Asia had been the envy of the world, they were suddenly imploding like a house of cards buffeted by a typhoon of their own making.

When Alan arrived at work that morning, he issued a statement putting the blame where it belonged—with the crony capitalism and inbred corruption that had finally undermined the surface prosperity of the past ten years.

"In a world of increasing capital mobility, there is a premium on governments maintaining sound macroeconomic policies," Alan said. He criticized the problem countries themselves for artificially propping up their currencies and financial markets and failing to break up the government-supported monopolies that controlled key industries, including the banking system. "As a consequence, these countries lost the confidence of both domestic and international investors."

With the tenth anniversary of the October crash of 1987 just weeks away, U.S. investors began to panic that a replay was all but inevitable. The Dow had soared above 8,000 for the first time just a few weeks earlier, but an avalanche of selling hit Europe and the U.S. markets, toppling stocks into a sickening tailspin. Once again, Alan was faced with a major decision: should he follow a laissez-faire strategy and let the markets sort things out by themselves, or intervene as he had done when the falling Mexican peso threatened to derail bourses throughout South America? It was the old moral-hazard-versus-unattractive-alternatives argument all over again.

Alan weighed ideology against practicality and came down on the side of expediency, as he had done throughout his public life.

Again he huddled with Rubin and Summers. Together, they formed a united front and urged Western and Japanese banks to extend their debts to the afflicted countries. They also urged Congress to approve an additional $50 billion for the International Monetary Fund to bail out Asia before the so-called "Asian flu" spread throughout the global economy.

"Larry and Alan are both very strong personalities," said Rubin, "smart as hell, and they both have views. I have views, too. Yet it worked out remarkably well, and it was very important. People don't realize how close we came to disaster. The whole system almost came off the rails."

The stock market regained its footing almost immediately and rocketed back through the 8,000 mark before the end of the year, posting another annual return in excess of 20 percent. The U.S. economy was now growing at a rate of more than 4 percent a year, well above the 2.5 percent level that had historically been considered inflationary. Corporate profits were accelerating, which was good for stock prices, and unemployment had plunged to levels not seen since 1970. Yet the tight labor market failed to generate the type of inflation that Alan and his fellow economists expected to see in such an environment. Many people were still left behind in this New Economy, but the spoils of prosperity were spreading to more and more workers with no inflationary consequences.

What was going on?

The more he crunched the numbers, the more Alan realized that the key to this economic sea-change could be attributed to two factors: falling commodity prices and, more important, a significant growth in the productivity of U.S. workers. The explosion of free enterprise overseas and the resulting increase in competition was largely responsible for the drop in commodity prices, and new technology was behind the enhancement of worker productivity at home. Alan understood that these changes were occurring independently of the Fed and the Clinton administration, but he was among the first to realize that they were more than a one-time event. Something real was taking place in the global marketplace that was unprecedented in human history. With the collapse of

233

socialist economies, capitalism had broken loose across the globe and transformed the old rules into a new economic paradigm. And, as the saying goes, paradigms are always shifting.

The global economy had shifted. Alan suggested that the emergence of the Internet and information technology could well turn out to be a "once or twice in a century" phenomenon. More and more, he was inclined not to let the Fed get in the way of this powerful new juggernaut, as long he carefully monitored inflationary trends and remained in front of the interest rate curve—that is, as long as the Fed kept short-term rates just high enough to restrain inflation before it got out of control.

"Greenspan's greatest achievement," said New York Federal Reserve Bank president William McDonough, "was that, as the intellectual leader of the Fed, he recognized what was going on first."

The economy had embarked upon a virtuous circle of sorts. With worker productivity high and profits growing, corporations invested more in their own businesses, encouraging consumers to buy more stocks and drive prices higher, which allowed companies to pump more money back into their enterprises. All this energy created a self-fulfilling process that was well on its way to producing the longest economic expansion in history. It was almost as though the economy had become a perpetual motion machine that would keep on going forever and ever—until the next traumatic event, like a crisis in one hot spot or another, threatened to blow it all to smithereens.

CHAPTER 31

I t soon became clear that the stock market was not a monolith. The broad averages, including the S&P 500, the Nasdaq Composite with its high component of technology shares, and the Dow Jones Industrial Average, masked what was really going on beneath the surface. All stocks were not going up equally. In fact, while technology and high-growth stocks were defying the law of gravity and rocketing to levels that bore no relationship to their intrinsic worth, many Old Economy stocks had entered bear markets of their own. Investors who had hung onto traditional portfolios composed of old-line companies in the industrial sectors of the economy were actually losing money, while those who had made the leap into the New Economy technology sectors were getting rich, or semi-rich, virtually overnight.

The sterling gains of the S&P 500, which comprised the top five hundred large-capitalization companies in the United States, were driven by the shares of only fifty companies, while more than four hundred stocks in the index were languishing. Contrast that with the even more robust performance of the Nasdaq Composite, 70 percent of which was made up of Internet and high-tech stocks, many of them with little or no earnings to support their lofty stock prices. These figures, perhaps more than any other that Alan analyzed each day, convinced him that the economy was indeed undergoing a radical transformation whose true dimensions no one fully understood as yet. The speculative fever surrounding startup Internet plays in particular troubled him immensely, but he could not deny that a new paradigm had come into existence—and it was shifting rapidly.

The broad stock market indices roared higher in a sharp trajectory during the first five months of 1998, crossing 9,000 on the Dow for the first time. When the FOMC met on May 20, Alan and the other central bankers sat around the immense mahogany table in the Fed's conference room. Most of them openly expressed their concern about the "unrealistic level" of stock prices; the torrid pace of economic growth, which was now accelerating at 6 percent a year; and the declining unemployment rate, which had recently dropped below 5 percent. A consensus seemed to be developing that the Fed needed to take preemptive action against inflation by raising short-term interest rates. To the amazement of just about everyone in the room, Alan—the preeminent hawk on inflation in the world—raised his hand to silence the group and called for caution.

Robert T. Parry, the San Francisco Fed chief who had long mirrored Alan's views on inflation, cited the low jobless rate and begged to disagree. Richmond Fed president J. Alfred Broaddus seconded Parry's view, stating that inflation would surely get out of hand unless the Fed acted soon. Fed governor Lawrence H. Meyer concurred with the dissenters, insisting that economic growth was too strong to be sustainable without fueling a rise in inflation. Alan suggested that they all adjourn for a coffee break, and when they returned to the conference table, Alan exercised his prerogative as Fed chairman to speak first. Addressing the group in his usual slow, low-key, confident manner, Alan argued that things were different this time, that the economy was undergoing a significant change, and that emerging new technologies were yielding productivity gains that would keep inflation in check. As long as worker productivity exceeded wage demands, it was possible for the economy to grow at a greater clip without triggering higher inflation.

It was a measure of Alan's persuasive skills that, when the assembled bankers voted on whether to raise rates or leave them where they were, they opted for the status quo. Broaddus cast the only dissenting vote. Alan's authority and conviction had carried the day, as he knew they would have to if he were to retain his effectiveness as Fed leader. When it came to a showdown, the process was completely democratic. Alan had only one vote, like all the others. The vote of the chairman of the Federal Reserve carried no more weight than the votes of the others.

"Alan rules the room," said former Fed vice chairman Manuel H. Johnson. "Until he makes a big mistake, he'll continue to get everything he wants."

"In a sense, Alan had become something of a dove," said another Fed source. "He has been willing to let the economy run faster than what a lot of people have been comfortable with. It's not uncommon for him to have a meeting where everyone disagrees with him but goes along with him in the end."

For Alan, it was a remarkable turnabout from his position of only a year or so before. The greatest inflation fighter since Paul Volcker had taken a position that put him pretty much in agreement with that expressed by President Clinton.

"I believe it's possible to have more sustained and higher growth without inflation than we previously thought," Clinton said at a press conference a month later.

Alan bristled, however, over any suggestion that he had become soft on inflation. His closest colleagues maintained that his views had not changed one iota since Reagan first appointed Alan more than ten years earlier. If Alan believed inflation was a serious threat, he would be the first to call for higher interest rates to preempt it. His values and goals had not changed, Alan said, but the economy had. Heightened global competition was restraining wage growth and limiting companies' ability to pass along higher costs, the primary components of the inflation index. In addition, computers, the Internet, and other labor-saving developments were boosting

productivity and allowing unemployment to decline without caus-
ing higher inflation. He had come to believe that the New Economy
was real, and that it was here to stay.

The other factor that entered the equation was the reduction in the
federal budget deficit that promised huge surpluses in the years
ahead. Politicians argued about which party was primarily responsible for the windfall in federal revenues that had begun to exceed
the hopes of even the greatest optimists. In 1998, when revenues
exceeded outlays for the first time in more than twenty-five years,
President Clinton asserted that "discarding the failed supply-side
economics of the 1980s" combined with his record tax hike in 1993
deserved the credit. House leader Newt Gingrich had a different
take on the matter, claiming that the Republican Party's "heroic
commitment to a balanced budget" made a surplus possible.

Alan knew that both men were wrong. Federal spending had
gone up significantly under Clinton, and the Congress controlled by
Republicans had proven to be as profligate as the Democrats who
preceded them. They simply had different priorities on how the
money should be spent. When he analyzed all the numbers, Alan
understood that the dynamic New Economy and its creation of
wealth for more and more Americans had made it possible for
Washington to have its cake and eat it at the same time. Tax revenues were up simply because the incomes of average Americans
had risen sharply. Middle-class Americans were fully employed and
enjoying lavish lifestyles, which overshadowed their usual concerns
about being taxed too heavily. Alan noted that, contrary to the
received wisdom, the budget deficit had actually begun to fall from
6 percent to 3 percent of gross domestic product (GDP) in the final
year of the Reagan administration.

"The amount of tax dollars paid by Americans soared when tax
rates were lowered in the 1980s because the lower rates produced
more income," said Federal Reserve Board member Lawrence Lind-
say, who worked closely with Alan. "Also, the economy grew faster in
the first few years following the Reagan tax cuts, which also boosted
revenues."

The economy slowed to a halt for several reasons under George Bush, who increased government spending by 28 percent above the inflation rate during his four years in office. Clinton was fortunate enough to be in office when the economy got moving again with the help of Alan and his cohorts at the Fed. Alan stayed as far away from the fray as it was possible for a Fed chairman to do, and kept his own counsel on the matter. In private, however, he chuckled at Clinton's good fortune and was fond of paraphrasing Woody Allen's apt observation that "ninety percent of life is just showing up."

Just as Reagan's military buildup, which helped topple the Soviet dictatorship, caused the deficit to soar in the mid-1980s, the so-called "peace dividend" that followed the Soviet collapse generated a half-trillion dollars in extra revenues from 1990 through 1998. The end of the Cold War enabled Clinton to increase spending on domestic social programs, catapulting non-defense outlays in real dollars and as a percentage of national output to the highest levels in U.S. history. Alan would have preferred that the administration rein in spending and limit the role of government in the economy, but he agreed with Milton Friedman that expenditures inevitably rise in tandem with the amount of money government has available to spend.

With so much profligacy and jockeying for advantage going on in the political arena, Alan's role as the nation's leading inflation fighter was more crucial than ever. Clinton had increased the size of government considerably during his first six years in office, but the economy had, fortunately enough, grown even faster. It had doubled in size over the past fifteen years and created thirty million new jobs, more than the rest of the industrialized world combined. To a great degree, exploding economic growth made Alan's job a bit easier than it was in 1987. The Fed could now afford to ease up on the monetary restraint it had to exercise during the deficit years, and the financial markets did much of the work of restraining or stimulating the economy. The New Economy put the Fed in the enviable role of playing referee, gently notching rates up or down to fine tune the economy when it was necessary.

In December 1998, the U.S. economy completed nearly eight full years of robust growth, one of the longest periods of economic expansion in history. Alan attributed this phenomenal achievement to global forces that had tilted much of the civilized world toward market capitalism. "For good or ill, an unforgiving capitalist process is driving wealth creation," Alan said. "It has become increasingly difficult for policy makers who wish to practice, as they put it, a more 'caring' capitalism to realize the full potential of their economies. As a consequence, increasingly, nations appear to be opting to open themselves to competition, however harsh, and become producers that can compete in world markets."

Privately, Alan was delighted about this eruption of competitive free-market forces throughout the world, which was made possible by technological advances. "What we may be observing in the current environment," he said, "is a number of key technologies, some even mature, finally interacting to create significant new opportunities for value creation."

Technology allowed investors to redirect their assets instantaneously from one market to another. "New technology has radically reduced the costs of borrowing and lending across traditional national borders," he said. Financial globalization has helped raise living standards and also "exposes and punishes underlying economic weakness swiftly and decisively."

Judging by his recent comments, Alan appeared to have made a complete about-face from his concerns about "irrational exuberance" expressed just two years earlier. Not even a new financial crisis overseas—this time in Russia, whose markets were imploding because of a lack of support from an underlying infrastructure— dampened his optimism. Alan coordinated his reaction to the situation in Russia closely with Rubin and his deputy secretary, Summers. Rubin was on vacation in the Virgin Islands when he first heard the news. Alan was playing tennis in Virginia, and Summers was home with his family. Almost simultaneously, the three men received an urgent call from the telephone operator at the Treasury, informing them of the Russian disaster. Summers came up with the best analogy to describe what was taking place.

"Global capital markets pose the same kinds of problems that jet planes do," he said. "They are faster, more comfortable, and they get you where you are going better. But the crashes are much more spectacular."

After conferring with the others, Alan dealt with the latest emergency as he had with the earlier crises, by lowering short-term interest rates from 5.5 percent to 4.75 percent by the end of the year. Following a sickening plunge in the autumn that dropped the Dow Industrials below 8,000, stocks rallied sharply in November and December to end 1998 with another impressive double-digit gain. Investors were once again in the best of all possible moods as they uncorked their champagne bottles to usher in the new year.

CHAPTER 32

While many of his former libertarian colleagues accused him of compromising his beliefs for the sake of political expediency, Alan maintained that his ideas had not changed since the 1950s. When he recommended to a Senate committee that economic regulations should all be "sunsetted," that is, given an expiration date, Senator Paul Sarbanes of Maryland accused Alan of "playing with fire, or indeed throwing gasoline on the fire."

"Do you also favor a sunset provision for the authorization of the Federal Reserve?" Sarbanes asked Alan, the sarcasm unmistakable in his voice.

"Yes, I do, Senator," Alan replied calmly.

"Do you actually mean," Sarbanes continued in disbelief, "that the Fed should cease to function unless affirmatively continued?"

"That is correct, sir."

"All right. The Defense Department?"

"Yes."

"Now my next question is, is it your intention that the report of this hearing should be that Greenspan recommends a return to the gold standard?"

"I've been recommending that for years," Alan reiterated his perennial position. "There's nothing new about that. It would probably mean there is only one vote in the FOMC for that, but it is mine."

In the wake of the Russian disaster, the stock market continued to soar virtually without letup during the early months of 1999, pushing through the 10,000 barrier on the Dow for the first time. Once they breached that mark, stocks barely paused for breath as they shot straight up another thousand points like a mountain climber determined to reach the summit—wherever that was—in the shortest time possible. No one was more delighted than President Clinton, who smiled broadly during a party on the South Lawn of the White House in late spring. Clinton posed for a photo op with Alan and Andrea. Afterward, Andrea chatted with friends while Alan stood off by himself, looking terrified that someone might approach and ask him about the stock market's torrid ascent.

"There's a tremendous difference between the public image that he so carefully creates," observed Democratic representative Joseph Kennedy of Massachusetts, "and the personal guy who is kind of fun to have dinner with. He tells great stories and has lived a life that bears very little resemblance to what he does today."

The setting accentuated the close and mostly cordial relationship that the Randian libertarian enjoyed with Clinton and the Democrats in the White House. No one was more surprised than Alan, who had long considered Republicans to be his natural political allies until he found himself locking horns with George Bush and his advisers seven years earlier. For his part, Clinton understood all too well that his place in history owed a lot to Alan's stewardship of the economy, which in turn would also have a major impact on the presidential race of 2000.

Alan failed to benefit personally from the lofty level of stock prices that were creating unprecedented wealth for many middle-class Americans. Figures released around this time revealed that his net worth had increased from the year before, but not by all that much. He continued to eschew stocks to avoid a potential conflict of interest, and invested his money instead in Treasury bills and money market accounts. As Fed chairman, he now earned $136,700 per year. Andrea, on the other hand, was not bound by the same strictures and had put most of her money in the stock market. She owned a block of shares in General Electric, the parent company of NBC, and also had substantial interests in Abbott Laboratories, Anheuser-Busch, Kimberly-Clark, and other stocks that put her net worth close to $2 million, not counting her real estate and retirement investments. All in all, Alan and Andrea were well off, but not as rich as outsiders might have expected.

In late June, despite his growing acceptance of the evolving New Economy, Alan again grew nervous about the threat of accelerating inflation. The economy was booming, stocks were skyrocketing, labor demands were rising, and commodity prices were also edging up, and all of these influences taken together were likely to be reflected in higher consumer prices in the months ahead. On June 30, Alan took the first of a series of preemptive steps to tighten monetary policy and boosted the bellwether Fed funds rate a quarter-point to 5 percent.

The rest of the year was going to be tricky in several respects, including the prospects of worldwide computer breakdowns as the calendar made the transition to the year 2000. The "Y2K bug" posed a real threat to the global economic system, even though most ordinary citizens chose to downplay its importance. Because of an old programming quirk, most computers could read only the last two digits of the year. As a result, governments, corporations, and various institutions throughout the world ran a serious risk that computers would interpret the transition to 2000 as a return to 1900. Since virtually *everything* depended on computers—financial transactions, energy distribution, telecommunications systems, and so forth—a computer meltdown could lead to global paralysis and widespread chaos.

Alan, Rubin, and political leaders from both parties worried that Americans could cause a run on the banks by withdrawing large sums of cash before midnight arrived on December 31. Alan was determined to make sure there was enough liquidity in the system to prevent that from happening.

"You have mentioned, or the Fed has mentioned that our financial institutions are doing quite well in dealing with the problem," said New York Senator Chuck Schumer during a Senate Banking Committee hearing. "A second and ancillary problem, but a serious one, is that citizens may be worried about what will happen and will take their money out of the financial institutions toward the second half of the year because they're worried about this. From what I understand, the Federal Reserve has set aside a certain amount of reserves for the end of 1999 to deal with that. As I understand, it's $50 billion."

"The concern that I have," said Alan, "is that people are going to draw too much out, and walking around with a lot of hundred dollar bills is not the safest way to keep your money."

"What advice would you give a citizen in December of this year about what to do with their savings account?" asked Senator John Edwards of North Carolina.

"I would say the most sensible thing is to leave it where it is. That's probably the safest thing. There's almost no conceivable way in which I can envision that computers will break down and records of people's savings accounts will disappear."

Alan went on to say that the $50 billion the Fed was prepared to pump into the banking system would be enough to handle any contingencies. He based that figure on the premise that one hundred million U.S. families might, in the worst-case scenario, withdraw an average of five hundred dollars per family as an insurance policy against a freeze on checking accounts and credit card payments. In the end, however, none of this came to pass. Well before the end of the summer, the overwhelming majority of financial institutions and major corporations announced that their computers were fully compliant with the Y2K transition, and they anticipated no problems. When the government assured the citizenry that their Social Security and benefit checks would go out on time, Americans turned their attention to more important matters—like whether they had enough champagne on hand to usher in the new year in style.

Alan also turned his attention back to his primary concern, that of the red-hot U.S. economy and the prospect of runaway inflation. He raised short-term rates on August 24, then again on November 16. By year's end, the Fed funds rate stood at 5.5 percent and the discount rate was 5 percent. When 2000 arrived with no major glitches, investors celebrated with a buying binge that drove stock prices to their fifth straight annual gain of more than 20 percent. The Dow Jones Industrial Average had risen more than 10,000 points since it hit rock bottom at 777 in August 1982. Average Americans were now better off financially than ever before. Alan no longer warned about irrational exuberance but, rather, he now agreed more or less with the views expressed by economist Lawrence Kudlow and many other Wall Street analysts who believed the New Economy was real.

"The value ascribed to any asset," Alan said during a speech in Jackson Hole, Wyoming, "is a discounted value of future expected returns, even if no market participant makes that calculation."

Markets do crash for all sorts of reasons, but they rarely get too far out of line with expectations for future corporate profits for long periods. A stock's present value depends on today's dividend and earnings per share, the anticipated future growth rate of dividends and earnings, and the risk premium investors demand over safer investments like Treasuries when they invest in volatile assets. At Jackson Hole, Alan made a strong case for respecting the pricing judgments of millions of investors who are knowledgeable about the financial prospects of the companies in which they invest. He had grown less concerned than he was three years earlier that stock prices would reach a level "at which it is hard to value them by any logical methodology," according to Gilbert Burck of *Fortune*.

President Clinton rewarded Alan's deft stewardship of the economy by appointing him to a fourth full term as Fed Chairman well before his third term officially expired. "Clearly, wise leadership from the Fed has played a very large role in our strong economy," the President said at a White House press conference in January.

"This chairman's leadership has been good, not just for the American economy and the mavens of finance on Wall Street. It has been good for ordinary Americans." At the time of Clinton's comments, unemployment was at a thirty-year low, consumer confidence was at a thirty-year high, and inflation was in check as the country enjoyed its longest period of growth since the 1960s.

"I welcome the appointment of Greenspan to another term," said Republican Senate Majority Leader Trent Lott. "He has served with a steady hand as the spirit and ingenuity of the American people have brought forth unprecedented economic prosperity."

Alan heaved a sigh of relief when stocks ran into stiff headwinds in March and April, with technology and Internet stocks in particular suffering a brutal pummeling. Investors were finally dumping the shares of companies with little or no earnings prospects and reinvesting the proceeds into companies with solid track records. It was a long-overdue correction, and it made Alan feel better about his growing belief that rational behavior eventually reasserts itself in the marketplace. Alan had lifted short-term rates two more times, on February 2 and March 21, and the cumulative effect of five rate hikes since June 1999 was finally slowing the robust economy. For good measure, he raised rates a sixth time on May 16, this time half a percentage point, which pushed the Fed funds rate up to 6.5 percent and the discount rate to 6 percent. In Alan's view, the long series of monetary tightening would be sufficient to defuse any fear of accelerating inflation.

He felt a sense of pride as he looked back over seventeen years of economic expansion, interrupted by only two quarters of contraction during the Bush presidency. Without taking too much credit for the vigor of the global economy, Alan knew that the monetary policy he had been implementing since 1987 was largely responsible for keeping the economy on track and avoiding some major potholes along the way. Occasionally, however, the old Alan returned, voicing doubts about the high valuations of stocks even when he appeared to accept the tenets of the New Economy.

"At some point, something has got to give, and we don't know what it's going to be," Alan said during his testimony about the ballooning U.S. trade deficit before the House of Representatives. "We don't know whether it'll be protracted over a very long period of time, in which case the adjustments will occur in the normal manner without any significance, or whether they will occur more abruptly."

Around the same time, Alan contradicted his earlier statements while testifying before the Senate when he asserted that higher worker productivity might actually trigger higher inflation. Previously, he and other champions of the New Economy had claimed that higher productivity was precisely what made it possible for the economy to grow rapidly *without* fueling inflation.

"You know, we're told to get productivity up," replied a clearly exasperated Senator Paul Sarbanes. "We get productivity up. The inflation prediction is very good. And yet the Fed is moving to tighten money to slow down the economy."

Sarbanes was not the only one expressing his confusion about Alan's conflicting remarks. "This is new," said economist Lawrence Kudlow. "No government official has previously argued that rising productivity causes inflation and therefore should be reduced."

"If the wealth effect continues to boost demand," asked Ed Yardeni, chief economist at Deutsche Bank, "then why can't productivity continue to boost supply" and keep inflation under wraps?

Alan insisted that he was not contradicting himself but simply musing out loud—a habit that he had supposedly overcome when he first realized how much of an impact his random thoughts had on global financial markets. On some level, he may have felt like Ayn Rand holding court on her philosophical throne, shrugging every now and again to make sure people were really paying attention to what he said.

CHAPTER 33

As the long presidential campaign dragged on through the summer and into the fall of 2000, Alan grew alarmed by the vast amounts of money both candidates promised to spend in the years ahead. Indeed, the Republican Congress had joined hands with the Clinton White House to end the fiscal year with a whopping increase in federal expenditures, and now Democrat Al Gore and Republican George W. Bush were talking about spending the entire projected budget surplus for the next ten years. Bush wanted to cut taxes as well. Alan knew that much of the ballyhooed surplus was due to luck, and could evaporate as quickly as it materialized.

"I believe most of us harbor doubts about whether the dynamics of the political process, some of which have been on display in the current budget deliberations, will allow the surpluses to continue to grow," Alan said in a speech to the libertarian Cato Institute on October 19.

June O'Neill, former director of the Congressional Budget Office, reinforced Alan's fears the same day. "There was a huge amount of luck involved in creating this surplus," she said. O'Neill attributed the surplus to three main factors: the surge in capital gains taxes from the massive increase in stock prices; more taxpayers pushed into the highest tax brackets, which had risen under Clinton; and a windfall from a cutback in military spending after the end of the Cold War.

Had the stock market risen more slowly during the 1990s or income been distributed more evenly throughout the workforce, the federal government would have been facing a deficit approaching $100 billion. In addition, if military spending had held steady at the level of 1990 instead of falling, the nation would have been struggling with a deficit of more than $300 billion instead of enjoying a surplus of $80 billion, according to the government's own estimates.

Alan knew that military spending would have to go back up under the next president, no matter who got in. He also knew that stock prices could not keep appreciating at the same rate of the past five years. In addition, with more and more wage earners being bumped into the top tax brackets, consumer demand would soon slow, which would have a negative impact on tax revenues. Taking it all together, both Gore and Bush were pledging to spend money that could evaporate into thin air virtually overnight. The rhetoric spewed by both major candidates during Campaign 2000 was especially banal, with both of them talking about spending projected trillion-dollar surpluses as though they had already occurred. If the winner in November followed through on *half* of the promises he had made during the campaign, Alan's job was going to become considerably more difficult during the remainder of his final term.

As Fed chairman, Alan could not publicly express his preference about which man he would rather see occupying the White House. Privately, however, Alan remembered all too well the problems he had had with George W. Bush's father less than a decade earlier, and he dreaded a repeat performance with the son. He had met George W. Bush on several occasions over the years, most recently at the Alfalfa Club's annual dinner in Washington in January 2000, but he had never engaged him in extended conversation. Alan worried about having to deal with the same cast of characters who had pressured him to lower interest rates before the 1992 election. Indeed, while Gore and Bush were still contesting who really won the election, Bush's running mate, Dick Cheney, was already firing a shot across the Fed's bow.

"We may well be on the front edge of a recession here," Cheney said on *Meet the Press* in early December. "I would hope that would change people's calculations with respect to the wisdom of the kind of tax cut that Governor Bush has recommended." The implication of his words was that the Fed needed to start thinking about lowering short-term rates to head off the recession Cheney and Bush saw looming over the horizon.

Alan did not agree with Cheney's dire forecast, but other observers were also growing concerned that the Fed's six hikes in short-term rates during the past eighteen months might have slowed the economy a bit more than anticipated. How ironic it would be if George W. won the election and took office while a new recession was taking hold, after Bush's father had held Alan responsible for the last recession when he was running for reelection. The last thing Alan needed was to get off on the wrong foot with the younger Bush.

In a speech before a group of community bankers in New York City a few days after Cheney made his comments, Alan conceded that "the pace of expansion of economic activity has moderated appreciably, in part as tighter financial conditions have had some impact on interest-sensitive areas of the economy." Alan admitted that "the wealth effect that spurred consumer spending is being significantly attenuated" as a result of the steep stock market decline.

"One must remain alert to the possibility that greater caution and weakening asset values in financial markets could signal or precipitate an excessive softening in household and business spending," Alan said. Shrewd politician that he was, Alan was laying the groundwork for the next round of monetary easing no matter which candidate occupied the White House in 2001.

Alan had long ago abandoned the notion that Republicans were the natural allies of libertarians. He had been able to find common ground with Bill Clinton and his team of financial advisers, particularly Rubin and Summers, whom he had come to regard as kindred spirits of sorts. Al Gore irritated Alan personally, as the vice president did just about everyone who came in contact with him. But Alan respected Gore's intelligence and believed he had a good sense of economic reality despite his campaign rhetoric. So, while Alan remained a registered Republican, he had managed to coexist peacefully with the Democrats he had worked and become friendly with during the past eight years.

The election ended in a virtual tie, with Gore taking the popular vote by about half of a percentage point and Bush winning the Electoral College by a nose if Florida went his way. The outcome was not known for more than a month as several recounts ended in dispute. Both candidates launched a legal and public relations blitz that became, in effect, a new campaign for popular support following the election. It came down to a question of which side could outmaneuver the other in the courts, and when the U.S. Supreme Court shut the door to further recounts, Gore was forced to concede. Finally, one of the tightest and most contentious presidential elections in U.S. history was over, and George W. Bush was declared the winner.

Alan surveyed the landscape and was a bit uneasy about what he saw. Bush lost no time in announcing his support for Alan during a CBS interview in December. President Clinton had "made the right decision in embracing Alan Greenspan," he said, "and I look forward to working with him." Alan, however, felt less than sanguine about the prospect of working with Lawrence Lindsey, who was likely to be named the new president's chief economic adviser. Lindsey had irked Alan during the campaign when he said that Alan privately endorsed Bush's economic plan, and he was later forced to back away from his statement following heavy criticism from Alan. Lindsey had also locked horns a bit with Alan when the obese economist served on the Fed board in the early 1990s and occasionally dissented from Fed policy. Lindsey voted against Alan four times during his tenure, a record that Lindsey later dismissed lightly.

"I had a ten percent dissent rate," he joked. "I had an independent mind, though I generally agreed with Greenspan."

Those close to Alan claimed that he regarded Lindsey with affection but also considered him to be a loose cannon of sorts, prone to shooting his mouth off at inopportune moments. Accordingly, Alan had kept him out of the loop on some key Fed deliberations, which annoyed Lindsey considerably. Alan knew that he would have to mend some fences to ensure a measure of tranquility during his final term as Fed chairman, but others began to speculate that Alan might have stayed around for one term too many.

The President-elect focused the spotlight on Alan when he visited the nation's capital for a series of meetings with Clinton, Gore, leaders of the House and Senate, and other key figures at the center of power. Bush's first tête-à-tête was a breakfast confab with Alan in Bush's suite at the Madison Hotel on Monday morning, December 18. Alan arrived around eight and met with Bush privately for about fifteen minutes before Dick Cheney and Larry Lindsey joined them for an extended discussion. The atmosphere was cordial and friendly. Bush and his team were clearly concerned that the economy was headed into a recession, but they were careful to avoid the appearance of putting pressure on the Fed to lower interest rates before the new administration was sworn in. Lindsey started off by bringing up Bush's economic agenda. Top on his list of priorities was the broad tax cut Bush had advanced during the campaign.

Contrary to what the media was reporting, Alan said that he was also in favor of cutting taxes and reducing the rate of government spending. He told them that the new administration stood a better chance of getting significant tax reform enacted if the economy appeared to be heading into a slump. Tax cuts would be viewed as a necessary tonic to jump-start economic growth. However, if the Fed cut short-term rates aggressively now, there was a danger that the economy would begin to accelerate too quickly, making substantial tax reduction more difficult to get through Congress. The Fed needed to steer a balanced course, keeping a wary eye on inflation while being careful not to tip the economy into a recession.

What everyone in the room understood, but what had to be left unsaid for obvious reasons, was that Bush would be better off accepting some pain early in his administration so that the Fed was not forced to start raising interest rates again when he was running for reelection. In other words, if a recession was coming, it was better to suffer through it during Bush's first year in office so that the economy, theoretically, would be back on an even keel before 2004. Alan also made it clear without saying so directly that it would be better to phase in the tax cuts over several years for the same reason. A large tax cut in 2001 was likely to stimulate the economy by the second half of the year, making it likely that the Fed would have to raise interest rates a year or two later to head off inflation. With phased-in tax reduction, the economy would be regaining a head of steam by 2003 or 2004 at the latest, when Bush would be campaigning for a second term.

The men were all smiles when the meeting broke up. Alan, masterful politician that he had become, was clearly in sync with the new team that would shortly take over the White House. Bush put his arm on Alan's shoulder as they exited the hotel, telling the phalanx of waiting reporters, "I talked with a good man right here. We had a very strong discussion about my confidence in his abilities."

Bush's seduction of Alan continued a few days later with the selection of Alan's long-time friend Paul O'Neill, former chairman of Alcoa, as treasury secretary. "We go back a long way," O'Neill said of Alan. "We've had lots of dealings with each other over the years that I've been at Alcoa and he's been at the Fed. I've made it a business, my business at his request, to come by on a fairly regular basis and tell him what I thought he was doing wrong and what I thought he was doing right, which I felt I had the privilege to do, being longtime friends and associates."

The Bush machine was already operating at full throttle before it was officially ensconced in the White House. If Alan felt any embarrassment about Bush's attempt to get him on board, he was careful not to show any signs of it. Some Wall Street observers read between the lines and predicted that Alan would not lose any time falling in step with the new administration's agenda. "Sometime in February or March," financial reporter Alan Murray wrote in the *Wall Street Journal*, "Federal Reserve Board Chairman Alan Greenspan will testify on Capitol Hill and declare a version of President Bush's tax-cut plan to be both 'reasonable' and 'prudent.'"

Indeed, it took Alan all of twenty-four hours to announce that the Fed had reversed course from fighting inflation toward protecting against excessive economic weakness—a signal that the Fed might be ready to start lowering short-term rates early in 2001.

Others in the financial industry wanted rates cut *now*, not later. Stocks had been plunging in value during the months leading up to the election and continued to slide during the electoral confusion that followed. Money managers thought Alan's Fed had gone too far with its tight monetary policy and believed it was long past time to ease up on interest rates.

"They should cut rates," said economist John Ryding of Bear Stearns. "Why wait? The case is straightforward. There are signs of excessive moderation."

"The drag on demand and profits from rising energy costs," said economist Alan Levenson, "as well as eroding consumer confidence, reports of substantial shortfalls in sales and earnings, and stress in some segments of the financial markets suggest that economic growth may be slowing further." Levenson shifted his forecast of a "soft landing" for the economy to a "hard landing," which was one step short of outright recession.

Stock prices, a fairly reliable harbinger of economic activity six to nine months down the road, finished the year with their first major losses in ten years. There was little doubt that one of Alan's goals was to let some air out of the stock market bubble. The broad S&P 500 Index had declined about 10 percent, a manageable correction in historic terms. Ironically, the so-called Old Economy stocks, otherwise known as value stocks, had fared best of all. However, the Nasdaq Composite, with its high component of technology shares, had suffered its worst loss ever—a sickening drop of nearly 40 percent for the year and more than *50* percent from its all-time high in spring 2000. Pricking the bubble was one thing, but a collapse of that magnitude ranked right up there with some of the worst crashes in stock market history. If Alan's plan was to remove some of the irrationality from investors' "exuberance," he now ran the risk of unleashing a bear market stampede that would be impossible to control if it continued much longer.

255

CHAPTER 34

T he bears were in total control on the first day of trading in the New Year. The next day, January 3, 2001, the Fed took the market by surprise and announced that it was cutting short-term rates half a percentage point because of its concerns about the economy. It was an extraordinary move, coming as it did between the Fed's scheduled meetings. Alan and his FOMC cohorts issued a press release, stating that it acted "in light of further weakening of sales and production, and in the context of lower consumer confidence, tight conditions in some segments of financial markets, and high energy prices sapping household and business purchasing power." Some Wall Street observers speculated that the Fed was close to panic.

"This says to me that Alan Greenspan is considerably—not just a little, but considerably—more worried about the health of the economy than the consensus forecasts," said Alan's old nemesis Alan Blinder, who had served as vice chairman of the Fed a few years earlier and had been briefly considered as Alan's replacement. "And if things are deteriorating as rapidly as Greenspan must think, this will not be enough to stop the deterioration," Blinder added, evidently relishing the opportunity to get in a dig at his former boss.

If there were any doubts that Alan was seriously worried about a recession, he erased them in his testimony before the Senate Budget Committee on January 25, 2001. "As far as we can judge, we have had a very dramatic slowing down," he said. "We are probably very close to zero at this particular moment."

Zero economic growth. Anything less would tip the country into recession if it occurred for two quarters in succession. What Alan left out of his testimony was that his *own* tight monetary policy dating back to June 1999 was primarily responsible for the contraction. It was not an altogether unwelcome development for the new administration in Washington. President George W. Bush could hardly be blamed for a slowdown that occurred in the final hours of the Clinton administration, and the gloomy situation reinforced Bush's claim that a tax cut was needed to stimulate growth. Alan jumped on the tax-cutting bandwagon with both feet during his testimony.

"Should current economic weakness spread beyond what now appears likely," he intoned somberly, "having a tax cut in place may, in fact, do noticeable good." Alan clearly was not going to have the same problems with the younger Bush that he had with the elder Bush.

Alan was growing more and more alarmed that the federal government would either spend the entire surplus or accumulate assets with its growing pile of cash. The government had to do *something* with the money; if it didn't spend it or give it back to the taxpayers, the only other alternative was to invest it in stocks, bonds, or real estate, which amounted to a subsidy of various investment markets. Alan had concluded that paying off the national debt and returning the excess cash to the taxpayers was preferable to government asset-gathering, which would expand the government's reach and lead to dislocations in the marketplace.

"Greenspan blessed the tax cuts as a way to synchronize debt reduction and accumulated surpluses, so that the surplus is inconsequential once the debt paydown has been completed," opined economist Alan Levenson. "He also gave approval to immediate action on crafting a tax plan regardless of the stage of the business cycle, since it is going to be necessary in any case. Implicitly, he opened the door for a discussion of privatizing Social Security as a way to fend off government accumulation of private assets."

Ironically, Alan had inadvertently done the new administration a favor by leaning too heavily on the side of monetary restraint and creating a situation that made Bush's economic plan all the more credible. With a massive slowdown taking place at the beginning of 2001, there was plenty of time to get the economy rolling again before Bush would be up for reelection four years later.

The economy continued to deteriorate, with fourth quarter GDP growth coming in at an annualized rate of about 1 percent. After the FOMC's regularly scheduled meeting on January 31, Alan announced that he was taking action once again, lowering short-term rates another half of a percentage point. The year was only a month old, and already short-term interest rates had come down a full point since the end of 2000.

"Consumer and business confidence has eroded further," the FOMC stated, "exacerbated by rising energy costs that continue to drain consumer purchasing power and press on business profit margins."

The tax bill that George W. Bush sent up to Congress in February had Alan's fingerprints all over it. While the Democrats were complaining that Bush's proposal was larger than the country could afford, it was only half the size of John F. Kennedy's bill in the early 1960s. As a percentage of the economy, the Bush proposal measured 1.1 percent versus 2 percent under Kennedy, and close to 3 percent during the Reagan years. In addition, Bush's tax relief—as Alan had suggested—was puny during his first two years in office; the bulk of the reductions wouldn't really kick in for several years.

At first glance, the tax package sounded "enormous," said Jim Glassman, senior economist at J. P. Morgan. "But if you look at the plan closely, relief starts small and scales in much later. This is certainly not going to be big enough—or soon enough—to rescue us from the current downturn."

Wall Street professionals and ordinary investors who hoped for a quick economic upturn, as well as a stock market rebound, were sorely disappointed. Many economists turned their wrath on the administration for not moving ahead with larger tax cuts sooner, and on Alan's Fed for not easing monetary policy faster.

"Greenspan's halo is slipping because the economy is slowing down and the stock market is falling," said Paul Kasriel, chief economist at the Northern Trust Company of Chicago.

Economist Robert Genetski of Chicago Capital was even more critical of Alan. The Fed's failure to lower short-term interest rates more significantly was "simply unconscionable," he said. "There's a total collapse in sales going on."

Alan had learned his political skills well over the years. Just as his advice to Bill Clinton had been calculated to benefit that president's 1996 reelection bid, so his advice to Bush was designed to jump-start the economy before the end of the new president's first term in office. Manipulating monetary policy was an art, not an exact science. There was always a risk that the Fed would err either on the side of monetary ease or restraint. But Alan had become a master high-wire financial aerialist during his fourteen years at the helm of the Fed, and no one doubted that he thoroughly enjoyed the role he played in the global arena. The big question was whether he could continue to rescue the economy from the brink of disaster as he had done so many times before, or whether he would make a fatal miscalculation during his remaining years as Fed chairman.

On March 20, then again on April 18 and May 15, Alan announced that the Fed was lowering short-term rates another half-point each time for a total of two and a half percentage points since the beginning of the year. "The risks are weighted mainly toward conditions that may generate economic weakness in the foreseeable future," he said. The three-month Treasury bill rate had already dropped to about 4.1 percent because of supply-and-demand factors. By lowering the Fed funds rate yet again in so short a period, this time to 4.0 percent, Alan and his colleagues were merely reacting to prevailing conditions in the marketplace. The Fed had fallen behind the curve instead of leading the way as it should have been doing. There was no doubt that Alan had overreacted on the side of tightening when the economy was booming and was now racing to catch up with a situation that deteriorated rapidly each day.

While the economy was not officially in recession—GDP growth for the first quarter of 2001 came in at a little more than 1 percent—the National Bureau of Economic Research released figures that indicated that the economy was approaching the "functional equivalent of recession." The bureau defined a recession as "a recurring period of decline in total output, income, employment, and trade" normally lasting from six months to a year. By this measure, two of the four major economic components reflected a recession in the spring of 2001. Industrial production was down 1.7 percent since August 2000, and manufacturing and trade sales were off 3.7 percent during the same period. Two more indicators—nonfarm employment growth and real disposable income—were also perilously close to signaling the onset of a recession. So, while official GDP growth was slightly positive for the fourth quarter of 2000 and the first quarter of 2001, the more technical indicators that Alan and other professional economists monitored were painting a darker picture. Hence, they were the real reasons behind the near-panic reductions in short-term rates by the Fed.

Economist Alan Levenson went so far as to say there was "an increasing likelihood that a recession has begun" in a report he wrote on May 31. He based his conclusion on data released in May by the Chicago Fed, revealing that an average of eighty-five separate measures of national economic activity had slipped into negative territory. In addition, jobless claims continued to rise steeply, revealing deteriorating conditions in the labor market. In short, Main Street America was clearly feeling the pinch regardless of what the official numbers issued by Washington stated about the health of the economy.

With moral support from Alan, both houses of Congress passed President Bush's tax-cut program in late May. In the end, it was a tepid, watered-down version of the one Bush had proposed during his campaign. Most of the key provisions were phased in over a period of ten years—meaning that if Bush lost his reelection bid in

2004, his successor was likely to jettison most of the reductions before they took place. Overall it was Reagan Lite, a bill designed to infuriate Bush's opponents while simultaneously disappointing his supporters. There was enough in it for everyone not to like, and Alan had to share some of the responsibility for ushering it into existence.

Economists of every persuasion, from the far left to the far right and all shades in between, agreed on one thing: The tax cut would not be nearly enough to spark the sputtering economy. That meant that only Alan and his colleagues at the Fed, relying on their arsenal of monetary tools, could save the economy from sinking further into recession. There was little doubt that their rate-cutting measures would succeed over time. If history was prologue to the future, the economy would begin to pick up steam by late 2001 or early 2002 at the latest, perhaps in time to give Bush and his Republicans some support during the off-year Congressional elections. The boom would continue, picking up from where it stalled out a year earlier.

Alan & Company continued to lower short-term rates through the summer of 2001, bringing the Fed funds and discount rates down to their lowest level in ten years, when George W. Bush's father was President. The stock market continued to slump, shaving the average wealth of Americans to the level of almost three years earlier. It was like the so-called "salami market" of the 1970s: every day investors lost another "slice" from their net worth. All thoughts of "irrational exuberance" were now a distant memory as the unemployment rolls continued to swell and the federal budget surplus evaporated into thin air because of declining tax revenues.

In the midst of the pervasive gloom, rumors began to circulate that Alan was planning to retire before his final term as Fed chairman expired in 2004. Some reports had him stepping down by the end of 2001 or during the first half of 2002.

"If Alan's planning to retire, it's news to me," said his wife, Andrea Mitchell. "He hasn't said anything to me about it."

An unnamed administration source was quoted as saying that the chairman, who was seventy-five years old, wanted to end his public career on a "high note." If true, the statement was laughable, considering that the economy was in its most perilous state since the last recession. While there was sharp criticism of Alan's recent performance by some Treasury officials, Alan was on good terms with key members of the Bush administration, including the President himself, treasury secretary Paul O'Neill, chief economist Lawrence Lindsey, and Vice President Dick Cheney. It was unlikely that Alan would leave the public stage while the economy was in the doldrums. However, most major economists were forecasting an economic revival by mid-2002. If Alan was planning to exit early, he was most likely to time his move to coincide with the next upturn, when he could truly say he was leaving on a "high note."

Suddenly, without warning, all speculation about Alan's imminent retirement faded from the public consciousness. The entire global dynamic changed abruptly on Tuesday morning, September 11, 2001. Two commercial airliners hijacked by a well-organized band of terrorists roared into the twin towers of New York's World Trade Center, turning the sleek structures into flaming mausoleums before they collapsed. A third hijacked plane slammed into the Pentagon, and a fourth crashed into an unpopulated field in Pennsylvania. The suicidal mission was the most devastating terrorist act in world history and succeeded in striking the twin symbols of U.S. strength: the heartbeat of the most dynamic economy on earth and the headquarters of the nation's military might. In the process, many human lives were obliterated in a flash and billions of dollars' worth of property was turned to rubble in lower Manhattan.

The United States of America was at war.

Alan returned immediately to Washington from an economic conference in Switzerland and announced that the Fed would take whatever actions were necessary to support the American and, indirectly, the European banking systems, as well as the economy at large. In the weeks that followed, the Fed chairman rose to the occasion once again, funneling tens of billions of dollars to the banks to ensure liquidity in the marketplace. While some speculated that the world economy might be mired in recession longer than expected as a result of the tragedy, others countered that government spending to rebuild the technological infrastructure would replace private demand as the major pillar of the economy. Defense spending was likely to boom, along with a restructuring of the Federal Aviation Authority and the air traffic control system. Wall Street had to replace its computer network, the communications industry needed to expand cellular phone capacity, and the energy industry would accelerate oil and natural gas production to provide adequate supplies for the coming war. The entire country was re-energized as it had not been for decades as Americans from every walk of life joined together to overcome the challenges ahead.

Alan made it clear that he was prepared to do his part to help the country recover. In a speech he delivered to the Institute for International Economics in the nation's capital on October 24, Alan sounded like John Galt in Ayn Rand's novel *Atlas Shrugged* when he denounced not only terrorists, but all those associated with the modern anti-globalization movement.

Globalization and free trade, he said, were the "antithesis of terrorism." He laid out his case for knocking down the final barriers to international trade and integrating economies across national borders. "Protectionism," Alan said, "will only slow the inevitable transition of our work force to more productive endeavors . . . if we hinder competitive progress, we will almost certainly slow overall economic growth and keep frozen in place younger workers whose opportunities to secure jobs with better long-term prospects diminish with time."

John Galt could not have said it better, and Rand would have been proud of her favorite protégé as she looked down from her perch in capitalist heaven.

The terrorist war on America seemed to have invigorated the seventy-five-year-old Fed chairman as he continued the battle, perhaps the final one of his career, to get the U.S. economy moving again. The Fed lowered short-term rates further through the end of the year, extending one of the most aggressive easing campaigns in its history. For all of 2001, the Fed cut rates a total of eleven times, dropping the Fed funds rate from 6.5 percent at the beginning of the year to 1.75 percent at the year's end. As 2002 got under way, a few glimmering signs began to emerge that the worst was over and the economy was starting to strengthen. Most economists did not expect a robust upturn. However, a consensus was forming that a slow recovery would be evident in the middle of 2002, and that by 2003 or 2004 the U.S. economy—the strongest engine of growth the world had ever seen—would be roaring ahead at full throttle. America had been bloodied but refused to be defeated.

Like the skyline of lower Manhattan, the very face of New York City itself, an era had ended and a new one was about to begin. For better or worse, the United States would never be quite the same again.

"What happens when King Alan goes?" some pundits began to speculate. "Imagine that Greenspan's successor decides to continue the monetary policy of the Greenspan era," speculated Harvard economist N. Gregory Mankiw. "How would he do it? The policy has never been fully explained . . . The only consistent policy seems to be: study all the data, and then set interest rates at the right level."

"The market acts as if it pretty closely understands the policy model the Fed uses," said William Poole, president of the St. Louis Fed. "There is a mystery, however. The Fed does not follow a . . . rule that can be written down as an equation or formula. How is it that the market and the Fed can so consistently agree on the interpretation of new information and its significance for policy actions?"

Poole answered his own question: "I don't know," he said.

Their points were good ones. Alan's formula for monetary policy existed largely in his own head. He read the same data that were available to other economists, but in the end the decisions he made were mostly intuitive. Whoever succeeded him as Fed chairman would make monetary decisions based on his, or her, own analytical abilities. Alan had already been Fed chairman longer than anyone except William McChesney Martin, who lasted nineteen years despite pressure to step down from both John F. Kennedy and Richard M. Nixon. Alan's current term would expire in August 2004, in the midst of the presidential election. More than likely, Alan *would* step down earlier and give President Bush plenty of time to name his successor.

King Alan was an unconventional economist by any measure. Part gold bug, part Austrian school free-market economist, part monetarist, with perhaps a residual dash of Keynesianism added for good measure, Alan had created his own school of economic theory that was fully understood only by himself. When Alan shrugged, the financial markets trembled, and sometimes they panicked. He was going to be a difficult, if not impossible, act to follow. It would take his successor a considerable time to establish the confidence in the U.S. financial system that he had built up over the years.

EPILOGUE

In reviewing Alan's performance as Fed chairman since he took over from Paul Volcker in 1987, I believe he will most likely have earned at least an A. History will rank him up there among the top men who held the job—surely heads and shoulders above his mentor Arthur Burns. The major question facing Fed watchers is whether the Federal Reserve and its control over monetary policy is the best way to monitor the nation's economy. Alan himself has never wavered from his view that a true gold standard constructed along the lines already discussed would eliminate the need for what he does. Most economists today regard that as an irresponsible, even reckless, position.

Is Alan right or wrong? Should all government programs and institutions be sunsetted—either continued or killed by the Congress after a set period, according to the needs of the time—as Alan suggested to an astonished Senator Paul Sarbanes during one of his confirmation hearings? That subject would make for a fascinating debate, for a different kind of book.

A more mundane question is whether the Fed, in the post-Greenspan era, will maintain the same clout that it had under Alan, or whether it will enter an era of faded glory. The Fed's job is to promote growth, fight inflation, and increase employment—somewhat contradictory objectives—through the use of its proprietary tools. "It's hard to hit three targets with one bullet, and easy to hit the wrong one," said author Martin Mayer, a scholar at the Brookings Institution.

Years ago the Fed fulfilled its mandate behind closed doors, and it took six months or longer for news of its policy decisions to filter out to the public. During Alan's reign, the Fed pretty much signaled its intentions before it actually took action, but in an age of instantaneous cash transfers, the central bank has less control over the nation's money supply than it did a while back. "The Fed, in other words, has much less real power than it had a generation ago," according to Mayer. "So it has become a highly theatrical enterprise, eager to seize attention and create attitudes . . . The spin-master is now out in front, announcing decisions and reasons for them while the market is open."

Others disagree. "The Fed still rules," said economist Alan Levenson. "The financial channels through which changes in the Fed funds rate are transmitted to the economy have doubtless changed over time . . . Yet this fact has far less to do with the effectiveness of monetary policy than with the channels of policy transmission."

In many ways, this is the same debate our founding fathers conducted during the early days of the Republic. Thomas Jefferson and his fellow Virginians distrusted the money men from New York and wanted to conduct the operations of government, such as they were, on a pay-as-you-go basis from tariffs and other nuisance taxes. Alexander Hamilton and the Federalists wanted to establish a central bank with the ability to raise money and finance operations through the capital markets. In the end, the Hamiltonians won, and we have been living with a central bank and extended banking system, in one form or another, for most of the past two centuries.

What it comes down to is that for better or worse, the Federal Reserve is not going to go away. It would take an economic collapse of cataclysmic proportions to dramatically change the way the United States conducts business. A more or less united Europe has established its own central bank, as has Japan, the globe's other major economy despite its decade-long period of intermittent recession. Ideology aside, barring a global depression that would destroy much of the wealth of the developed world, central banks will continue to rule the marketplace, and the Federal Reserve will remain the most powerful central bank of all for the foreseeable future.

For that reason more than any other, it is critical that someone of Alan's stature and intellect remain at the helm of the nation's most important financial institution.

NOTES

Part One: All That Jazz

Chapter 1

Background on the early days of Washington Heights came from material supplied to the author by the Washington Heights-NYC Committee. Information on Greenspan's early years and family history came primarily from interviews with Greenspan's cousin Wesley Halpert, from *Greenspan* by Justin Martin, and from other books and articles cited in the Acknowledgments section. Greenspan's interest in baseball was documented by Wesley Halpert, and the history of the Brooklyn Dodgers was supplied by the National Baseball Hall of Fame.

Chapter 2

Much of the material in this chapter dealing with Greenspan's fascination with the 1939 World's Fair and his social life in junior high school came from interviews with Wesley Halpert and other sources close to the family. Material on the changing demographics of Washington Heights came from the author's recollections of growing up in the area. The history of George Washington High School was supplied by the George Washington High School Alumni Association, and other information about the school came from interviews with Mark Lutsky, who still taught there in 2000.

The material on Henry Kissinger came from interviews with sources close to Mr. Kissinger. The details about Greenspan's political interests when he was a teenager, and his reaction to *Time's* designation of Stalin as "Man of the Year," were reviewed and verified by Greenspan.

Chapter 3

Greenspan's musical debt to Bill Sheiner and association with Stan Getz were confirmed by Greenspan. The history of Juilliard was supplied by the school's trustees. Information about Greenspan's classes at the uptown campus and his fascination with the Village Vanguard were reviewed and confirmed by Greenspan. The history of the Village Vanguard was supplied by *The Night Owl*. Material dealing with singer Harry Belafonte came from interviews with sources close to Mr. Belafonte. Greenspan's intellectual debt to David Hilbert, and his thoughts about politics, economics, and FDR's final years were confirmed by Greenspan.

Chapter 4

Quotes from Leonard Garment dealing with Greenspan's tenure with the Henry Jerome orchestra came from interviews with sources close to Mr. Garment and from his book *Crazy Rhythm*. Material and quotes from Henry Mandel came from an interview with the musician, and quotes from Henry Jerome came from interviews with the former bandleader. Greenspan's realization that he was not in the same class as some of his fellow musicians, and his discovery of *The Fountainhead,* was confirmed by Greenspan. Recollections of Greenspan at NYU came from interviews with Greenspan's lifelong friend Robert Kavesh. The philosophical environment at NYU at the time came from conversations with Murray Rothbard, the leading Misesnian economist in the United States before his death, and was confirmed by Kavesh. Greenspan's intellectual ambivalence about economics during this period was confirmed by Kavesh and Greenspan.

Chapter 5

The history of John Maynard Keynes was supplied by the University of St. Andrews in Scotland. Greenspan's characterization of the U.S. economic environment in the 1940s came from a speech delivered by Greenspan to the Conference Board in New York City on October 16, 1996. Information about Greenspan's physical and social development, and his interest in sports, was provided by Robert Kavesh and confirmed by Greenspan. The history of the National Industrial Conference Board was supplied by the

Conference Board. Quotes attributed to Pierre A. Rinfret came from interviews with Mr. Rinfret. Material about Arthur Burns came from Pierre Rinfret's personal papers, interviews with Robert Kavesh, and sources close to Milton Friedman, and was reviewed and verified by Greenspan.

Part Two: The Randian

Chapter 6

The description of Greenspan's first car and his starting salary came from sources close to Greenspan, and the details were reviewed and confirmed by Greenspan. The material dealing with Greenspan's meeting with and marriage to Joan Mitchell came primarily from interviews with the artist and others close to the couple. The details about Ayn Rand were provided by several sources: interviews with Barbara Branden and Nathaniel Branden, as well as their respective books, *The Passion of Ayn Rand* and *Judgment Day*; conversations with early Rand disciples, including Murray Rothbard, Leonard Peikoff, and George Reisman; and the author's personal observations. The parallels between Objectivism and the scholastic philosophy of Thomas Aquinas were provided by Jesuit philosopher James Sadowsky. Greenspan's impressions of Rand's Saturday night discussion groups were reviewed and confirmed by Greenspan. Details about Rand's aversion to facial hair and her other eccentricities were provided by Barbara Branden and Murray Rothbard. Nathaniel Branden's changing views about Greenspan's Keynesian underpinnings were confirmed by Mr. Branden.

Chapter 7

The material dealing with Greenspan's marriage to Joan Mitchell came from interviews with the artist, Barbara Branden, and others close to the couple. Nathaniel Branden's comments on the marriage were detailed in his book *Judgment Day*. The information about Greenspan's renewed interest in Ayn Rand and her philosophy was provided by various members of her "Collective" and confirmed by Greenspan. The information about Greenspan's involvement with William Townsend came from several sources: *Washington Post* reporter Linton Weeks; "The Fountainhead: Alan Greenspan Faces the Biggest Challenge of His Career" by John Cassidy, *The New Yorker*, May 1, 2000; Nathaniel Branden; *Greenspan* by Justin Martin; and various books cited in the Acknowledgments section.

The details about the early years of Townsend-Greenspan were provided by interviews with Pierre Rinfret, Barbara Branden, and Robert Kavesh.

Chapter 8

Further material about Townsend-Greenspan came from interviews with Robert Kavesh and sources close to John R. Taylor. The insights on the influence of the Taylor Rule on the Fed funds rate came from David Wessel, reporter for the *Wall Street Journal*. Greenspan's views of the Taylor Rule were reviewed and confirmed by Greenspan. Other details about John R. Taylor were supplied by the Hoover Institution and the Federal Reserve Bank of St. Louis. Comments about Greenspan's relationship with various members of Rand's inner circle came from interviews with Barbara Branden, material supplied by R. W. Bradford, and various sources close to Rand. The material about Edith Efron came from conversations with Ms. Efron. Greenspan's opinion of *Atlas Shrugged* was provided by Barbara Branden and Nathaniel Branden in their books. Rand's view of Arthur Burns came from sources close to Rand.

Chapter 9

Greenspan's letter to the *New York Times* appears in *Greenspan* by Justin Martin. Greenspan's evolving relationship with Rand came from interviews with Barbara Branden and from various sources close to Rand. Greenspan's "fundamental agreement" with Rand's philosophy was confirmed by Greenspan. Von Mises's opinion of economic forecasting was provided by Murray Rothbard. Murray and Joey Rothbard's relationship with Rand came from conversations with the Rothbards, Leonard Liggio, and others close to Rand. The details about John Hospers and Edith Efron came from various publications. Rand's views about homosexuals came from her own writings and were widely known by her disciples. The appeal of Objectivism for "fallen-away Jews and Catholics and Protestants" is based on the author's personal observations. Greenspan's continuing fondness for Rand despite her eccentricities has been acknowledged by Greenspan on numerous occasions. The information about the death of William Townsend was supplied by the Social Security Administration and by former employees of the firm who prefer to remain anonymous. The material about Arthur Burns came from the personal papers of Pierre Rinfret and from Kevin L. Kliesen, an economist with the Federal Reserve Bank of St. Louis.

Chapter 10

The details regarding the formation of the Nathaniel Branden Institute came from various sources: *Judgment Day* by Nathaniel Branden; *The Passion of Ayn Rand* by Barbara Branden; interviews with Murray Rothbard and others close to Rand; and the author's personal observations. The information about Objectivists who moved on to greater accomplishments came from interviews and conversations with Robert Bleiberg, Martin Anderson, Ira Levin, and F. Clifton White. Greenspan's essay on the gold standard appeared in *Capitalism: The Unknown Ideal*, and his detailed views on the subject were confirmed by Greenspan. Greenspan's fortunes at Townsend-Greenspan and his investment activities are based on interviews with Robert Kavesh and the personal papers of Pierre Rinfret. Greenspan's morning soaks in the tub have been noted by various sources, including Andrea Mitchell and Greenspan. Objectivist reactions to the election of 1960 are based on interviews with various Objectivists and the author's personal observations. Dorothy Kilgallen's quote appeared in the *New York Journal American*. The information about Ayn Rand's break with Bennett Cerf appears in Cerf's book *At Random*.

Chapter 11

Greenspan's views of the antitrust laws first appeared in *The Objectivist* and have been reiterated in various statements by Greenspan over the years. Greenspan's comments about the fascistic nature of the New Deal appeared in *The Objectivist*. Greenspan's interest in Leisha Gullison is discussed in books by Barbara Branden and Nathaniel Branden and was confirmed by Greenspan. Nathaniel Branden's adulterous relationships with Patrecia Gullison and Ayn Rand have been well documented by both Brandens. The characterization of the environment surrounding the breakup is discussed in the Brandens' books and is also based on the author's personal observations. The statement attacking the Brandens that was signed by Greenspan and others first appeared in *The Objectivist* and has been reprinted in various publications over the years.

Part Three: The Adviser

Chapter 12

The details surrounding Greenspan's reunion with Leonard Garment are reported in Garment's book *Crazy Rhythm*. The information about the conservatives who gravitated to Nixon is based on interviews with F. Clifton White and other sources close to Leonard Garment and Richard Nixon. The profile of Nixon came from interviews with F. Clifton White. Nixon's attitude toward Jews is based on excerpts from the secret tapes released after Nixon's resignation from the presidency. The material dealing with Greenspan's involvement with Nixon's policy advisers is based on interviews with various Nixon associates and was confirmed by Greenspan. Greenspan's conversation with Robert Kavesh came from interviews with Kavesh. The profile of George Romney is based on interviews with F. Clifton White and the author's personal observations. Greenspan's preference for Reagan over Nixon was confirmed by Greenspan. The reasons behind Nixon's selection of Spiro Agnew as a running mate came from interviews with F. Clifton White and the author's personal observations.

Chapter 13

Greenspan's role during Nixon's transition period came from interviews with F. Clifton White and sources close to Martin Anderson. The information about Nixon putting pressure on Arthur Burns to pursue an easy monetary policy was provided by several sources: Steven Horwitz, Allen J. Matusow, and Pierre Rinfret. Greenspan's reaction to Burns's capitulation to Nixon was confirmed by various sources close to Greenspan. The profile of John Connally came from interviews with F. Clifton White and the author's personal observations. Milton Friedman's criticism of Nixon is based on speeches he made over the years and his columns in *Newsweek*. Herbert Stein's view of Nixon is based on interviews with Stein. Greenspan's comments about the perils of state intervention in the economy were confirmed by Greenspan. Greenspan's reaction to antiwar demonstrations in Washington, D.C. came from interviews with several people close to Greenspan. The details surrounding the demonstrations are based on the author's personal observations and the writings of Norman Mailer.

Chapter 14

The profile of Herbert Stein is based on interviews with Stein and the personal papers of Pierre A. Rinfret. The ideas of the supply-siders around Nixon came from interviews with Jack Kemp and Jude Wanniski and from the writings of Arthur Laffer. Arthur Burns's complicity in Nixon's political agenda has been widely documented over the years in various publications. The details surrounding Nixon's final days in office are based on various sources: interviews with F. Clifton White and sources close to Henry Kissinger, various books written about the period, and the author's personal recollections. Possible reasons for the break-in at Watergate came from interviews with White.

Chapter 15

Greenspan's reaction to Burns's phone call is based on interviews with Robert Kavesh, and various sources who worked at Towsend-Greenspan. Greenspan's testimony before the Senate Banking Committee is on the public record. Greenspan's concerns about his testimony were confirmed by Greenspan. President Ford's and Seidman's views of Greenspan came from interviews with sources close to both men. The information dealing with the FBI's investigation of Greenspan is based on interviews with Joan Mitchell Blumenthal and former FBI agents. Ayn Rand's comments following Greenspan's swearing-in as chairman of the Council of Economic Advisers were widely reported by the media. Rand's infatuation with Gerald Ford is based on the author's personal observations. Greenspan's advice to Ford came from interviews with William Simon and sources close to Seidman. The profile of Simon is based on interviews with the former treasury secretary. Details about Ford's economic priorities came from interviews with Simon and from Simon's private papers.

Chapter 16

The profile of Barbara Walters was based on interviews with Ms. Walters. Information about Greenspan's lack of prowess at tennis and golf is based on interviews with Robert Kavesh, William Simon, and sources close to Gerald Ford, William Seidman, and others close to the Ford administration. The details surrounding the contest between Ford and Reagan for the 1976 Republican presidential nomination came from interviews with F. Clifton White and Ronald Reagan. Ford's reaction to his defeat is based on interviews with sources close to the former President and his public statements following the election. Greenspan has reiterated his views about a gold standard, and the necessity for maintaining a central bank in the absence of a gold standard, many times over the years.

Chapter 17

Carter's economic record is based on the consensus views of leading U.S. economists who have written on the subject. The details surrounding the

1980 primaries and the issues affecting the presidential campaign are based on the author's recollections. The information about the arguments surrounding the size of Reagan's tax cut came from several sources: Jack Kemp; sources close to Milton Friedman, Murray Weidenbaum, and Martin Anderson; and the author's personal observations. Laffer's bell curve was widely discussed by the media at the time. The traditionalists' disillusionment with the supply-side direction taken by Reagan came from interviews with various sources close to Reagan. The details about the several schools of free-market economic philosophy are based on papers published by the Cato Institute and the author's understanding of the issues. The details about Reagan's first one hundred days in office came from the writings of William Niskanen, interviews with Jack Kemp and others close to Reagan, and the author's own research.

Chapter 18

The circumstances leading to Reagan's 1981 tax cut were reported in my own book, *The New Tax Law and You* (NAL, 1981) and are based on various sources, including interviews with Jack Kemp and people close to Martin Anderson and Milton Friedman. Alan Greenspan's opinion of Reagan is based on interviews with several individuals close to Greenspan who prefer to remain anonymous. The information about Ronald Reagan's creation of the National Commission on Social Security Reform was supplied by various sources, including the Social Security Administration and the Cato Institute. Comments about the Chilean privatization of its own social security system are based on a speech given by L. Jacobo Rodriguez, delivered in Portugal in 1997. James Baker's role in hosting the commission's meetings came from interviews with F. Clifton White and sources close to Mr. Baker. The details surrounding the death of Ayn Rand are reported in *The Passion of Ayn Rand* by Barbara Branden, *Judgment Day* by Nathaniel Branden, and the author's recollections. The details about her funeral were widely reported in the *New York Times* and other publications. Several sources close to Greenspan discussed with the author how the irony of Rand's death occurring on Greenspan's birthday resonated powerfully with Greenspan.

Chapter 19

The disastrous outcome of Greenspan's chairmanship of the National Commission on Social Security Reform is based on interviews with

F. Clifton White, the writings of William Niskanen, and data supplied by the Cato Institute. Greenspan's own comments about the work of the commission were widely reported at the time. Greenspan's reiteration of his views about a gold standard were reported by Dan Ascani, president of Global Market Strategists. The details about Greenspan's developing relationship with Andrea Mitchell came from interviews with sources close to Ms. Mitchell and A&E's biography of Greenspan. The information about Townsend-Greenspan's deteriorating financial health is based on the personal papers of Pierre Rinfret and on interviews with various individuals who worked with Greenspan at the time and prefer to remain anonymous.

Chapter 20

Greenspan's relationship with Charles Keating was covered in detail by various news sources, including Fox Market Wire and the Associated Press. The profile of Keating came from articles published in the *Washington Post*, *The New Yorker*, and other publications. Greenspan's comments about his humiliation over his support of Keating were reported by the same sources. Details about Greenspan's and Andrea Mitchell's social life in Washington, D.C. came from interviews with sources close to Judy Woodruff, Alan Hunt, Judy Mackey, Martin Anderson, and others.

Part Four: The Chairman

Chapter 21

The details about the economy under Presidents Jimmy Carter and Ronald Reagan came from various sources: the Federal Reserve, Merrill Lynch, Goldman Sachs, William Niskanen, and the author's own analysis. The information about the developing strain between Paul Volcker and Reagan's advisers, as well as their favorable assessment of Greenspan, is based on interviews with sources close to James Baker, Don Regan, and Ronald Reagan who asked not to be identified. The history of the Federal Reserve has been covered in detail in various books cited in the Acknowledgments section. Greenspan's opinion of his predecessors is based on interviews with various sources close to Greenspan. The description of the Marriner S. Eccles Federal Reserve Board Building is based on the author's observations.

Chapter 22

Greenspan's statements upon his appointment as chairman of the Federal Reserve were widely published at the time. The views of his supporters and detractors are based on interviews with various senators and representatives who asked not to be identified. The outcome of the final vote is on the public record. The theory of the Phillips curve came from British economist A. W. Phillips in the late 1950s and was further developed into its present form by Edward Phelps and Milton Friedman. According to J. Bradford De Long, professor of economics at the University of California at Berkeley, it has been all but discredited today. Many others, including conservative economist Lawrence Kudlow, share this view about the Phillip's curve. Details about the economic and financial conditions prevailing during Greenspan's early days at the Fed are based on the author's personal analysis. Information regarding Gerald Corrigan's role during the 1987 crisis came from interviews with sources close to Mr. Corrigan. White House alarm about Greenspan's rate hikes is based on interviews with sources close to Beryl Sprinkel, Michael Darby, and James Baker. Greenspan's comments during his interviews with David Brinkley and Sam Donaldson appeared in various books cited in the Acknowledgments section. Initial opinions of Wall Street analysts about Greenspan came from private conversations with various analysts.

Chapter 23

The portrait of Greenspan monitoring market conditions is based on interviews with various sources at the Fed who prefer to remain anonymous. Remarks made by Beryl Sprinkel and James Baker came from interviews with sources close to both men. During the market crash of 1987, the author was responsible for keeping abreast of minute-to-minute developments. The details about Greenspan's visit to Dallas appeared in several books cited in the Acknowledgments section and in other publications. Comments made by Sprinkel came from interviews with sources close to the economist. The analysis of the role played by program traders and arbitrageurs is based on the author's own work.

Chapter 24

The comments made by Andrea Mitchell about her relationship with Greenspan came from interviews with sources close to Ms. Mitchell. Greenspan's testimony before the Senate Banking Committee is available on various government web sites. Henry Gonzalez's harsh criticism of the power of the Federal Reserve has been well documented over the years. The information about the mounting tension between Greenspan and the Bush administration came from various sources close to Bush, including F. Clifton White and others who asked not to be identified. Remarks made by D'Amato, Darby, Rahn, and Sprinkel came from interviews with sources close to them. Susan Estrich made her remarks about Michael Dukakis during a television interview with Katie Couric. The profile of Nicholas Brady is based on the author's personal observations, conversations with various Wall Street analysts, and interviews with several advisers inside the Bush administration. President Bush's own comments were widely reported at the time. News about Brady's cancellation of his weekly lunches with Greenspan appears in various books mentioned in the Acknowledgments section.

Chapter 25

The information about the Bush administration's displeasure with Greenspan's monetary policy is based on interviews with sources close to Brady, Darby, and Boskin. Greenspan's comments about the causes of the recession were delivered in his testimony before the Senate Banking Committee in 1992. Michael Boskin's comments about the recession and his evaluation of the economic impact of environmental and disability laws appeared in a paper he wrote for the Cato Institute. Greenspan's assessment of Bush's economic record is based on interviews with economists close to Greenspan who asked not to be identified.

Chapter 26

Senator D'Amato's remarks about Greenspan were widely reported in various publications at the time. The information about Greenspan's confusion over the death of artist Joan Mitchell came from interviews with various people close to Greenspan and his first wife. The effect of the worsening economy on Bush's reelection campaign is based on the author's personal observations. The comments about Bush's dismal campaign came from interviews with Bill Rusher and F. Clifton White. The details about Greenspan's first meeting with Bill Clinton appeared in Bob Woodward's book *The Agenda*. Rubin's remarks are based on interviews with sources close to Rubin.

Chapter 27

In *The Agenda*, Bob Woodward makes too much of Greenspan's alleged endorsement of Clinton's economic package. In reality, Greenspan believed deficit reduction was critical, but he had always favored cutting government spending to achieve the goal. However, he was realistic enough to understand that Clinton would rely heavily on higher taxes along with some moderation in federal spending, so Greenspan reluctantly went along with the package as the best he was likely to get. Greenspan's embarrassment over being seated between Hillary Clinton and Tipper Gore has been widely discussed. The comments made by John LaWare and other economists about the compromising situation came from interviews with sources close to LaWare. Greenspan's comments about Clinton's final economic package are on the public record. The issue of the erasing of the FOMC tapes and Henry Gonzalez's reaction is based on interviews with Gonzalez. Greenspan's opinions of Gonzalez and D'Amato came from interviews with sources close to Greenspan who asked not to be identified. The exchange between Greenspan and Senator Paul Sarbanes occurred during Greenspan's regular testimony before the Senate Banking Committee.

Part Five: The Boom

Chapter 28

The information about Alan Blinder undermining his own credibility is based on conversations with fellow Wall Street analysts. The discussions about the "moral hazard" of bailing out Mexico during the so-called peso crisis came from interviews with sources close to Robert Rubin and Alan Summers, and from various Wall Street analysts. The details surrounding the death of Alan's mother came from interviews with Wesley Halpert and others close to Greenspan. The information about the death of Alan's father was supplied by the Social Security Administration. The historical measures of stock valuations are based on the author's own research.

Chapter 29

The details surrounding the comments made by Elaine La Roche were provided by the Bond Market Association. Alan's remarks about the Social Security system at the Abraham Lincoln Award ceremony were provided by the Union League of America and the National Center for Policy

Analysis. Alan's comments about "irrational exuberance" to the American Enterprise Institute for Public Policy Research were widely reported by the media. Comments made by J. Bradford DeLong came from the professor's papers. The conclusions reached by the Congressional Advisory Commission on the Consumer Price Index are on the public record. Similar conclusions were reported by the National Center for Policy Analysis. Lawrence Chimerine's remarks came from interviews with the economist. The criticism directed at Alan by Senators Jim Bunning, Paul Sarbanes, and Phil Gramm is on the public record.

Chapter 30

The details about Alan's proposal and marriage to Andrea Mitchell were reported by CNN and other media. The comments about the marriage made by Judy Woodruff and Al Hunt came from interviews with sources close to both parties. Andrea Mitchell's remarks about Alan are based on interviews with sources close to Ms. Mitchell. Alan's early morning routine of soaking in the bathtub while reviewing economic reports was confirmed by Ms. Mitchell on several occasions. The estimates of Alan's net worth are based on figures released by Alan to the media every year. The comments about Alan made by Arthur Levitt and Robert Solow came from interviews with sources close to both men. The details about the so-called Asian Flu or Asian Contagion are based on the author's own research. Alan's comments about the situation were made in a speech he gave to the Cato Institute. William McDonough's comments about Alan's recognition of the evolving New Economy came from interviews with sources close to Mr. McDonough.

Chapter 31

The analysis of stock market conditions is based on the author's own research. The details about the Fed's deliberations over interest rates came from interviews with Fed sources who asked not to be identified. The analysis of the events leading up to the creation of the federal budget surplus is based on several sources: interviews with sources close to Lawrence Lindsey, information published by Stephen Moore of the Cato Institute, and the author's own research. Greenspan's comments about the New Economy were widely reported by the media. The details surrounding the handling of the Russian crisis came from interviews with sources close to Robert Rubin, Lawrence Summers, and the Fed.

Chapter 32

The exchange between Greenspan and Senator Paul Sarbanes came from material supplied by R. W. Bradford. Representative Joseph Kennedy's comments about Greenspan are based on interviews with sources close to the congressman. An assessment of Greenspan's net worth is published every year. Preparations for Y2K were widely reported by the media. In 1999, the author served on a Y2K task force for a major financial institution. Greenspan's comments about stock valuations came from a speech he delivered in Jackson Hole, Wyoming. Greenspan's appointment to a fourth term as Fed chairman was widely covered by the media. Greenspan's remarks about the trade deficit and his exchange with Senator Paul Sarbanes are part of the public record. Lawrence Kudlow's and Ed Yardeni's reactions to Greenspan's remarks are based on interviews with the economists.

Chapter 33

Greenspan's and June O'Neill's analyses of the reasons for the budget surplus were published by the Cato Institute. Greenspan's wariness about a new Bush administration came from interviews with various sources close to Greenspan who asked not to be identified. Dick Cheney's dire economic forecast was widely reported by the media. Greenspan's cordial relationship with leading Democrats was covered in detail by Bob Woodward. Information about Greenspan's testy relationship with Lawrence Lindsey is based on interviews with sources close to both men. The details about Greenspan's meeting with George W. Bush, Dick Cheney, and Lawrence Lindsey came from sources close to Lindsey who prefer to remain anonymous. Paul O'Neill's comments about Greenspan were reported by the media. Alan Murray made his comments in an article he wrote for the *Wall Street Journal*. The economic assessments of John Ryding and Alan Levenson came from conversations with both economists.

Chapter 34

Alan Blinder's remarks about the shift in Fed policy came from interviews with sources close to the economist. Greenspan's comments to the Senate Budget Committee are part of the public record. Greenspan's concern about the federal government gathering too many assets was widely reported by the media. The various economists' remarks are based on discussions with them. The statement that Bush's tax plan had Greenspan's "fingerprints all over it" is based on interviews with sources close to the Bush administration. Andrea Mitchell's comment came from a statement she made to Don Imus. Remarks made by Mankiw and Poole are based on statements made by both men.

Epilogue

Ranking Greenspan's place in history is the author's own assessment. Quotes attributed to Mayer came from an article written by him, and comments made by Levenson are based on an interview with him. The concluding remarks are the author's opinion.

INDEX

Aesthetic Realists, 23-24
Agnew, Spiro, 96-97
agriculture, 169, 196
Ailes, Roger, 92
Alcoa, 113, 254
Aldrich-Vreeland Act of 1908, 164
altruism, 50, 51, 53, 69, 81–82
American Bankers Association, 178
American Continental Corp.,
    155, 156
American Economic Review, 63
American Enterprise Institute for
    Public Policy Research, 223
American Society for Esthetics, 73
Americans with Disabilities Act,
    194–95
Anderson, John, 130, 131
Anderson, Martin, 78, 92, 98, 100,
    101, 110, 131, 132, 136, 137,
    157–58

anti-Semitism, 93, 100, 232
antitrust laws, 84, 115, 167,
    168–69
Archer, William, 138, 139
Armstrong, William, 138
Asian markets collapse, 231–32
atheism, 70, 73, 83, 116, 229
Atlas Shrugged (Rand), 67, 70–71,
    74, 263
A train (subway), 7–8
automobile industry, 120, 135,
    172, 203

Baker, Howard, 138
Baker, James, xvi, 126, 138, 157,
    162–64, 167, 172, 173,
    177–78, 181
balanced budget. *See* budget,
    balanced
Ball, Robert M., 138

285

Fisher, Irving, 6
FOMC. *See* Federal Open Market
    Committee
Forbes magazine, 181
Ford, Gerald R., xiv, 115–27, 137,
    168–69
forecasting. *See* economic
    forecasting
Forest Hills (Queens), 48, 55
Forster, E. M., 35
For the New Intellectual (Rand), 82
Fort Tryon Park, 4
Fortune magazine, 246
Fountainhead, The (Rand), 31, 32,
    49, 51, 52, 67
Fraunces Tavern, 113
free market
    Burns's view of, 42–43, 75–76
    Carter critics and, 129
    global economy and, 234,
        240–41
    gold standard and, 79
    Greenspan's view of, 8, 26, 27,
        66, 72, 115, 152, 168, 169,
        216
    Keynesian interventionism vs.,
        27, 34, 35
    New Economy and, 233
    Nixon's political expediency vs.,
        101
    Rand's belief in, 31, 50, 51, 66,
        71, 72, 73
    tax cuts and, 106
    utilitarian arguments, 31–32
Friedman, Milton, xv, 42, 75, 101,
    131, 132, 136, 139, 172–73,
    239
Fuller, Mary Falvey, 138

Gainsbrugh, Martin, 39
Gardiner, John, 229
Garment, Leonard, 28, 29, 32,
    91–92, 93, 98
gasoline shortage, 128, 130
Gates, Thomas, Jr., 98
Genetski, Robert, 259
George Washington Bridge, 8, 10
George Washington High School,
    15–17, 23, 24, 30
Getz, Stan, 21, 29
Gillespie, Dizzy, 24, 25, 29
Gingrich, Newt, 238
Gingrich Revolution, 211
Ginsburg, Ruth Bader, 230
Glassman, Jim, 258
Glass-Owen bill (1913), 165
global economy, 233–34, 237,
    240–41, 244, 247, 263
Goldsmith, Nathan and Anna
    (grandparents), 6, 7, 9, 10,
    11, 14, 19, 20, 23
gold standard, 79–80, 84, 94, 100,
    114, 127, 152, 164, 167, 243,
    266
Goldwater, Barry, 93, 95, 132
Gonzalez, Henry, 185, 208–10,
    211
Gorbachev, Mikhail, 153
Gordon, Max, 23
Gore, Al, 170, 202, 249, 250, 251,
    252, 253
Gore, Tipper, 207
Gould, Joe, 24
government spending
    budget deficit and, 206
    Bush (G. H.) administration
        and, 239